D0906490

SUPERCARS

MASTERPIECES OF DESIGN AND ENGINEERING

RICHARD DREDGE

THUNDER BAY
P·R·E·S·S

San Diego, California

Thunder Bay Press

An imprint of the Advantage Publishers Group
5880 Oberlin Drive, San Diego, CA 92121-4794
www.thunderbaybooks.com

Copyright © Amber Books, 2006

Copyright under International, Pan American, and Universal Copyright Conventions.
All rights reserved. No part of this book may be reproduced or transmitted in any form
or by any means, electronic or mechanical, including photocopying, recording, or by any
information storage-and-retrieval system, without written permission from the copyright holder.
Brief passages (not to exceed 1,000 words) may be quoted for reviews.
All notations of errors or omissions should be addressed to Thunder Bay Press,
Editorial Department, at the above address. All other correspondence (author inquiries,
permissions) concerning the content of this book should be addressed to Amber Books
at the address below.

Library of Congress Cataloging-in-Publication Data available upon request

ISBN-13: 978-1-59223-559-9
ISBN-10: 1-59223-559-X

Editorial and design by
Amber Books Ltd
Bradley's Close
74–77 White Lion Street
London N1 9PF
England
www.amberbooks.co.uk

Project Editor: Sarah Uttridge
Designer: Hawes Design
Picture Research: Richard Dredge and Terry Forshaw

Printed in Singapore

1 2 3 4 5 10 09 08 07 06

Contents

The Supercar Experience

It used to be easy to define a supercar – and perhaps it still is. But where there used to be a ready formula that involved power and speed, along with jaw-dropping looks, the goalposts have moved. Until the start of the 1980s, any car that was capable of topping 257.4km/h (160mph) or which packed 400 horses under the bonnet, was something very special indeed. They were also very expensive, often impractical and styled without a thought for function over form.

While there used to be a distinction between grand tourers and supercars, the boundaries have now blurred. As a result, modern cars such as the 455.9kW (612bhp) Mercedes CL65 AMG can cross continents comfortably while still being ferociously quick.

As the 1980s turned into the 1990s, there was a huge increase in the number of supercar projects attempting to reach fruition, fuelled by advances in materials and technology – as well as a buoyant economy. This was the era of carbon fibre, multiple turbochargers and electronics, along with fat bonuses to pay for it all. The biggest changes arrived by the end of the decade though, with family saloons and estate cars being engineered to cope with the sort of speeds that only a few years previously had been the sole preserve of mid-engined impractical exotica. Prestige manufacturers such as Audi, Mercedes, BMW and Jaguar were building cars that could transport five people and their luggage across continents at 250km/h

(155mph). The speeds would have been higher too, if they hadn't entered into a gentlemen's agreement to limit the maximum velocities of their cars to a mere 250km/h (155mph).

21st Century Changes

Then the 1990s turned into the twenty-first century and that's when things started to go completely ballistic. Not only did new supercar makers emerge which were more than capable of threatening the existence of the establishment, but at the same time the bar was raised even further. This was the era of the 321.8km/h (200mph) club, with there being no shortage of contenders for entry. Companies such as Pagani and Koenigsegg appeared from nowhere, with beautifully engineered cars that were amazing to drive and offered even more style than many of the well-known supercar builders. The gauntlet was well and truly thrown down.

The problem with this new breed of supercar maker was the lack of attainability of their products – although that's just part of the appeal of any hypercar, of course. When the twenty-first century arrived it brought with it an important new phenomenon though – the affordable and practical supercar. While that term affordable may be relative, the practicality isn't. For Heaven's sake, we now have estate cars that pack 500 horses and are capable of 289.6km/h (180mph) – while also despatching the 0–97km/h (0–60mph) dash in five seconds or so. Even practical four-seater coupés such as the Mercedes CL65 AMG can generate over 447kW (600bhp), offering 0–100km/h (0–62mph) in four seconds or so. It's not that long since such statistics were strictly the domain of extreme hypercars that only companies such as Lamborghini or Ferrari could produce.

Bugatti aims to produce the greatest supercar of all time, with its Veyron. The company hasn't held anything back in trying to produce the world's fastest car, but it's not a car with the finesse of the McLaren F1. The car uses four turbos and 16 cylinders.

While load carriers such as the Audi RS6 or Mercedes E55 may be ludicrously fast and immensely practical, there's one area in which they'll never be able to compete with established supercar makers, and that's the visual drama. But there's another realm in which they score highly, and that's usability. They have complicated transmissions that are simple to use. Their engines are powerful but clean, reliable and not even slightly temperamental. To be fair, by the time these family cars were on sale, even the contemporary hypercars were far more usable and much better built than their predecessors. With modern electronics and engine management systems they were clean, tractable at low speeds and totally driveable throughout the rev range – yet could still produce anywhere between 296 and 592kW (400 and 800bhp) without a murmur.

To keep such powerful cars usable, alongside the engine development there also had to be evolution of the rest of the drivetrain. Components such as gearboxes, tyres and braking/suspension systems had to be engineered to cope with 444kW (600bhp). Perhaps that's the most impressive way in which the supercar has evolved over the last half a century; after all, there were cars with around 296kW (400bhp) by the late 1960s. But the chassis design of such vehicles held them back – now it's easy to exploit such power (and much more). In fact it's so easy to exploit it that the quest for ever more power continues unabated. As engine design takes a leap forward, so does chassis construction. Perhaps the Bugatti Veyron is the

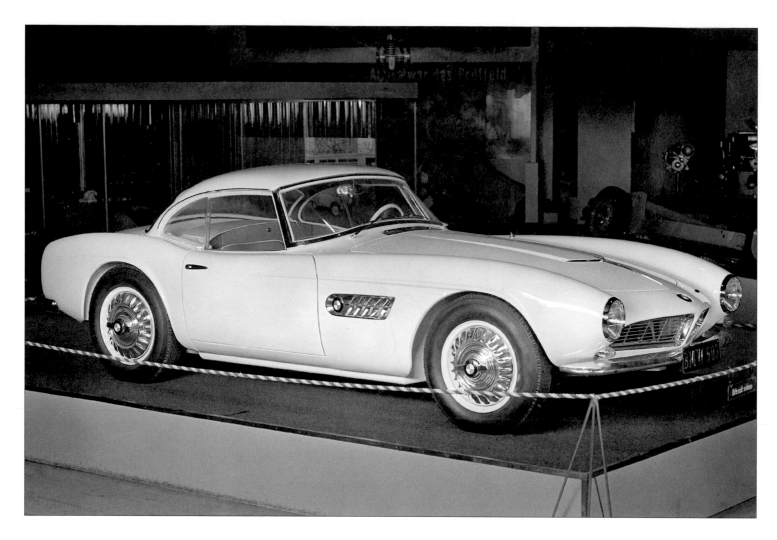

In the 1950s, things were very different. The BMW 507 attempted to bridge the gap between the world of the supercar and that of the grand tourer. Fitted with a 3.2-litre (195.2ci) V8 engine, the car was capable of 217.2km/h (135mph), but it wasn't especially spacious.

pinnacle of that evolution; after all, trying to tame its near-740kW (1000bhp) engine has caused such problems that one has to ask whether anybody will ever try to beat it. With four-wheel drive, carbon brakes and traction control systems galore, getting so much power to the tarmac in a reliable fashion has virtually stumped the company's engineers. All of which begs the question as to what the point of it all is, when to attempt a top-speed run you have to call out the factory's engineers and they have to come and swap the tyres over for you!

In the beginning

With its massively complex chassis, the Veyron is a far cry from the cars which bore the Bugatti name in the 1920s and 1930s. And while those first cars were pretty quick, they weren't the earliest attempts at a supercar. From the time that Karl Benz and Gottlieb Daimler built the very first cars powered by internal-

combustion in the mid-1880s, the die was cast. It wouldn't take long for increasingly powerful cars to be built, for motorsport to get going, and for makers to jump onto the performance and luxury bandwagons.

As early as the Edwardian era there were vehicles that were the supercars of their day; Vauxhall's Prince Henry along with cars from Sunbeam, Stutz and many more were capable of 128.7km/h (80mph) or more. When the more affordable family cars of the time were able to muster a top speed of 64.3km/h (40mph) on a good day, such top speeds were incredible. Indeed, at the start of the twentieth century there were those who claimed that anybody travelling at speeds of 160km/h (100mph) would die because the body wouldn't be able to withstand the strain. But it wasn't long before such speeds were possible, although for a long time they were the exception not the rule.

While the Edwardian era had been a period in which car design and engineering moved up a gear, it was the 1920s and especially the 1930s that were to leave a more permanent mark on the history of the supercar. Not only were increasingly powerful engines being built, but this was also the heyday of the independent coachbuilder. Some of the most glamorous cars ever made were produced in the 1930s, with marques such as Duesenberg, Alfa Romeo and Mercedes all building massively powerful cars that have become some of the most collectable machines of any kind ever created. Then there were cars from marques such as Bentley and Bugatti, the former producing thunderous supercharged behemoths that were likened to lorries on account of their tremendous dimensions. Meanwhile, Mercedes was building its SS, SSK, SSKL and 540K models, with supercharged engines that could propel the cars to speeds of over 160km/h (100mph). They were fantastically exclusive cars that only the most wealthy would ever be able to purchase – both when the cars were new and also now they're collectors' items.

World War II halted supercar development for a few years, but some of the technology used in military and aeronautical environments filtered into top-end road and racing cars once the 1940s were over. Mechanical fuel injection was fitted to the Mercedes 300SL gullwing for example, while supercharging became more and more popular – even though it was nothing new. In time the turbocharger would become equally popular, although it wasn't fitted to a production car until the late 1960s, when Chevrolet fitted it to the Corvair – a car that would go down in history as one of the most dangerous cars ever designed.

As consumerism took hold in the 1950s, luxury goods became increasingly popular and all sorts of companies began building bespoke – and expensive – cars. By the time the 1960s were half-way through there were all sorts of tiny outfits around the globe, attempting to churn out high-performance cars. In Spain there was Pegaso while in France, Facel Vega production was underway. On a larger scale, Germany was busy putting together Mercedes 300SLs, BMW 507s and Porsche was building the 356 – then later the 911. At this stage, Italy wasn't hogging things when it came to building fast cars. Lamborghini didn't get going until the latter half of the 1960s and Ferrari wasn't as well established as it is now – although it was already a force to be reckoned with.

Meanwhile in Britain there were all sorts of fascinating projects getting off the ground – many of them utilizing powerful American V8s to give them plenty of grunt. It was a formula that had worked for Allard, which had been building V8-engined cars since the early 1950s. The AC Cobra and Sunbeam Tiger were two such cars; vehicles which weren't

While it's long been credited with being America's only true supercar, the Chevrolet Corvette got off to a very shaky start. Despite a small initial production run, Chevrolet's dealers were still left with cars they couldn't sell – leading to a radical rethink.

The E-Type Jaguar was claimed to be the world's first affordable production sportscar capable of 241.3km/h (150mph). Fifty years on, the modern equivalent is now artificially restricted to 249.4km/h (155mph) as part of a gentleman's agreement.

lacking in the engine stakes. Sadly they were (at least initially) all too lacking in the chassis department, which meant driving them was solely the domain of those who had no sense of self-preservation. But not all British supercars were scary – some were surprisingly civilized. The first genuine 241.3km/h (150mph) production sports car had been launched at the 1961 Geneva motor show: the Jaguar E-Type. With its svelte lines and relatively affordable price tag, suddenly supercars weren't completely out of reach.

While Europe has long been the focus of the supercar world – at least in terms of producers – America's first supercar was already over a decade old by the time the mid-1960s had arrived. The Chevrolet Corvette had been launched in 1953, and despite very poor sales initially, General Motors decided to stick with it. At first the Corvette was barely even a supercar – its top speed was just over the magic ton and it wasn't that great to drive, so it was no surprise that Ford's Thunderbird outsold it by a ratio of five to one. Yet not only has the Corvette gone on to become

one of the all-time motoring icons, but those early cars are among the most collectable cars around, thanks to their rarity.

By the end of the 1960s, any supercar worth its salt had its engine positioned behind the passenger cell – here was a completely new breed of high-performance car that put dynamics ahead of everything else. The Ford GT40 had pioneered this design in the early 1960s, but that was a race car that happened to be built in tiny numbers for the road. It was the Lamborghini Miura, the chassis of which made its debut at the 1966 Geneva motor show, which created the new template for supercar design. Although at first many people thought the car (and the company) was just a flash in the pan, it was the car that started it all. By the time the 1970s rolled around, in the eyes of many, if a supercar wasn't mid-engined, it wasn't worth bothering with.

Small can be super too
While the cars in this book focus on the most expensive, most powerful and most prestigious models ever made, biggest doesn't necessarily mean best. There's a whole raft of supercars out there that are much less powerful than those featured in these pages, but much smaller, lighter and far more nimble.

Cars such as the Ariel Atom, Grinnall Scorpion or Caterham Seven weigh around a third of the typical V12 Ferrari or Lamborghini. So although they may pack rather less power, it's the power to weight ratio that matters, and with a third of the weight but maybe half of the power, they automatically have a superior power to weight ratio.

One of the key things, though, is that a supercar isn't just about straight-line speed; it's no good being outrageously fast in a straight line if everything goes out the window at the first bend. What's needed is a car that can accelerate quickly, cruise at high speeds, corner impressively so the high speeds can be maintained – and stop impressively too. Apply these criteria to some of the early mid-engined supercars and it doesn't take long to work out that many of them fell very short on one or more of these yardsticks. While acceleration and straight-line speed were no problem for many of the exotic cars being produced during the 1960s, their crude suspension systems and primitive brakes led to the demise of many drivers who simply ran out of road because the cars weren't capable of cornering properly or pulling up from high speeds.

One of the main exponents of the light is best strategy was Colin Chapman, who founded Lotus. His cars were successful because he knew that by saving weight wherever possible, everything else could be kept simple. A car weighing half a ton rather than a full ton didn't need such hefty (and therefore weighty) brakes. It also didn't need such a large engine because its power requirements were that much lower. This in turn led to greater agility and better economy – after all, sports cars should be more about driving fun than anything else, and that wasn't derived purely from high speeds.

The appearance of glassfibre in the 1950s was the catalyst for many low-volume sports cars – and by chance it's also a very light material. While its strength isn't very good, glassfibre is easy to mould to whatever shape is wanted. Without the need to invest in expensive tooling, it's just the ticket for the company that wants to build cars by the dozen rather

The first supercar to introduce four-wheel drive was the Audi quattro, which made its debut in 1980. With grip levels unlike anything seen before, the car was able to dominate the World Rally Championship; it also heralded the dawn of a new era in road cars.

than by the thousand. It was this wonder material that allowed Colin Chapman to produce perhaps the greatest driver's car of its time – the Elan. It wasn't especially fast, but it was especially light and nimble – which also meant it was cheap to run. It was a formula that worked in the 1960s and it's every bit as relevant now, with cars such as the Elise and Exige benefitting from low weight and just moderate power levels to deliver a thrilling driving experience.

Another factor to consider is that as our roads get ever more crowded, it becomes harder and harder to exploit a car's usable performance. It's when this is borne in mind that a mind-bending top speed becomes irrelevant – whether a car can do 321.8km/h (200mph) or 482.7km/h (300mph) at the top end, if it's impossible to ever get above 160km/h (100mph), it all becomes irrelevant. As a result, the focus will increasingly be on making cars enjoyable and incredibly capable at much lower speeds.

The first examples of such cars evolved from rally weapons, with the Audi quattro leading the way with its launch in 1980. This was followed within half a decade by the Lancia Delta HF Integrale, and by the end of the 1990s there were some incredibly capable – and even more affordable offerings produced by

Among the most nimble and capable of all modern supercars is the Subaru Impreza. It'll accelerate to 100km/h (62mph) from standstill in less than five seconds and can do around 241km/h (150mph), yet it's capable of carrying five people and their luggage.

Japanese car makers Mitsubishi and Subaru. Just as Audi and Lanica had done, they were entering the World Rally Championships with saloons such as the Lancer and Impreza, and realized that by packing as much technology into them as possible, the cars would become unbeatable – on the road as well as the track. As power outputs crept up closer and closer to 296kW (400bhp), more and more electronic gadgetry was used to keep the power under control. By keeping weight to a minimum and constantly evolving the engines, tremendous power outputs could be realized without the need to sacrifice reliability.

All this development was focused on giving the cars eye-popping acceleration and even more impressive stopping capabilities, while also allowing them to seemingly defy the laws of physics when it came to cornering abilities. By taking this route it allowed the cars' owners to exploit the chassis at relatively low speeds, as the cars weren't initially capable of especially high speeds anyway. But of course as the various models evolved, power outputs rose along with top speeds – which allowed these cars to offer a very real threat to some of the established supercar brands. At least in terms of abilities, if not image…

The future

With the twenty-first century barely underway, the demands on our oil reserves are greater than ever. Despite this, luxury and performance cars are selling in larger numbers than ever before. With supercars

more usable than they've ever been, more and more people are buying high-performance cars for regular use, while there are more collectors than ever before. So the future is certainly bright, but that doesn't mean things can continue forever as they currently are.

The whole point of supercars is that they are at the cutting edge of technology. Whether it's engine design, construction or materials, the high price of a supercar is at least partly justified by the necessarily high costs of being the first to use a new technology. What the future holds in terms of materials remains to be seen, but surely one of the most likely routes supercar makers will be forced to take is an investment in alternative-fuel propulsion.

While it's unlikely that we're ever going to see an electric Ferrari, there's a good chance that at some point we'll see a hybrid supercar from one of the big car makers – but not necessarily one of the bigger supercar makers. There's also a decent chance that the diesel supercar isn't too far away, although when Mercedes experimented with such a formula in the 1970s, it came to nothing. A series of C-111 prototypes used various engine configurations

This was the future of the supercar according to Mercedes in the early 1970s. The C-111 series experimented with different forms of propulsion including diesel and rotary petrol engines. The series could have been very successful, but Mercedes decided to focus on practical cars instead.

including diesel, but the world wasn't ready for it and the project quietly died.

Of course the fundamental issue is that while the diesel engine would still be using fossil fuel for power, by taking the oil-burning route there would automatically be better fuel consumption. Not only this, but diesel engines are inherently more torquey, and it's torque which gives acceleration while power merely increases the top speed. As the environmentalist and road safety movements gather pace, there's every chance that there will be legislation to restrict the top speeds of cars, forcing supercar makers to maximize the driving pleasure at lower speeds. If that sounds like a recipe for depression, it isn't. Way back in the 1960s, Colin Chapman proved that for a car to be super, there was no need for ultra-high speeds.

1950–1969

With World War II gradually fading into the past, the days of austerity were disappearing extremely quickly. Motorsport was becoming increasingly popular once again and a by-product of this rediscovered popularity was a raft of supercars that were at the very forefront of technology.

While in the early 1950s Ferrari had only just got going, companies such as Mercedes and Jaguar were already well established – and they would lead the supercar charge throughout the 1950s with models such as the 300SL and the D-Type.

The 300SL and the D-Type are featured on the following pages; there were plenty of other cars we could have chosen but which didn't make it. The D-Type had a rival from within its own ranks; the XK range offered glamour and performance while also being relatively affordable. That last trait certainly couldn't be levelled at the offerings of Ferrari or Maserati, but they definitely had style and pace. It was a similar story over at Aston Martin, which was busy building the DB2/4.

Meanwhile, over in Germany Porsche was busy developing the longest-lived of all the supercars – the 911. From very humble beginnings the car was

Although the mechanical layout of the 911 isn't one that many would suggest is ideal, the car has gone on to become the most enduring supercar ever. It offers pace, practicality and reliability in one stylish package – how could Porsche ever kill it off?

developed ever further to become a four-wheel drive monster that could humble all but the very fastest of supercars. Despite this it remained eminently usable and reliable, characteristics that couldn't be levelled at many of its rivals.

In America the muscle car was king, and while some of the power outputs were little short of comical, there was no doubt that vehicles such as the Dodge Charger Daytona and Ford Shelby Mustang GT500 were serious pieces of kit. Brutal they may have been, but they were also incredibly fast.

Perhaps the greatest surprise of the 1960s was the emergence of Ford as a maker of fully fledged supercars. Not only that, but supercars that could take on and beat Ferrari at its own game, which was endurance racing. Then at the other end of the scale there were tiny outfits trying to produce world-beaters – which is just what AC did with its Cobra, thanks to rather a large dose of help from the American Carroll Shelby. In fact, if there's one thing that hasn't changed in the world of supercars over the decades, it's the diversity of offerings – and long may that continue.

AC Cobra

The Cobra looks far more aggressive than the Ace thanks to those flared wheel arches. The 427 got even wider, with front and rear tracks increased by around 101mm (4in) to improve roadholding still further.

Roll hoops weren't fitted to all Cobras; they were installed for the 427 S/C (Street/Competition) model, which was a racer modified for road use. This ploy helped AC get rid of unwanted competition cars.

The first Cobras ran on wire wheels, but these couldn't cope with the massive torque they had to transmit to the tarmac. Halibrand alloy wheels were then fitted, which were also used by the GT40s.

An aluminium body, made by hand, was one of the key characteristics of a Cobra. From the twenty-first century, a carbon fibre option was available from the factory – which is even lighter but stronger.

One of the main ingredients is a V8 engine, for maximum power and torque. The first car featured a 4.3-litre (262.3ci) powerplant, but by 1965 this was a full 7 litres (427ci).

Take a look through any kit car magazine and you'll see that the market is swamped with lookalikes of AC's brutal Cobra – and for good reason. Not only is it one of the most beautifully aggressive cars ever designed, but it's also got a reputation for being an unattainable monster that's incredibly tricky to drive. For most people, the only taste of Cobra driving they'll ever get is if they build one themselves. That's exactly what Carroll Shelby did with the original, in

It's no wonder that the Cobra has gone on to become the most copied supercar ever, with curves like those. You can look as hard as you like, but you're not going to find any straight lines anywhere.

1962, when he transplanted a 192.4kW (260bhp), 4260cc (256ci) Ford V8 into an AC Ace. It was a simple formula; take one civilized British sports car and shoehorn a powerful V8 into it, creating a machine that was far more than the sum of its parts.

European V8 sports car

The Cobra wasn't the first British car to be fitted with raw American power; it was a formula that had served Allard well since the early 1950s. When Carroll Shelby wanted a car to beat Ferrari in circuit racing during the 1960s, he could see the Ace's potential. Shelby had already been at the sharp end of motor

racing, having raced for years and won Le Mans for Aston Martin in 1959. By 1960 he'd been forced to retire from racing because of heart problems, so Shelby set himself two goals. The first was to construct a successful V8-powered European-styled sports car – and the second was to beat Enzo Ferrari at his own game. This second ambition was because of a personal grudge harboured by Shelby, after he'd been approached by Ferrari to become a works driver. When Shelby wanted to talk terms he was treated in Ferrari's usual offhand manner, so the partnership turned sour before it had even begun.

When Shelby retired from racing he had no idea how he'd put his V8-engined car into production. He approached various car makers such as GM, Jensen, Aston Martin and Healey, but none were interested apart from Donald Healey. Unfortunately, his new partnership with BMC (British Motor Corporation) meant such co-operation was impossible, which was when Shelby turned to AC. The company was based in Surrey, and it had a reputation for building sports cars. But its product range was getting long in the tooth – the Ace had been launched in 1953. Its six-cylinder engines were equally ancient – what was needed was a healthy dose of V8 power.

Shelby heard of AC's problems and contacted the company, suggesting that he transplant an eight-cylinder engine into the Ace. AC was keen to progress the project, even though Shelby had no idea whose engine he'd use. That conundrum was soon solved when Shelby got talking to Dave Evans, head of Ford's NASCAR racing programme. Evans had at his disposal some examples of Ford's all-new V8 engine that had been introduced in the 1961 Fairlane.

The Cobra's interior was predictably spartan, but it featured everything you needed to make sure it was all working properly. And being very simply engineered, the chances are that it would keep working properly.

Although the powerplant was a cast iron unit, thanks to its thin-wall casting technology it was virtually as light as an alloy item.

Design overhaul

With the engine sorted it was a case of beefing-up the Ace's bodywork and coming up with a chassis that could take the torque. By January 1962 the prototype was ready and within a year the car had won its first races. That was when the Cobra went on sale in Ford dealerships, in a bid to boost the company's image – although the really big boost came in October 1963 when the 427 (7-litre) engine was first installed.

These first 427-powered cars were virtually impossible to drive thanks to their huge power and incredibly crude chassis. The answer was to introduce an overhauled design, with much more strengthening and coil-spring suspension. It was still a brute, but at least it was slightly more driveable!

More than four decades on the car is still in production, although AC has gone through some tumultuous times in between. It now has a carbon fibre body and is supplied in kit form only, so it's ironic that a modern-day owner has to go out and source their own powerplant – although it would be a travesty to fit anything other than a V8!

AC Cobra	
Years of production	1962–8
Displacement	4727cc (284ci)
Configuration	Front-mounted V8
Transmission	Four-speed manual, rear-wheel drive
Power	200.5kW (271bhp) @ 6000rpm
Torque	423.9Nm (314lb ft) @ 3400rpm
Top speed	218.8km/h (138mph)
0–60mph (0–97km/h)	5.5sec
Power to weight ratio	210.1kW/ton (284bhp/ton)
Number built	1137

Bizzarini GT Strada 5300

Those swoopy lines were penned in-house, although they were refined by Giorgetto Giugiaro during his time with Bertone.

Those gorgeous Campagnolo alloy wheels measured 381mm (15in) across, and were made of lightweight aluminium alloy. They were 152.4mm (6in) wide at the front and the rears were an inch wider.

Although the GT Strada was heavily based on the Iso Grifo, the Bizzarini featured a bodyshell made of alloy to keep the weight down — it was also more suited to low-volume production.

The Bizzarini's V8 engine was supplied by Chevrolet — it was normally seen in the Corvette. With a capacity of 5.3 litres (323.3ci) (hence the car's name), power and torque were more than enough. It was easiest for Bizzarini to buy the engine and gearbox as a unit, direct from Chevrolet. As a result, the four-speed transmission is also the same as the Corvette's.

Double wishbones with coil springs and telescopic shock absorbers were fitted at the front. The rear featured trailing arms with a de Dion tube, Panhard rod, coil springs and telescopic shock absorbers.

With a CV as impressive as Giotto Bizzarini's, it's hard to see how an attempt to produce his own supercar could fail. He'd been instrumental in some of the most prestigious Italian supercars ever seen; Ferrari's 250 GTO, Lamborghini's V12 engine and the Iso Rivolta, the world's first monocoque supercar. The Rivolta had been developed into the Grifo, and it was this car that was to prove the basis for Bizzarini's own supercar, the GT Strada.

Bizzarini had first become involved with the Iso company when it asked him to help design and develop its first car, the Rivolta. This was later

Those scoops behind the rear wheels had strong overtones of the Ferrari 250GTO about them, while there was little chance of seeing anything useful through that sharply sloped rear window. But those curves were something else!

rebodied as the Grifo, a far more exotic-looking car – which was just how Bizzarini liked things. Bizzarini then started to race a competition version of the Grifo (most notably at the 1964 and 1965 Le Mans races), and it was this that led him to start building the car under his own name.

In a smart move (which did little to help his relationship with Iso), Bizzarini registered the Grifo name so that Iso could no longer use it. A deal was consequently done to sell the name back to Iso in return for enough parts for Bizzarini to build 50 road cars with his own name on them. Why Iso didn't just come up with a new name for its sports car isn't recorded – but it would have been the obvious thing to do!

Lightweight chassis

Although there are quite a few visual similarities between the Grifo and the GT, the body was completely redesigned. Also, while the Iso featured steel panelling, the Bizzarini's bodyshell was made of lightweight alloy. This not only helped improve the power to weight ratio, but it was also better suited to the tiny production numbers involved – typically, just two or three cars would be produced each month.

Bizzarini GT Strada 5300

Years of production	1965–9
Displacement	5354cc (321.2ci)
Configuration	Front-engined V8
Transmission	Four-speed manual, rear-wheel drive
Power	270.1kW (365bhp) @ 6000rpm
Torque	508.9Nm (377lb ft) @ 3500rpm
Top speed	275.1km/h (171mph)
0–60mph (0–97km/h)	6.0sec
Power to weight ratio	216kW/ton (292bhp/ton)
Number built	139

To get the project going, Bizzarini rented a factory in Turin. He hired a team to build the chassis for him, but once constructed it was clear that they were too brittle for the torque that the 5.3-litre (323.3ci) V8 was producing.

After some hasty re-engineering the car was offered for sale during 1965. The suspension was by coil springs all round with wishbones at the front and a de Dion rear axle. The Corvette's four-speed manual gearbox was fitted, but there were all sorts of options available to buyers. The idea of the Strada was that it was built on a bespoke basis, so the engine could be tuned to suit the buyer; it was also possible to choose the rear axle ratio. In standard form, however, there was 270.1kW (365bhp) on tap and 508.9Nm (377lb ft) of torque – enough to catapult the car from a standing start to 60mph (97km/h) in around six seconds.

American sales

By 1966, Bizzarini was ready to start selling his cars in America. A deal was done with US importer John Fitch, and while the cars were essentially the same mechanically, the bodyshells were made of glassfibre instead of the previous alloy. The other significant difference between the European and American models was the fitting of independent rear suspension for US cars in place of the de Dion set-up which was seen elsewhere.

In 1967, Bizzarini had a brush with bankruptcy, but was baled out by a group of 'investors'. The problem was that they didn't invest anything – they merely took even more money out of the company. The problem was that it was cash the company didn't have, so it was only a matter of time before everything went belly-up. That finally happened in 1969, after a claimed 139 GTs had been built – although the real number is probably significantly lower than this.

However, that's not the end of the Bizzarini story. The marque was revived in 1990, with the BZ 2001GT. Based on the Ferrari Testarossa, the car was developed in conjunction with US property developer Barry Watkins – but it proved stillborn after the car was universally shunned.

Wherever you looked on the Bizzarini there was some form of adornment. There was no shortage of scoops, slats and ducts to either feed cooling air to the engine or the brakes, or to channel hot air away.

Dodge Charger Daytona

The Charger Daytona featured lots of detail changes over the standard car, such as aerodynamic fairings for the windscreen surround, a different roof and new rear window. The brakes and suspension were also uprated.

There were two engines available in the Charger Daytona; a 277.5kW (375bhp) 7.2-litre (437ci) unit or a Hemi that displaced 7 litres (427ci). Whichever unit was fitted, the car was capable of nearly 321.8km/h (200mph).

Chrysler's designers reckoned that decreasing the drag by 15 per cent would be equivalent to increasing power by 62.9Kw (85bhp). That's why the shovel nose was grafted on – which added 457mm (18in) to the car's length.

Buyers of the Charger Daytona could specify a manual gearbox or an automatic. If they chose the latter it was a Torqueflite three-speed unit; the manual offered a choice of four ratios.

That rear wing was essential to provide the downforce necessary as the car crept closer to 321.8km/h (200mph). A small one was fitted initially, but the boot lid couldn't be opened; the answer was to fit a 584mm (23in) high fin.

The Charger Daytona was all about going fast – nothing else mattered. For that reason the aerodynamics had to be spot on, which was why the sloped nose was grafted on, although the pop-up headlamps didn't help when switched on!

If you're a film or TV fan you'll know all about Vanishing Point, Bullitt and The Dukes of Hazzard. All cult viewing – and all featuring a Dodge Charger. But all three featured not just any old Charger; central to all of them was a second-generation model, built for just four years between 1967 and 1970. It was chosen for good reason; here was a car that looked dramatic, had masses of performance on tap – and was also successful in competition.

The Charger story started in 1957, the year in which America's big three (General Motors, Ford, Chrysler) officially agreed with each other to withdraw factory backing in motorsport. That meant there was no oval or drag racing allowed, but by the mid-1960s Chevrolet had started to surreptitiously sponsor motorsport. Ford followed suit, which left Chrysler

feeling rather left out. The result was an order in 1964 for Chrysler's engineers to come up with an outstanding powerplant that would go down in history as an all-time great. The response was the 7-litre (427ci) Hemi, which was loosely based on the Chrysler Firepower V8 that had been produced between 1951 and 1958.

When the engine was unveiled, it was claimed to produce 307.1kW (415bhp) with a single four-barrel carburettor, and a massive 314.5kW (425bhp) when equipped with a pair of carbs. The thing was, these figures were the claimed outputs – the real figures were actually rather higher. Not like Chrysler to understate the case…

Racing success

The powerplant was unveiled in February 1964, just before the Daytona 500 race. While all the other teams were struggling to top 273.5km/h (170mph), the Hemi-powered cars were sitting at 281.6km/h (175mph) for lap after lap. It was no surprise therefore, that a Hemi-powered car took first place, with the next four cars also packing Hemi engines.

Such success sent Ford and Chevrolet running to motorsport officials, complaining that this was not the done thing. Their complaints fell on deaf ears, but NASCAR officials did decide that any engine which powered a racer car would have to be available (in some form) in a road car. Chrysler was furious, and withdrew from motorsport for the 1965 season – leaving Ford to win 48 out of the 50 races. Then there was a change of heart – Chrysler reckoned it might as well put the Hemi into a road car, then thrash Ford and Chevrolet on America's race tracks. And that's just what it did, taking the 1966 season…

Road car version

To be eligible for racing the Hemi, the engine had to go in a road car, which is where the Charger came in. Launched in 1966, this was a fastback version of the medium-sized Coronet with a choice of 5.3- or 6.3-litre (323.3 or 382.4ci) V8 engines. For 1967 there were initially few changes to the fastback Charger, but then in August of that year came the news; there was to be a new model, headed by a R/T (Road and Track) version that packed a 7.2-litre (437ci) engine. That model was the Magnum, but there was also a 7-litre (427ci) Hemi option available, which had a four-barrel carburettor.

These top two engines were only available when the car was ordered in R/T specification, which meant they were thinly disguised racers for the road. They also didn't carry the normal warranties while the cost was a whopping extra 30 per cent over the standard models. All this was because the R/T cars were what Chrysler termed speciality vehicles, which were effectively homologation specials. And they were certainly outrageously fast; as well as topping nearly

Dodge Charger Daytona	
Years of production	1969
Displacement	7211cc (432.6ci)
Configuration	Front-mounted V8
Transmission	Four-speed manual, rear-wheel drive
Power	277.5kW (375bhp) @ 4600rpm
Torque	648Nm (480lb ft) @ 3200rpm
Top speed	321.8km/h (200mph)
0–60mph (0–97km/h)	4.8sec
Power to weight ratio	160.5kW/ton (217bhp/ton)
Number built	504

257.4km/h (160mph), they could sprint to 60mph (97km/h) in less than five seconds.

Then came the knockout punch; the Charger Daytona of 1969. The previous year hadn't been a good race season for Chrysler, so the company resolved to build something more aerodynamic – and the Daytona was the result. With its lengthened (and more slippery) nose, plus a 584mm (23in) high rear wing, the car certainly had presence. It also offered success to a certain degree, but not as much as Ford's cars – the blue oval took 29 wins against Chrysler's 22. This was when Chrysler gave up, ushering in a new era in conservatism with its cars. Things would never be the same.

The proportions of the Daytona were completely wild, with the bonnet seemingly going on forever. That pointed nose cone added 457.2mm (18in) to the length while the rear spoiler was the largest ever seen on a production car.

Ferrari 250GT SWB

While the road cars were equipped with a 108.1-litre (23.78-gallon) fuel tank to allow for some luggage space, the racers didn't need such practicalities. That's why they were fitted with enormous 154.5-litre (34-gallon) tanks.

The SWB was built to win races, which is why the final drive ratios could be tailored to suit the circuit being tackled. There were seven different ratios available, offering theoretical top speeds of between 201.1 and 267.1km/h (125mph and 166mph).

To help keep the front brakes cool air ducts were built into the nose. These fed air to the brakes which was then exhausted via the vents behind the front wheel arch. There were also such vents at the rear.

Of the 163 cars built, 74 were racers and the other 89 were road cars. The competition versions featured side windows made of plastic (to reduce weight) while road cars took conventional glass.

Giving the 250 its name was an all-alloy V12 engine, located in the car's nose. With each cylinder displacing 250cc (15.3ci), the total capacity was 3 litres (182.1ci) – with total power being 207.2kW (280bhp) at 7000rpm.

Few would disagree that Ferrari can be credited with having produced some of the most beautiful cars ever built, but surely the most attractive design of all must be the 250GT SWB. While many of Ferrari's creations are brutally aggressive, the 250GT SWB merely looks muscular with perfect proportions and all those gorgeous curves.

The 250GT SWB (Short Wheelbase Berlinetta) came about because of changes in the rules for motor racing during the 1950s. Speeds were extremely high and

Seen in profile, it's hard to fault the lines of the 250GT SWB. There's just the right amount of subtle aggression to show the car means business, while overall there's an understated look. Not like the modern Ferraris...

there was a fear that safety was being compromised. This fear was borne out by the terrible disaster at the 1955 Le Mans race, when over 80 people died. The decision was consequently made to force companies to develop racers that resembled cars that could be bought for the road. Up to this point, too many racers were single or twin-seaters that bore little resemblance to anything a customer could buy for the road.

Racers and road cars

Such a scenario suited Ferrari perfectly, as it was positioned to sell cars that looked like the ones winning races around the world. It already built the long wheelbase 250GT Berlinetta, so engineering a spin-off from this wouldn't prove to be a problem. The SWB was ultimately derived from a particular version of the 250GT called the Tour de France, named after the famous road race, which Ferrari had won each year from 1956 to 1961.

During 1959, Pininfarina built seven examples of the Tour de France which featured a more rounded nose. While these weren't identical to the final SWB models, they incorporated most of the features seen in

Ferrari 250GT SWB

Years of production	1959–62
Displacement	2953cc (177.1ci)
Configuration	Front-mounted V12
Transmission	Four-speed manual, rear-wheel drive
Power	207.2kW (280bhp) @ 7000rpm
Torque	274Nm (203lb ft) @ 5500rpm
Top speed	225.3km/h (140mph)
0–60mph (0–97km/h)	6.5sec
Power to weight ratio	162.8kW/ton (220bhp/ton)
Number built	163

the SWB when it broke cover later that year. The debut of the 250GT SWB took place at the 1959 Paris salon, the car having been built by Scaglietti, and predictably, the car went down a storm. Because the car was now 200mm (7.8in) shorter than the car it was based on, it looked much more lithe. All that reduction was in the wheelbase, making the car more nimble while also helping to make it more aerodynamic as well as lighter.

The 60-degree V12 engine wasn't new, but it was a revised version of the unit seen in the standard 250GT. Displacing 3 litres (183ci), there was up to 207.2kW (280bhp) at the driver's disposal along with 274Nm (203lb ft) of torque. It was fitted with seven main bearings and both the block and heads were constructed from alloy. Whereas the earlier engine featured spark plugs on the inside of the V, the new powerplant featured them on the outside. This allowed for quicker plug changes during races, but it also meant the combustion process was more complete. Feeding the V12 was a trio of twin-choke Weber carburettors, but serious racers doubled the carb count in a bid to throw as much petrol into the engine as possible. Because of the bespoke nature of the car, it was also possible to request specific camshaft profiles and even compression ratios. The result of all this work could be as much as 207.2kW

(280bhp), although lesser cars generated closer to 117.6kW (240bhp). Whatever the power output, the engines were always the epitome of reliability, which is what mattered the most in racing.

The Paris Salon

When the car was unveiled at the Paris Salon, it was a racer. But the car had also been developed to be sold as a road car which could also be raced if required. This particular version carried Lusso badges, which meant there were a few more creature comforts fitted, while power was also slightly down, at 117.6kW (240bhp). One of the other key differences was with the materials used; road cars featured a bodyshell made mainly of steel, while the racers incorporated much more alloy in their construction. To reduce weight further, plastic side windows were fitted and the interior trim was ditched.

By the time production ended in 1962, 163 250GT SWBs had been built. Of these, 74 were racers while the other 89 were road cars. However, the 250GT SWB paled into insignificance against what was to follow – the legendary 250GTO.

The well-stocked dash allowed the driver to keep tabs on what was going on under the bonnet. Despite the very high prices that Ferrari charged for its cars, it wasn't particularly well put together though.

Ferrari 365 GTB/4 (Daytona)

There was no monocoque construction for the Daytona. Instead there was a conventional chassis built from square tubes that were welded together. This arrangement meant the bodyshell wasn't required for torsional stiffness.

Mounted at the front was a V12 engine, displacing 4.4 litres (267ci). There were four gear-driven overhead camshafts and each cylinder displaced 365cc (21.9ci), which is how the car took its official title of 365GTB/4.

VRY 506H

Graypaul Motors Ltd

At first the Daytona was fitted with four headlamps under plexiglass covers. But they weren't legal for the US market, which is why the system was replaced by more conventional pop-up units.

To help with the weight distribution, the five-speed gearbox was mounted at the back of the car in unit with the rear axle. It was connected to the engine via a torque tube, in which ran the propshaft.

In true racing tradition, the wheels weren't bolted on – instead they featured knock-on spinners. Owners could choose from Borrani wire wheels or Cromodora alloys, which were 381mm (15in) in diameter.

Nobody can deny that the Ferrari 365GTB/4 (also unofficially known as the Daytona) is one of the most arresting supercars ever designed. When it was launched in 1968 it was also one of the most capable. But even before it had turned a wheel, the car was old-fashioned. The way forward for ultra-high performance cars was with the engine behind the driver and passenger, yet the Daytona still featured an engine located in the car's nose. It may have helped no end when it came to packaging, but that was hardly the most important thing in a car of this nature. Compromises were the last things that were needed, and Lamborghini had shown the way with its Miura that was already two years old when the new Ferrari broke cover.

Weight distribution

Despite the traditional layout of the Daytona, it still had a weight distribution of 52:48 front:rear, so it wasn't as though the balance was completely out of kilter. But where Ferrari had initially assumed that Lamborghini would never be a serious rival, its cutting-edge designs showed that Ferrari could no longer rest on its laurels. While the 365GTB/4 was little more than an update of its predecessor the 275GTB/4, what was really needed was a completely new car. But that wouldn't arrive until 1971, when the Boxer made its first appearance.

By mounting the engine as far back as possible in the nose, while also locating the gearbox at the back of the car, Ferrari managed to achieve almost perfect weight distribution. It also helped that the V12 powerplant was an all-alloy unit, helping to keep its weight to a minimum. After all, it wasn't as though the engine was physically small, with its 4.4-litre (267ci) displacement. The unit was also mounted as low down in the frame as possible, to help ensure the centre of gravity wasn't any higher than it needed to be. This was facilitated by using a dry-sump system instead of a conventional wet-sump, which helped to reduce the height of the engine while also avoiding the possibility of oil surge during high-speed cornering.

Straight from the decade that taste forgot, the Daytona's interior wasn't especially easy on the eye, with that two-tone colour scheme. But despite this, it was beautifully designed and very classy with lots of leather and chrome.

With 261.2kW (353bhp) available, along with 430.6Nm (319lb ft) of torque, it was no surprise that the Daytona had a top speed of around 273.5km/h (170mph). If that seems quick now, in the late 1960s it was a phenomenal speed for a road car. That meant the very best engineering had to be incorporated elsewhere in the car to allow it to be as usable as possible. To that end there were ventilated disc brakes both front and rear, which worked extremely well; they had to be punished severely before they began to suffer from fade. Measuring more than 279mm (11in) across, these brakes were made possible by the use of 381mm (15in) wheels. Two styles of wheel were available, depending on the owner's preferences. Along with more modern alloy wheels, there were also traditional Borrani wire wheels on offer.

The suspension also had to be pretty decent to cope with the sorts of forces generated by spirited driving of the Daytona. That's why unequal-length double wishbones were employed, with coil springs and telescopic dampers. These were joined by anti-roll bars at the front as well as the rear.

Coupés and convertibles

Although the factory claimed that the Daytona tipped the scales at around 1272kg (2805lb), when magazines weighed the car independently, they found that the real weight was around 25 per cent more. With this in mind it's even more impressive that the car was capable of despatching the 0–60mph (0–97km/h) sprint in under six seconds while the quarter-mile dash could be dismissed in less than 14 seconds. As well as the coupés which rolled

While everybody considers this to be the classic Daytona look, retractable headlamps were only fitted from 1971. For the first few years of production, faired-in headlamps were fitted – but few of these cars remain.

off the production lines, there were also around 100 spyders (convertibles) built, which have gone on to become extremely collectable. Even rarer though are the competition models which were built by the factory for entry in endurance racing at the hands of privateers. With 296kW (400bhp) available, the top speed rose to a genuine 289.6km/h (180mph). But these cars were still quickly outclassed by the mid-engined beasts that by then had begun to dominate.

Ferrari 365 GTB/4 (Daytona)

Years of production	1969–73
Displacement	4390cc (263.4ci)
Configuration	Front-mounted V12
Transmission	Five-speed manual, rear-wheel drive
Power	261.2kW (353bhp) @ 7500rpm
Torque	430.6Nm (319lb ft) @ 5500rpm
Top speed	280km/h (174mph)
0–60mph (0–97km/h)	5.4sec
Power to weight ratio	162.8kW/ton (220bhp/ton)
Number built	1406

Ford GT40

From start to finish the Ford small-block V8 was fitted. Initially it displaced 4.2 litres (254.9ci), but this was quickly enlarged to 4.7 litres (282.5ci). By the time the final cars were built for the last two seasons, they displaced 5 litres (303.5ci).

Ford decided not to position the radiator at the rear of the GT40, close to where the engine was located. Instead, the nose housed the radiator, with the coolant pipes running the length of the car.

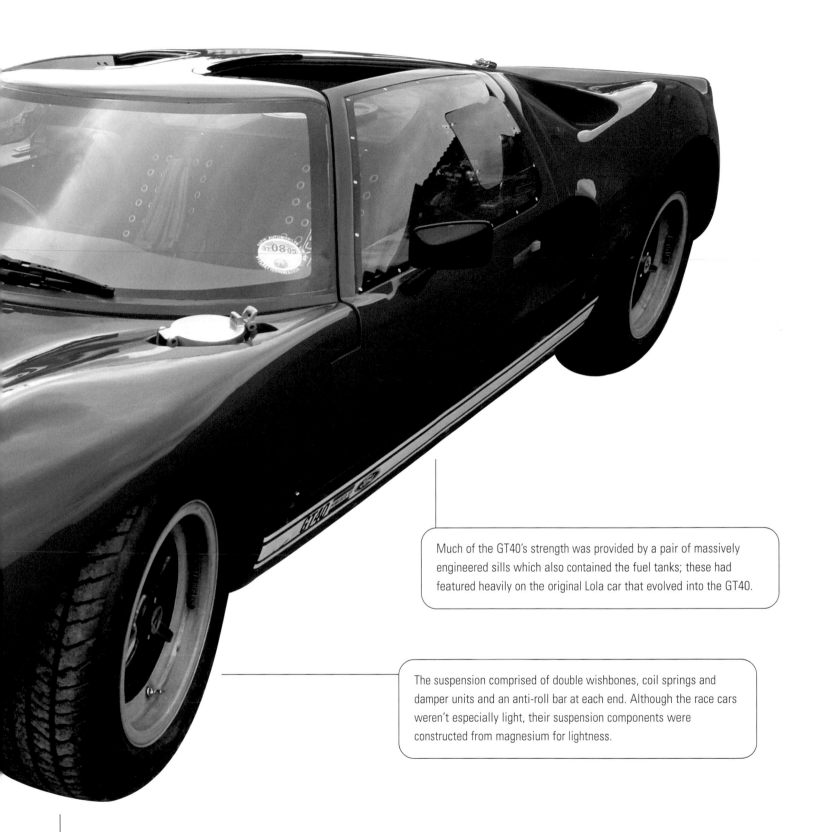

Much of the GT40's strength was provided by a pair of massively engineered sills which also contained the fuel tanks; these had featured heavily on the original Lola car that evolved into the GT40.

The suspension comprised of double wishbones, coil springs and damper units and an anti-roll bar at each end. Although the race cars weren't especially light, their suspension components were constructed from magnesium for lightness.

The Halibrand alloy wheels offered immense strength with great lightness. The first GT40s had been fitted with wire wheels, but these were distorted too easily by the levels of torque they were asked to transmit.

If you were much over 1.8m (6ft) tall, you could forget being able to clamber into the GT40's cockpit. Not only was there very little in the way of headroom, but access was terrible thanks to the massively wide sills.

Ford built the GT40 with one aim in mind – and that was to put an end to Ferrari's domination of endurance racing. When Ford had approached Ferrari in a take-over bid during 1963, things were going very well until the last minute. Assuming the deal was in the bag, Ford's directors were furious that all their efforts had come to nothing, which is why they determined there and then that Ferrari would have to be taken down a peg or two.

It was decided from the outset that the car would be built in the UK, because that's where the most talented race-car engineers and designers were located. The car would be powered by an American Ford V8 engine, which would be the usual large, unstressed unit that could easily be tuned to develop huge amounts of power for the circuit. The car was designed at Ford's American design centre, in Dearborn. But its construction took place in the UK; the glassfibre body panels were constructed in England while the cars were assembled in Slough, at Ford's Advanced Vehicle factory.

Design

The GT40 was based on a Lola V8-powered prototype which had been designed by Eric Broadley. It had run in the 1963 Le Mans 24-Hour race, but had retired; despite this, Ford reckoned the car would provide just the basis it needed for its own endurance racer. Lola's race car provided the strong steel monocoque around which were hung the glassfibre panels. The car was initially known as the GT, but because it stood all of 40in high it became known as the GT40; the carbon copy that Ford produced four decades later stood 44in higher, but would be known simply as the GT.

Sitting in the middle of the GT40 was a 4.2-litre (254.9ci) Ford V8, but once production (if you can call it that) got under way, this was soon changed to a 4.7-litre (282.5ci) unit to give more power and torque. There was double wishbone suspension all round, along with coil springs and damper units. An anti-roll bar was also fitted front and rear, while disc brakes hauled the car down from the 321.8km/h (200mph) top speeds that the racers were capable of.

Although the GT40 was designed as a race car, Ford realized the PR potential of making some road cars available for wealthy customers. While the GT40 didn't make an especially civilized road car, it did offer immense performance as well as jaw-dropping looks. However, despite the GT40's Le Mans success throughout the 1960s, sales were very hard to come by – not helped very much by the list price of £6450. This was at a time when a decent house would have cost around the same!

Le Mans

Ford first ran GT40s at Le Mans in 1964, but success was conspicuous by its absence – although Phil Hill did manage to notch up a fastest lap during the race. A new strategy was needed, and that was delivered by Ford's new competitions manager – Carroll Shelby. He increased the displacement of the V8 to 7 litres (427ci) with new MkII cars, but the biggest change was to come with a move in production to the US. These so-called J models were based around a bonded honeycomb chassis, in a bid to reduce weight – the original GT40 was not a light car. But because of the change in production, none of the cars were ready for the 1966 Le Mans race. Instead a mixture of MkI and MkII cars were campaigned – with a trio of MkIIIs crossing the line together, to give Ford its first Le Mans win.

Although some GT40s were built for the road for selected wealthy customers, it was usually the race track that was the true home of the car.

Ford GT40

Years of production	1964–9
Displacement	4738cc (284.2ci)
Configuration	Mid-mounted V8
Transmission	Five-speed manual, rear-wheel drive
Power	226.4kW (306bhp) @ 6000rpm
Torque	444.1Nm (329lb ft) @ 4200rpm
Top speed	263.9km/h (164mph)
0–60mph (0–97km/h)	5.3sec
Power to weight ratio	227.1kW/ton (307bhp/ton)
Number built	133 (all types)

In 1967, JW Automotive took over Ford's Slough facility, to focus on building road-going cars. The J model racers would continue to be built by Ford in the US, and it would be these which would take on Le Mans. In 1967 Ford decided to quit while at the top, but in private hands the GT40 went on to win in 1968 and again in 1969, with the Gulf Oil-sponsored 'Mirage' cars.

Ford Shelby Mustang GT500

The extra pair of driving lights set into the radiator grille were actually the high beams for the standard lights. The outer pair of glasses were for dipped beam only, a configuration which was illegal in some US states.

The nose of the Shelby Mustang was 76mm (3in) longer than standard, to make it look a lot more menacing. The radiator grille was also recessed more deeply for added aggression.

The GT500 didn't appear until 1967, which was the year that Ford extended the roofline to the rear of the Mustang. This gave Shelby the perfect opportunity to blend a rear spoiler into the panelwork.

People who had bought the Mustang GT350 felt that it was too uncompromising for the road, not least of all with its ultra-stiff suspension. As a result, the GT500 had softer suspension for greater comfort.

The GT500's weight was quite a problem, as it tipped the scales at 1493kg (3292lb). The original Mustang weighed 1136kg (2504.8lb), but the GT500 had only 32.6kW (49bhp) more power. It was also nose-heavy, with 57 per cent of the weight at the front.

When it went on sale in 1964, the Ford Mustang became the fastest-selling car in history. In its first year in the showrooms, a whopping 418,812 found buyers and by the end of the second year of sales, a million had been sold. There was a huge range of options and engines available – no two Mustangs needed to be the same, and the car could be all things to all people – a shopping hack, a sports car or something flash for the weekend if the drop-top option was chosen.

The world first saw the first Mustang at the April 1964 New York World's Fair – here was an affordable car that buyers could personalize, with powerplants ranging from mild to wild. For the faint-hearted there were straight-sixes on offer, in 2.7-litre (163.8ci) and 3.27-litre (198.4ci) flavours. Anyone with a stronger constitution could opt for a V8 – if a 4.2-litre (254.9ci) unit was too tame it was possible to buy a 4.7-litre (289ci) one instead, with either two-barrel or four-barrel carbs. True power junkies opted for the Hi-po 289 (known as the K-Code option), which was a 4.7-litre (285.2ci) V8 with enough tweaks for it to give 200.5kW (271bhp) – and if that wasn't enough, there was always the Shelby GT350 from 1965. This was based on a 289 Hi-po but was even more powerful.

SSCA Championships

The Mustang GT350 had been created towards the end of 1964 with the express intention of winning the 1965 SCCA (Sports Car Club of America) Championship, raising Ford's sporting profile in the process. It was the work of Carroll Shelby, who by this stage was masterminding Ford's domination of the Le Mans 24-Hour race. Shelby had already had incredible success with Ford's V8 engines in his Cobras, so he suggested to Ford that he should modify the Mustang to take on the then-unbeatable Corvettes. Ford happily accepted and the result was the Shelby

The appearance in 1967 of a more aggressive roofline paved the way for an even more fierce version of the Mustang. Few complained that the GT350 available previously was too slow, but that didn't stop Ford upping the power.

Mustang GT350, which used the same engine as found in the Cobra 289. Liveried in the American racing colours of white with two blue stripes, they were raced with a lot of success in both American and European events.

Weight and fuel economy

For 1967 the Mustang bodystyle was altered, with the roofline sloping all the way to the back of the car. The change brought with it a new model to the Shelby line-up; the GT500. It featured a 7-litre (427ci) engine, pumping out well over 259kW (350bhp). Where the early Shelby Mustangs were very competition-oriented, the 1967 and 1968 cars were more of a combination between performance and luxury.

Ford Shelby Mustang GT500

Years of production	1967–9
Displacement	7013cc (420.7ci)
Configuration	Front-mounted V8
Transmission	Four-speed manual, rear-wheel drive
Power	262.7kW (355bhp) @ 5400rpm
Torque	567Nm (420lb ft) @ 3200rpm
Top speed	225.3km/h (140mph)
0–60mph (0–97km/h)	7.2sec
Power to weight ratio	176.1kW/ton (238bhp/ton)
Number built	4123

Suspension rates were softer, with less harsh anti-roll bars and Gabriel shock absorbers in place of the previous Koni items. While this increased the comfort levels, it did little for the handling – not least of all because the GT500 was more nose-heavy than previous models. While the GT350 had weighed 1273kg (2806.9lb), the GT500 was a hefty 220kg (485.1lb) more. The problem was that much of this extra weight was concentrated at the front, wrecking the balance of the car in the process. While the GT350 had featured a weight distribution of 53:47 front:rear, the GT500's was 57:43.

Another problem the GT500 had was that of its thirst. While fuel was cheap, buyers didn't like the idea of a car that guzzled fuel at the rate of around 10mpg – or even 6mpg as one magazine managed to achieve. Despite this, at the end of 1968 a more

While the GT500 didn't look much different from lesser derivatives of the Mustang, the basic car's lines were exactly right anyway. There was just the right amount of aggression, with that stubby nose and haunches over the rear wheels.

powerful GT500 KR was launched, which featured the 428 Cobra Jet engine. Production of the Shelby Mustangs ceased at the end of 1969, when Ford's own high performance had mostly taken over.

The Mustang remains in production, although it has as much in common with the original as the new Beetle does with its 1940s namesake. But with Ford celebrating its centenary in 2004, things started to look a bit more rosy – as part of its drive to cash in on its past, the Mustang concept was earmarked for production. As it was more than 30 years since there had been a pretty Mustang, it was long overdue.

Iso Grifo

When the Grifo was introduced, many of its rivals weren't especially efficient aerodynamically. Although the Grifo wasn't particularly sleek, some attention to detail had been paid, such as with the flush-fitting door handles.

There was a choice of either alloy or wire wheels. In both cases they were knock-on items rather than the more conventional bolt-on ones. Whichever type was chosen, the wheels were 381mm (15in) in diameter.

In profile, the Grifo was reminiscent of the Jensen Interceptor, not least of all because of those vents that sat just behind the front wheel arches. They were essential to allow the engine to keep cool.

The Grifo used good old-fashioned Chevrolet Corvette power, courtesy of a 5.4-litre (327.7ci) V8 mounted in the nose. It was a low-tech overhead valve unit, but it still pushed out 259kW (350bhp) at 5800rpm.

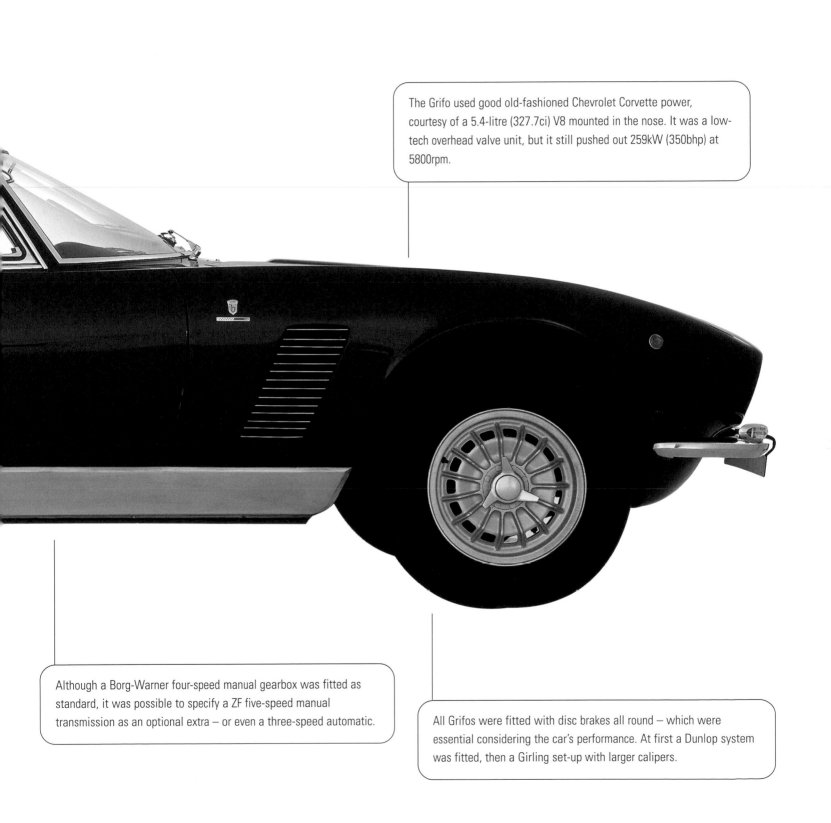

Although a Borg-Warner four-speed manual gearbox was fitted as standard, it was possible to specify a ZF five-speed manual transmission as an optional extra – or even a three-speed automatic.

All Grifos were fitted with disc brakes all round – which were essential considering the car's performance. At first a Dunlop system was fitted, then a Girling set-up with larger calipers.

There's usually something about supercar makers that flies in the face of reason. Many of those who start up a supercar company do so after they've made their fortunes elsewhere. People such as Ferruccio Lamborghini and David Brown (of Aston Martin fame) should really have known better, frittering away huge sums of money just to build a car with their own name on the badge. That's exactly what Renzo Rivolta did, when he decided to produce a supercar that was amazingly fast but didn't need the constant attention of a mechanic.

Rivolta had made his fortune selling bubble cars, trucks and scooters – modes of transport for the masses. His new venture would be the complete opposite, with bespoke bodywork and plenty of power – with a consequent high price. The motive power would be provided by Chevrolet, courtesy of its Corvette V8 engine in 5359cc (321.5ci) form. Even in basic form this could develop 222kW (300bhp) and 486Nm (360lb ft) of torque – and a change from solid to hydraulic tappets would see an instant increase to 270.1kW (365bhp)

With strong overtones of the Bizzarini 5300GT Strada, it wasn't difficult to tell how the Iso Grifo was made up. Those lines just had to be Italian, but with American V8 power there was an extremely muscular stance.

Design

The design was entrusted to Nuccio Bertone's styling house. It was a newcomer to the company who was given the task of coming up with a suitable shape; that person was Giorgetto Giugiaro, who has since become a legend in the world of car design. Although the Grifo's rivals were invariably based around a spaceframe chassis, the Iso used monocoque construction. The main structure for this was a steel punt, around which were steel panels. Independent suspension was fitted at the front, with double wishbones and coil spring/damper units. However, at the back there was a de Dion layout with radius arms and a Watts linkage. The transmission was borrowed from the Corvette; this was a four-speed item but a ZF unit equipped with an extra ratio was available as an optional extra.

By 1962 the Grifo was ready for its debut at the Turin motor show. Its name meant griffon, the mythical beast with an eagle's head and a lion's body, and the car was a sensation. But it took another three years to engineer the car to a stage where it was ready to be delivered to the first customers. Once it was ready, the first press cars were also lent out, and the car proved to be every bit as good to drive as it was to look at. A top speed of 262.3km/h (163mph) was immediately clocked up along with a 0–60mph

(0–97km/h) time of just 6.6 seconds – and a 0–100mph (0–160km/h) sprint in just 15.5 seconds.

Stagnation

Things were looking promising – until Renzo Rivolta died in 1966, leaving the company to his son Piero. This was when the rot set in, as the new head of the company embarked on a series of failed projects, the most disastrous being a move into Formula One in the early 1970s. While he was busy trying to build his

Quilted leather was very much in vogue when the Grifo was designed – at least where Italian sports cars were concerned. Thanks to the relatively high roof line there was also plenty of space in the Grifo's cabin.

empire, in reality it was falling apart around him. The Grifo was neglected, and with its design not having really progressed in a decade, sales plunged. The only significant external titivation the car received in its life was a redesign of the nose, although even this wasn't as major as it sounds. The previous exposed lights remained, but instead of staying visible all the time, they were hidden behind flip-up panels which partly obscured them.

At least the mechanical side was developed a bit more, with the arrival of a 5.7-litre (345.9ci) engine, first from Chevrolet and later from Ford. There was even a 7-litre (427ci) (and later 7.4-litre/449.1ci) powerplant offered, which reputedly allowed the car to crack 289.6km/h (180mph). But what didn't reach production was the convertible version of the car, which had been shown at the 1964 Geneva motor show. Perhaps if that had been introduced, things might have been different. Instead, the company struggled on to 1974, when it finally gave up and closed its doors. That was until 1990, when the Grifo badge was resurrected by a new company – which never even got out of the starting blocks.

Iso Grifo

Years of production	1964–74
Displacement	5359cc (321.5ci)
Configuration	Front-mounted V8
Transmission	Four-speed manual, rear-wheel drive
Power	259kW (350bhp) @ 5800rpm
Torque	486Nm (360lb ft) @ 3600rpm
Top speed	262.3km/h (163mph)
0–60mph (0–97km/h)	6.4sec
Power to weight ratio	202kW/ton (273bhp/ton)
Number built	413

Jaguar D-Type/XKSS

The rear fin was essential to maintaining stability when the car was running at very high speeds on circuits such as Le Mans, which the D-Type was built especially for.

There were disc brakes at the front as well as the back. Jaguar had pioneered the use of disc brake technology with the C-Type, with the Dunlop system being carried over onto the D-Type.

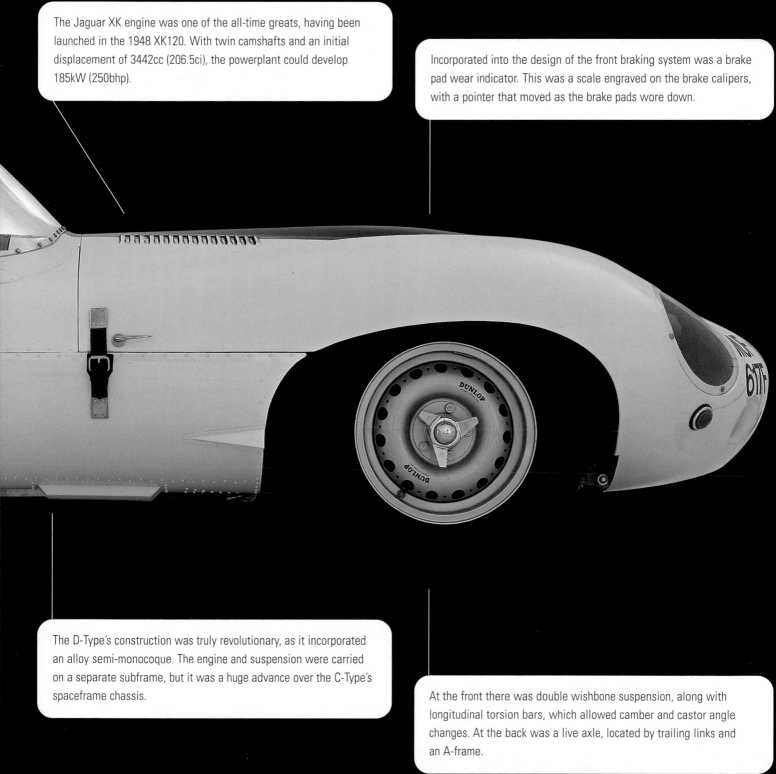

The Jaguar XK engine was one of the all-time greats, having been launched in the 1948 XK120. With twin camshafts and an initial displacement of 3442cc (206.5ci), the powerplant could develop 185kW (250bhp).

Incorporated into the design of the front braking system was a brake pad wear indicator. This was a scale engraved on the brake calipers, with a pointer that moved as the brake pads wore down.

The D-Type's construction was truly revolutionary, as it incorporated an alloy semi-monocoque. The engine and suspension were carried on a separate subframe, but it was a huge advance over the C-Type's spaceframe chassis.

At the front there was double wishbone suspension, along with longitudinal torsion bars, which allowed camber and castor angle changes. At the back was a live axle, located by trailing links and an A-frame.

Despite the D-Type now being one of the world's most desirable classics, Jaguar couldn't sell them initially. So it came up with the XK SS, which was based on the D-Type and better suited to road use.

There was nothing revolutionary about the D-Type, if each of its key features was taken in isolation. But as a package, this car broke the mould because it was the first time that innovations such as semi-monocoque construction, disc brakes and aerodynamic design were all rolled together into one package.

The C-Type Mk2

The D-Type project had started in 1953, known as the XK120C Mk2, or the C-Type Mk2. The C was short for Competition, and the plan was to introduce the XK120's mechanicals into a purpose-built bodyshell that was both light and aerodynamic. The C-Type had also done this, but with the D-Type the aim was to go several steps further. The C-Type had already won Le Mans in 1951 and 1953, so its successor had to be every bit as competitive – which it was.

Jaguar was obsessed with winning Le Mans, which in the 1950s was the most prestigious race in the world. The company wanted to prove its prowess as a maker of sporting cars, and the French endurance race offered the perfect opportunity to do just that.

The D-Type was first seen publicly in October 1953, when test driver Norman Dewis drove the car at 289.6km/h (180mph) on a closed Belgian motorway. Within months it was at Rheims for further testing then in June 1954 it made its Le Mans debut. Until this point the car didn't have an official name, but with its predecessor having been called the C-Type, it didn't take long to come up with a solution.

Jaguar D-Type/XKSS

Years of production	1953–7
Displacement	3442cc (206.5ci)
Configuration	Front-engined straight-six
Transmission	Four-speed manual, rear-wheel drive
Power	185kW (250bhp) @ 6000rpm
Torque	326.7Nm (242lb ft) @ 4000rpm
Top speed	239.7km/h (149mph)
0–60mph (0–97km/h)	5.2sec
Power to weight ratio	182.7kW/ton (247bhp/ton)
Number built	87 (inc 16 XKSS)

Whereas the C-Type had mechanical fuel injection, the D-Type was fitted with a trio of Weber carburettors. But the basic powerplant was the same; Jaguar's famed straight-six XK unit in 3442cc (206.5ci) form. However, the D-Type was a huge advance over the C-Type in just about every possible respect. It had more power but less weight, while it was much more aerodynamic to enable even higher speeds to be attained. However, the most significant difference between the cars was the construction; the D-Type's semi-monocoque was a huge step forward over the C-Type's spaceframe as it was much stiffer and stronger.

The exterior design was also a big leap forward, with that fantastically curved nose and huge rear fin. It was the work of ex-Bristol aircraft designer Malcolm Sayer, who had joined Jaguar in the early 1950s and who went on to design the C-Type, D-Type and E-Type – as well as the ill-fated XJ13.

When the D-Type appeared at the 1954 Le Mans, it was the first event in which the car was raced in anger. Although two of the cars were retired because of gearbox and brake problems, the third car nearly

The D-Type was built for endurance racing, and it was on the track that it was most at home. With that fantastically aerodynamic bodyshell and brilliant Jaguar engineering, the car conquered Le Mans four times in a row.

claimed a victory, but was narrowly beaten by a Ferrari. But it didn't take long for the car to clinch its first win, which was at Reims in July 1954.

Modifications

There were various modifications for the 1955 season, including longer noses to improve the aerodynamics. While Jaguar went on to win Le Mans that year, it was after the worst motor racing accident of all time, when over 80 spectators were killed. It was a hollow victory. By August 1955, Jaguar was offering the D-Type as a roadgoing production car. At a cost of nearly £4000 it wasn't cheap, but it was one of the most beautiful – and fast – cars on sale at the time.

Jaguar returned to Le Mans in 1956, but fared badly with its factory-backed cars – although a privately entered car did win the race ahead of both Aston Martin and Ferrari. At this point Jaguar decided to call time on its Le Mans support, but a D-Type still won in 1957, in private hands.

From 1957 the XKSS was also available, which was a D-Type underneath but it featured a redesigned bodyshell that looked less like a race car. With a full-width windscreen, folding cloth roof and a bit more interior trim, the XKSS was more civilized – it even had a proper cockpit instead of the split item sported by the D-Type.

Lamborghini Miura

One of the most distinctive features of the Miura's design was its pop-up headlamps, which were hinged at the front rather than the back. It was an uncommon arrangement, with most rival cars having them rear-hinged.

The radiator was mounted at the front, although the engine was at the back. Despite the car's very low nose, there was still room for the spare wheel at the front – although it was mounted very far back.

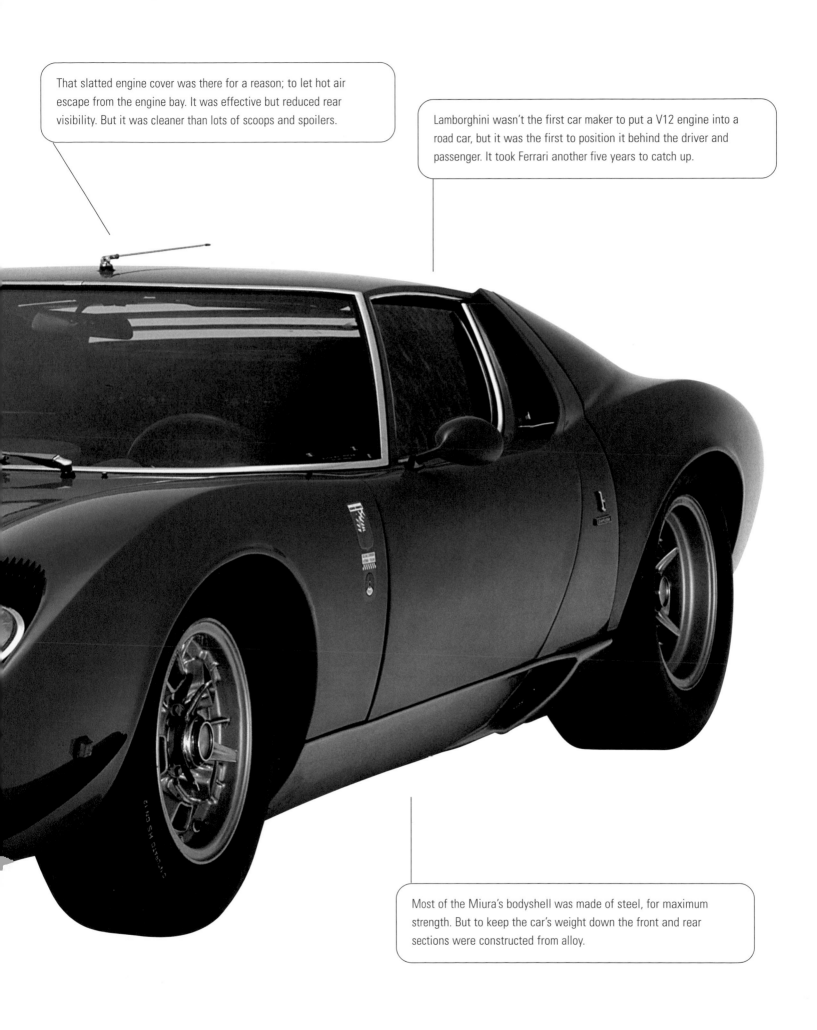

That slatted engine cover was there for a reason; to let hot air escape from the engine bay. It was effective but reduced rear visibility. But it was cleaner than lots of scoops and spoilers.

Lamborghini wasn't the first car maker to put a V12 engine into a road car, but it was the first to position it behind the driver and passenger. It took Ferrari another five years to catch up.

Most of the Miura's bodyshell was made of steel, for maximum strength. But to keep the car's weight down the front and rear sections were constructed from alloy.

Enzo Ferrari wasn't an easy man to get on with, and when Ferruccio Lamborghini fell out with him, the gauntlet was thrown down. Until then Lamborghini had made his money building tractors and air-conditioning systems. He had several Ferraris, and when the company's creator was less than helpful over a recurring fault with one of them, Lamborghini resolved to prove that a supercar didn't have to be temperamental.

Although Lamborghini's first cars (the 350GT and 400GT) weren't especially dramatic, his first mid-engined supercar was perhaps the most innovative supercar ever devised. It threw away the rulebook in terms of mechanical layout, and created a new formula that has become the standard for supercars ever since.

Rear-mounted powerplant

Ferruccio Lamborghini wanted to show from the outset that supercars could be modern and based on then-current race car technology. With the most successful racing cars having their powerplants mounted behind the driver, it made sense that

Every so often a car comes along that rewrites the rule book. The Miura was one such car, with its engine sitting just ahead of the rear axle – its contemporaries all featured a powerplant over the front wheels.

the most dynamic road cars should also be using this popular layout.

Bearing in mind that the Miura was only the second model line to come out of the fledgling company, it was even more impressive that Lamborghini managed to pull it off successfully. It helped that the press was already on Lamborghini's side; the arrival of the 350GT and 400GT only two years earlier proved that this new company was set to be no mere flash in the pan. Not that the company wouldn't go through major upheavals on a regular basis!

The Miura was first shown at the 1966 Geneva motor show, creating a storm because it borrowed nothing from existing supercars. Sitting behind the two occupants was a transversely mounted V12 that featured a quartet of camshafts and was capable of generating a very healthy 259kW (350bhp). That was enough to take the car up to nearly 273.5km/h (170mph), with the 0–60mph (0–97km/h) dash being discarded in less than seven seconds.

Lamborghini's aim was to replicate race car practice for the road throughout the car as much as possible. That's why there was double-wishbone suspension all round as well as massive disc brakes. The car also featured a semi-monocoque, which was strong enough to protect the occupants in the event of a crash (unless driven flat-out into a bulldozer, as in *The Italian Job*!).

The styling was the work of junior designer Marcello Gandini, who was working for the Bertone styling house. But it was the engineering that allowed Gandini to excel so spectacularly – which is where Gianpaolo Dallara came in. He was Lamborghini's genius engineer who worked out how to package everything – this really was a car that pushed the boundaries of what was possible. Getting a V12 engine to fit into the available space, along with a gearbox and final drive was no mean feat. Dallara hit on the idea of mounting the powerplant sideways and incorporating the gearbox into the sump (just as had been done in the humble Mini). Once this had been done it was relatively simple to position the final drive behind the engine/gearbox combination, with the whole shooting match then sitting between the cabin and the rear axle. It's been done many times since, but in the mid-1960s there was nothing like it.

Upgrade

The first incarnation of the Miura was known as the TP400, shorthand for Trasversale Posteriore 4-litre. The Miura name also started the trend for naming Lamborghini's models after bulls; reference to Ferruccio Lamborghini's Taurean star sign. By 1970 it was time to upgrade the car, the result being the 273.8kW (370bhp) Miura S. This had a far more flexible powerplant, with a flatter torque curve so it wasn't as peaky. But it was the final incarnation of the breed that's now the most sought after – the SV. Not

It's rumoured that the Miura's transversely positioned powerplant was prompted by the arrival of the Issigonis-designed Mini in 1959. Whether or not that's true, there's no denying that the Miura was just as revolutionary.

only did it have a very fruity 284.9kW (385bhp) engine (enabling it to allegedly crack 281.6km/h / 175mph), but the gearbox arrangement was significantly improved. For a first attempt at a mid-engined supercar, the Miura was a pretty good effort. But Lamborghini's follow up, the Countach, was even more spectacular…

Lamborghini Miura

Years of production	1966–72
Displacement	3929cc (235.7ci)
Configuration	Mid-mounted V12
Transmission	Five-speed manual, rear-wheel drive
Power	273.8kW (370bhp) @ 7700rpm
Torque	386.1Nm (286lb ft) @ 5500rpm
Top speed	276.7km/h (172mph)
0–60mph (0–97km/h)	6.7sec
Power to weight ratio	211.6kW/ton (286bhp/ton)
Number built	763

Maserati Ghibli

The front-mounted V8 engine was fitted with four camshafts, which were chain-driven. Generating 251.6kW (340bhp), the unit was developed from the one seen in Maserati's racing cars of the 1950s and 1960s.

To haul the Ghibli down from the massive speeds it was capable of, there were ventilated disc brakes at the front with twin calipers. Disc brakes were also fitted at the back, but they were solid rather than vented ones.

The front suspension followed classic race car practice, with unequal length wishbones joined by coil springs and telescopic dampers. There was also an anti-roll bar fitted in order to keep things tidy on the bends.

While an alloy bodyshell would have made sense to keep weight down, the Ghibli's panels were constructed of steel. As a result it tipped the scales at a hefty 1699kg (3680.1lb), decreasing the power to weight ratio.

At the back the suspension was surprisingly crude, with a live axle mounted on semi-elliptic leaf springs. To improve things there were also radius arms with a Panhard rod along with an anti-roll bar.

Very few mainstream cars in the 1960s were fitted with five-speed gearboxes – they were reserved for ultra-expensive motors such as the Ghibli. They were fitted to allow for much more relaxed high-speed cruising.

While it's always been the British that have a reputation for classy interiors swathed in leather, the Italians have also been able to do a pretty good job as well. Nowhere is this more apparent than in the Ghibli.

If you wanted something flash in the late 1960s, but you didn't want to be predictable, Maserati was the place to go. The Miura and Daytona were hardly what you could call common, but they were the cars that everybody wanted – the Ghibli was the less obvious choice, even if it was hardly what you could call discreet. It was also rather old-fashioned compared with its two Italian rivals, both of which could boast 12-cylinder powerplants compared with the Maserati's mere eight. But that didn't matter; with looks to die for and a fantastic racing pedigree, nobody could argue that the Maserati wasn't a fully paid-up member of the supercar élite.

First appearance

The Ghibli was first shown to the public at the 1966 Turin Salon – the same year that the Miura also broke cover. After the Lamborghini, the Maserati seemed rather passé, even if nobody could call it dull. A front-engined V8-powered supercar hardly broke the mould after the daring mid-engined Miura, but the Ghibli went on to outsell its two key rivals so it was

clearly sought after in its day. It was also designed by Giorgetto Giugiaro, never a bad claim to fame.

It was 1967 before the first cars were delivered to their eager first owners, the Ghibli name having been taken from a hot desert wind. The car featured a tubular steel frame, over which was stretched steel panelling. It was Ghia which built the cars – the company later being acquired by Ford to build its own supercar, the Pantera.

Maserati Ghibli

Years of production	1967–73
Displacement	4719cc (283.1ci)
Configuration	Front-engined V8
Transmission	Five-speed manual
Power	251.6kW (340bhp) @ 5500rpm
Torque	440.1Nm (326lb ft) @ 4000rpm
Top speed	257.4km/h (160mph)
0–60mph (0–97km/h)	6.6sec
Power to weight ratio	148kW/ton (200bhp/ton)
Number built	1274

Although the steering was by recirculating ball (rather than the more precise rack and pinion), the car was great to drive with much better handling than many expected. Disc brakes at each corner went some way to ensuring the driving experience was reassuring, but the leaf-spring rear suspension was the fly in the ointment. At least there were unequal length wishbones at the front, following the classic race car practice.

V8 engine

Perhaps one of the reasons why the Ghibli is so often overlooked is the fact that it's powered by a V8. At this level another four combustion chambers are normally expected, but with 4.7 litres (285.2ci) to draw on, the Ghibli driver isn't really left needing more power. After all, with over 300 horses on tap, performance wasn't weak – even if it wasn't quite on a par with the Miura or Daytona. Maserati claimed the car was able to top 280km/h (174mph), but the reality was somewhere closer to 257.4km/h (160mph). It was also capable of despatching the 0–60mph (0–97km/h) sprint in 6.6 seconds, as well as the standing quarter in 14.5 seconds – so nobody could accuse it of being a slouch.

The standard transmission was a five-speed ZF gearbox, although an automatic was available. That

was something that its rivals couldn't claim, and it also hinted at whom Maserati thought was likely to buy the car. Rather than being an outright sports car, it was marketed as more of a grand tourer – which was why the car was so much more successful in the US than either the Lamborghini or the Ferrari. In keeping with its grand tourer image, the Ghibli has plenty of luxury equipment such as air-conditioning, electric windows, centre-lock alloy wheels and leather trim.

In 1969 a Spyder version of the Ghibli went on sale, the lines once again penned by Giugiaro. Although it was universally acclaimed, it was generally felt that Lamborghini and Ferrari still had the edge in terms of image. That led to the introduction of the Ghibli SS in 1970, with a longer-stroke version of the V8. That took the displacement to 4930cc (295.8ci), with peak power being increased to 262.7kW (355bhp) in the process. But the big news was the flatter torque curve, making the car more driveable so it was even more comfortable on long journeys. But the Ghibli's heyday was already over, and the final car rolled off the production lines in 1973.

The Ghibli has always been overlooked in favour of rivals from companies such as Ferrari or Lamborghini. Yet with lines like those of this Spyder version, nobody could accuse the car of looking anything other than sensational.

Mercedes 300 SL Gullwing

The weight was kept down by using aluminium where possible for the panels. Accordingly, the doors, bonnet and boot lid were all alloy. In the case of the doors, this was essential just so they could be opened and closed!

One of those power bulges in the bonnet was unnecessary – it was there just to balance the one on the other side. That was there to allow the fuel injection system to fit underneath.

Those gull-wing doors weren't a part of the original design. But the bulky sill structures didn't allow conventional doors to be used, meaning a radical solution needed to be found.

Disc brakes were never fitted to the 300SL in coupé form, but the Roadster was available with them from 1961. Instead, the coupé featured massive finned aluminium brake drums.

Those side air vents and the brows on the wheel arches didn't feature on the first cars. They came later, and were there purely for the sake of styling – although Mercedes claimed the brows had some aerodynamic benefit.

Although the 300 SL had a reputation for being at the cutting edge when it was first seen in 1954, in some ways it wasn't really that advanced technically. Sure, it had mechanical fuel injection, but there were still drum brakes all round and elsewhere it was generally conventional. Where it was anything but conventional was in its construction; here was a road car with a spaceframe chassis and those crazy gull-wing doors which nobody else had tried before. They also wouldn't feature on a road car for a long time after...

The 300 SL was initially seen in 1952 as a lightweight sports racer. The 300 denoted the engine's 3.0-litre (182.1ci) capacity while the SL stood for Super-Leicht, or super-lightweight. Being a race car, the issue of cost didn't really figure in the 300 SL's development. So when the decision was made to produce a road-going version, once again it was decided that build costs wouldn't be too much of a factor. But with a cost of $7500 when it was launched in the US in 1955, buyers could have had a pair of Corvettes for rather less money. Affordable it wasn't, but then few supercars ever are...

Running gear

The 300 SL's running gear was largely borrowed from the 300-series of saloons, albeit with some very significant changes along the way. That meant the suspension utilized swing axles at the rear, which could lead to some pretty hairy experiences on the limit. Enter a bend too quickly and the car could quickly snap its tail out – lift off the power mid-bend and your fate was pretty much sealed unless you were spectacularly skilled at the wheel.

Everywhere you look on the 300SL there's another stylistic touch, whether it's a scallop or a grille – yet it doesn't look like an especially fussy design. In this profile shot, it's also easy to see just how massive the sills are.

The 3.0-litre (182.1ci) straight-six mounted up front featured a single overhead camshaft, and in standard form it was capable of producing a healthy (but hardly sensational) 128.7kW (174bhp). When tuned it was possible to extract well over 149kW (200hp) from the same engine, and with the right rear axle ratio, with 240 horses on tap, the car was capable of exceeding 257.4km/h (160mph). Pretty impressive for a car that went on sale less than a decade after the end of World War II!

Mercedes 300 SL Gullwing	
Years of production	1954–7
Displacement	2996cc (179.7ci)
Configuration	Straight-six
Transmission	Four-speed manual, rear-wheel drive
Power	177.6kW (240bhp) @ 6100rpm
Torque	292.9Nm (217lb ft) @ 4800rpm
Top speed	225.3km/h (140mph)
0–60mph (0–97km/h)	8.8sec
Power to weight ratio	1293kg (2,850.5lb)
Number built	1400 Gullwings, 1858 Roadsters

The thing is, the 300 SL road car could very easily have never happened. The car had been incredibly successful in 1952, winning Le Mans, the Berne Grand Prix and the Carrera Panamericana. Having proved the reliability of its cars in endurance racing, Mercedes decided to focus on Grand Prix racing in 1954. But US car importer Max Hoffman had other ideas. He told Mercedes that if it produced a roadgoing 300 SL, he would order up to 1000 of them for sale in America. He knew they would sell whatever the price. Consequently, Mercedes showed a prototype road car at the 1954 New York motor show – and it was an instant hit. It was the world's fastest road car, and those sensational looks guaranteed it classic status before the first car was even sold.

Cost

Although the car was on everyone's wish list, that's where it had to stay for most people – it was simply too expensive for the majority of potential buyers. By 1957 around 1400 examples had been built, which is when the 300 SL Roadster superseded the coupé. To allow for conventional doors the chassis had to be redesigned, although losing the roof meant there had to be considerable stiffness on offer. Strengthening the chassis took its toll on the kerb weight, but to partly compensate the powerplant was retuned to liberate a few more horses – however, the open car was never as quick as the coupé.

To make the high-speed handling much safer the rear suspension was redesigned, although it still incorporated swing axles in its design. By the time the Roadster appeared, the 300 SL was getting outdated in some ways – it was now seen as a tourer rather than a sports car. To keep it ahead as long as possible there were disc brakes fitted all round in 1961. But from 1963 there would be an all-new, much more modern (and affordable) range of SLs on offer.

Considering the 300 SL has gone on to become known as the GullWing, it's surprising that so few other manufacturers have incorporated such a door design into their own cars. Instead, they generally opt for beetle-wing designs instead.

Porsche 911

That shape is instantly recognizable from any angle, despite the fact that there have been several all-new cars since the 911 was first seen in 1963. It's easy to see that the car was a development of the VW Beetle, with that hunched back over the rear engine.

The key ingredient with any 911 has always been the flat-six engine, which has gradually grown in size and sprouted turbochargers along the way. As a result, power has grown to over 296kW (400bhp), while top speeds have risen accordingly.

Another key element that arrived fairly soon after the 911 first appeared is the oversized rear spoiler. The classic whale-tail spoiler of the 1975 Turbo has grown and grown, to become a twin-fin spoiler on some models.

There have been numerous bodystyles available over the years, the main one being the famous coupé. But from 1982 there was also a full cabriolet on sale and in 1965 the first Targa had been launched, with a removable roof section.

The 911 is a driver's car, which is why most of the ones sold have featured a manual gearbox. But Porsche offered the unpopular Sportomatic in the 1960s; nowadays the Tiptronic sequential manual transmission is common.

The thought of anything other than rear-wheel drive was anathema to Porsche's engineers when the 911 was launched. But as four-wheel drive gained acceptance, it became logical to fit it to the 911 from 1990.

This modern interpretation of the 911 features a beautifully laid out dashboard that works wonderfully. Early cars weren't so great, with scattered switchgear that was an ergonomic nightmare – not in keeping with Porsche's image.

How can the Porsche 911 be summed up in just two pages? Here's the longest-lived supercar ever, launched more than 40 years ago, and which has been through dozens of iterations. Yet despite the current models sharing nothing at all with those first cars of 1963, the 911 has always been instantly recognizable as the most practical and durable high-performance car ever.

Origins

The 911's roots are based in the 356 of 1948. This was the car that set the rear-engined layout which the 911 would adopt from its launch in 1963. When it was first shown, the car carried the 901 badge, but Peugeot objected, claiming that all three-digit numbers containing a zero in the middle belonged to the French manufacturer. Porsche relented, and from that point on the rear-engined sportster carried 911 badges. Whereas the 356 had featured just four cylinders, the 911 would carry six from the outset – although there was a four-cylinder version of the car available, called the 912. Both cars would be air-cooled, just as the 356 had been and the Beetle before it.

The 911 was designed and engineered by Ferdinand Porsche's two sons, Butzi and Ferry. Their brief was to take the 356 and iron out its failings, the chief one being potentially lethal handling. The problem with the 356 was that on the limit its handling was completely unpredictable, so the 911 received an all-new suspension. But in the wrong hands the car could still break away very quickly, with no chance of ever catching it.

Even those first cars were fitted with five-speed manual gearboxes and disc brakes all round. The steering was also very sharp while the torsion bar suspension was relatively forgiving and also compact. There was initially a 96.2kW (130bhp), 2-litre

Porsche 911	
Years of production	1963–
Displacement	3600cc (216ci)
Configuration	Rear-mounted flat-six
Transmission	Six-speed manual
Power	201.2kW (272bhp) @ 6100rpm
Torque	340.2Nm (252lb ft) @ 5000rpm
Top speed	270.3km/h (168mph)
0–60mph (0–97km/h)	5.2sec
Power to weight ratio	147.2kW/ton (199bhp/ton)
Number built	N/A

(121.4ci) engine, which was enough to take the car to 209.2km/h (130mph). By 1965 there was a world first; the Targa top was introduced. This featured a lift-out roof section and a folding PVC rear window – the definitive model with a glass rear window wouldn't appear until 1968. For 1969 there was a capacity increase to 2.2 litres (133.5ci), bringing with it an increase in both power and torque. By 1974 the engine had grown in size once more, this time to 2.4 litres (145.6ci).

After this, the legends came thick and fast. The Carrera 2.7 RS of 1972 introduced the rear spoiler to the 911, although at this stage it was a relatively small item. Built for just a year, the Carrera RS was capable of 249.4km/h (155mph); the following year, the 2.7-litre (163.6ci) powerplant was standardized for the whole range. However, the rear spoiler fitted to the Carrera RS would look tiny in comparison with the one fitted to the Turbo of 1974. Unveiled at the Paris motor show of that year, this was the model that would really catapult the 911 into the supercar world. The problem was, although it was viciously fast, the engine suffered from horrific turbo lag. There would be nothing, then all of a sudden the turbo would kick in and the car would be hurled towards the horizon – it was completely unpredictable to the novice driver.

The ultimate incarnation of the 911 used to be the 2.7 RS model from 1973, but this changed once the GT3 was launched. With more power and less weight than regular 911s, it was astonishingly fast – and eminently usable too.

Later versions

The 911 continued to be developed but during the late 1970s it looked as though the car's time had come. Porsche soldiered on with it, first launching the SC, then introducing the cabriolet in 1982. This was sold alongside the Targa, and throughout the 1980s it was the 911 that represented the worst excesses of yuppiedom. As the boom peaked in 1989, the timing was right for the new 911, codenamed the 964 with its new panels and bumpers. It would be this model that introduced four-wheel drive to the 911, which would stay when the last of the air-cooled models was launched in 1989. Code-named 993, it featured a new multi-link rear suspension.

For 1997 there was a complete change; the 996 featured water cooling and was entirely new structurally. A massive leap forward, this was superseded in 2004 by another all-new car, the 997. Apart from the concept, this latest car shares nothing with that first car – but it's instantly recognizable as a 911.

1970–1979

While time has been kind to most of the supercars of the 1970s, it's amazing that any of them ever actually saw the light of day. If there was one business that you didn't want to be in during this decade, it was building very expensive and thirsty cars.

The 1970s brought huge turmoil in the form of oil crises and global recession, threatening the very existence of every supercar maker. It was a grim time for companies such as Aston Martin, Lotus and Lamborghini, which regularly teetered on the brink of bankruptcy. Despite this, there were plenty of supercar projects in progress throughout the decade, as people looked forward to better times. However, many of these projects faltered before they had even got going, and even existing supercar offerings were threatened when companies such as Lamborghini and Aston Martin were forced to call in the receivers. The near-demise of Lamborghini nearly took the BMW M1 project with it, as the Italian company was initially supposed to have been building the German car; when the costs continued to escalate it would have been very easy for BMW to have just pulled the plug on the project.

Built for rallying, the Lancia Stratos featured one of the most amazing wedge shapes ever seen. When viewed in profile the car looks remarkable – and it's no less incredible when viewed from overhead.

It was the earliest years of the 1970s that were the bleakest; by the mid-point the worst was over and things were looking brighter. Despite this, there was little stability at any of the major supercar makers – that wouldn't happen until they had all been acquired by the major conglomerates a couple of decades later. As a result, build quality continued to be patchy at best while development work was frequently carried out by the marques' loyal supporters.

Lamborghini lurched from one owner to another, yet managed to continue to develop new models although no money was coming in. AC more or less went into hibernation while Aston Martin stopped building cars for a few years as it tried to find some sort of financial stability. Monteverdi, which you'll also find in these pages, hardly existed at any point, and once Ford had tired of De Tomaso, it was a similar tale for the Italian marque. In fact there was little in the way of good news for supercar makers in the 1970s – so it was no surprise they were all glad to get the decade out of the way and move on to the 1980s.

BMW M1

A slatted cover was fitted above the mid-mounted engine. Made of matt-black plastic it didn't restrict visibility especially, but did help to allow hot air to escape from the engine bay.

The slots below the rear side window on the driver's side were there to provide air for the engine's induction system. Those on the other side were there to channel cooling air into the engine bay.

The suspension was double-wishbones with coil springs and dampers at the front. At the rear there were semi-trailing arms, which give more variation in camber than double-wishbone set-ups.

Those polished lines are attributed to Giorgetto Giugiaro, but the M1 was very closely based on the Turbo concept of 1972. That was penned by BMW's then styling chief, Paul Bracq.

Although the M1's silhouette was about as far removed as possible from the classic saloon shape, there was still room for the BMW grille. This cooled the radiator and oil cooler, which were in the car's nose.

While there were no superfluous ducts, scoops or spoilers on the M1, there were some aerodynamic and cooling aids. The discreet front air dam was essential to control the flow of air underneath the body.

When you look at the BMW M1 in a twenty-first century context, its specification isn't especially impressive. After all, a 204.9kW (277bhp) straight-six is well and truly trumped by so many of BMW's own saloons nowadays that it seems positively tame. However, while the M1's silhouette goes some way to making up for this horsepower deficiency, when the car was first put on sale in 1979 it was more than competitive. The M1 may have sported just six cylinders, but nobody could argue with a 0–60mph (0–97km/h) time of 5.5 seconds or a top speed of 260.7km/h (162mph).

Designed for the racetrack

When work on the M1 began, its purpose was to fight BMW's corner on racetracks around the world. As such it clearly had to be competitive, but it also had to be civilized in road trim as 400 road cars would have to be built if the car was to qualify for Group 4 racing. The man behind the project was Jochen Neerpasch, who had been a successful sports car racer before becoming head of motorsport at Ford, then BMW (and later Mercedes). When Neerpasch joined BMW, the company's race cars were based on the

The M1 has become something of an enigma, thanks to its rarity and that it's BMW's only attempt at a mid-engined supercar. Since the days of the M1, BMW has focused instead on making saloons that can go even faster.

roadgoing CSL 'batmobiles'. He argued that what BMW needed was a car designed for the racetrack from the outset – and the basis for the car had already been designed.

In 1972, BMW's then head of design Paul Bracq had created a styling study called the Turbo. This dramatic gull-winged car featured a mid-mounted turbocharged 2-litre (121.4ci) engine, and while the mechanicals were all wrong, its basic lines were just what Neerpasch wanted. What was envisaged was a development of the 3.5-litre (212.4ci) straight-six that powered the already successful BMW touring cars, and when Neerpasch proposed this to the company's board, the project was given the green light.

Once the decision was taken to progress, BMW needed to get the cars designed and built in a hurry. Giorgetto Giugiaro soon came up with the goods in terms of design, and Lamborghini was chosen to construct the necessary 400 cars. The company was struggling to make ends meet, but had huge experience of exotic car construction. But it didn't take long for the project to fall behind schedule, with the money running out far more quickly than had been planned and the target weight being overshot by miles. As a result, the car ended up being developed and built all over Italy. Italdesign (run by Giorgetto Giugaro) produced the bodyshells and the cars were finally assembled by Baur in Stuttgart, Germany.

Without looking forced, BMW managed to incorporate its classic double-kidney grille into the nose of the M1. The classic 'hockey-stick' window line didn't make it into the M1's design though – unsurprisingly.

Problems

By the time the M1 surfaced, it was over-budget, overweight and running late. But that was just the start of BMW's troubles – the formula that it had been designed to compete in had been scrapped, so the car was redundant. The answer was to negotiate a series of Procar support races at European Formula One meetings, with 24 M1s competing against each other.

With the car not getting the chance to prove its worth against rivals such as the Porsche 911, BMW struggled to sell the road cars it had built. While the car was spectacular, it was deemed to be perhaps a little too neatly finished and with just six cylinders (the same as a 911, remember) it was seen as inferior to the eight-cylinder Ferraris and Lamborghinis available elsewhere. But the available performance was very strong and the car was superbly balanced.

The key to the M1's talents was its classic race car construction, with a spaceframe chassis and double-wishbone suspension at each corner. There was a five-speed manual gearbox, servo-assisted ventilated discs at each corner and a limited slip differential to get the power down. It's a tragedy for BMW that the M1 could have been so much more successful in racing if the timing had been right. But even if the Group 4 series hadn't been canned, there's still a chance the car would have failed because it was simply too heavy to be competitive. But that only made it a better road car.

The M1 was built specifically to make BMW competitive on race circuits around the globe. Here it is in action at Monaco, in a Procar race to support the Grand Prix there.

BMW M1	
Years of production	1979–80
Displacement	3453cc (207.1ci)
Configuration	Mid-mounted straight-six
Transmission	Five-speed manual, rear-wheel drive
Power	204.9kW (277bhp) @ 6500rpm
Torque	322.6Nm (239lb ft) @ 5000rpm
Top speed	260.7km/h (162mph)
0–60mph (0–97km/h)	5.5sec
Power to weight ratio	145kW/ton (196bhp/ton)
Number built	454

De Tomaso Pantera

The interior was a typical Italian mish-mash that was an ergonomic disaster but looked great with its leather trim and sweeping dash. The semi-reclining driving position wasn't comfortable, but it felt the part.

There were disc brakes all round, originally solid, later ventilated. As the car evolved, vents were fitted ahead of the rear wheel arches, to aid with brake cooling, but they were more cosmetic than functional.

The Pantera used monocoque construction, because using a separate chassis would have led to too much flexing. A stiffer bodyshell improved the handling, but the early examples were poorly produced.

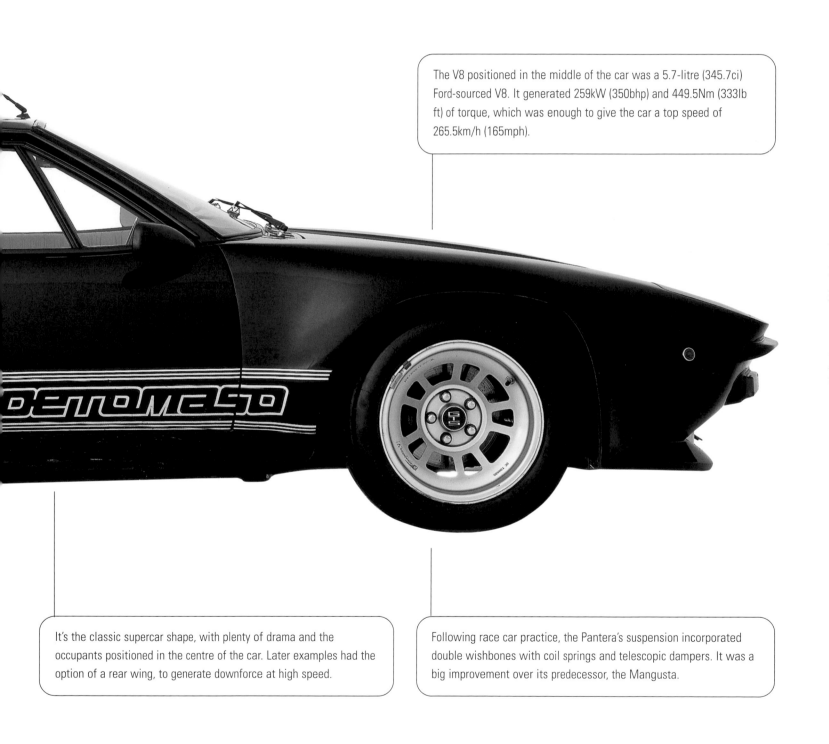

The V8 positioned in the middle of the car was a 5.7-litre (345.7ci) Ford-sourced V8. It generated 259kW (350bhp) and 449.5Nm (333lb ft) of torque, which was enough to give the car a top speed of 265.5km/h (165mph).

It's the classic supercar shape, with plenty of drama and the occupants positioned in the centre of the car. Later examples had the option of a rear wing, to generate downforce at high speed.

Following race car practice, the Pantera's suspension incorporated double wishbones with coil springs and telescopic dampers. It was a big improvement over its predecessor, the Mangusta.

Having enjoyed huge success in the showroom on the back of its Le Mans successes with the GT40, Ford realized that as the 1970s dawned, what it needed was an image booster. Although the GT40 had been mid-engined, the arrival of the Miura in 1966 turned the supercar world on its head. The breed would never be

This later version of the Pantera was fitted with an ungainly bodykit, which was all the rage during the 1980s. The earlier car's design was far purer without the massive rear wing and the unsubtle wheelarch extensions.

the same again after the appearance of the Lamborghini, and Ford had to compete with its own mass-produced (in relative terms) mid-engined design.

With rival General Motors regularly producing styling studies that suggested a mid-engined Corvette was a possibility, Ford wanted to get something into production as quickly as possible. The company was even more determined once American Motors produced its AMX/3 supercar proposal in 1969. Here was an exotic-looking supercar with its engine positioned behind the driver – at what was expected to be a relatively affordable price. Ford had to do something – and quickly.

Outsourced development

The fastest and easiest way of getting a completely new car into production was to outsource its development. The two key people at Ford (Henry Ford II and newly appointed company president Lee

De Tomaso Pantera

Years of production	1971–93
Displacement	5763cc (345.7ci)
Configuration	Mid-engined V8
Transmission	Five-speed manual, rear-wheel drive
Power	259kW (350bhp) @ 6000rpm
Torque	449.5Nm (333lb ft) @ 3800rpm
Top speed	265.5km/h (165mph)
0–60mph (0–97km/h)	5.4 sec
Power to weight ratio	177.6kW (240bhp/ton)
Number built	9000 approx

Iacocca) both knew Alejandro De Tomaso, who they reckoned could engineer a car for them and get it into production. De Tomaso already had a pair of supercars on his CV; the four-cylinder Vallelunga and the V8-powered Mangusta. Both had appeared during the 1960s and both were powered by Ford engines; the Vallelunga by a 1600 Cortina unit and the Mangusta by a 4.8-litre (291.3ci) unit in Europe (but the US got a 5-litre (303.5ci) powerplant).

In 1967, De Tomaso had bought the Ghia design house. This allowed him to design and engineer low-volume production cars more quickly than a lumbering giant such as Ford could manage, which is why he was commissioned to come up with the goods. Because the project was bankrolled by Ford, there was no question as to who would supply the engines; a 5.7-litre (345.9ci) V8 was selected from the outset, mated to a ZF five-speed manual gearbox.

Launch

By 1970 a prototype car was on show at the New York auto show. Called simply the 351, it had been styled by Ghia's Tom Tjaarda with the chassis development carried out by ex-Lamborghini engineer Gianpaolo Dallara, the man behind the Miura's chassis development. The longitudinally installed V8 was placed ahead of the rear axle line, but behind the driver, while the brakes were all-disc. Following race car practice there were double-wishbones and coil springs at both ends along with rack and pinion steering to keep everything as sharp as possible.

The car went on sale in 1971, christened Pantera (Panther) by Ford. Although early cars were badly built (and subsequently recalled), things settled down. Development continued with impact bumpers being fitted in 1972; in the same year the Pantera L (for Luxury) made its debut. The 290 debuted in the same year, with a 3-litre (182.1ci) V6 borrowed from the Capri – but just one was produced. Six examples of the GT4 were also made in 1972: painted red and black, they had wider wheels and wheel arch extensions. These were similar to the GTS, introduced in 1973 as a regular production model. The Pantera 270 was shown in 1973, using a 2.7-litre (163.8ci) Ford V6. A reaction to the fuel crisis, the car remained a one-off.

Next was the GT5 which was introduced in 1982. A GTS with rear wing, bigger front air dam and an improved interior, it was joined by the GT5-S in 1984. The GT5 featured all the body addenda of the GTS, but in metal instead of plastic, and the wheel arch extensions were riveted to the wings. The wheel arch extensions were integrated into the GT5-S's bodywork.

1991 saw the introduction of a much-facelifted new Pantera. Penned by Marcello Gandini it was wider with new suspension and brakes. But the project stalled before it had even got off the ground – just like the all-new Pantera that was proposed in 2001.

The Pantera offered the perfect mix of Italian styling with American engineering. Those Campagnolo alloy wheels were typical Italian fare, but when the throttle was booted it was clear where the mid-mounted V8 came from.

Ferrari Boxer

The use of a boxer engine (which is much less tall than a conventional unit) meant the powerplant could be mounted relatively high in the chassis without the car's centre of gravity being unacceptably high.

By mounting the engine higher in the chassis, the Boxer's five-speed manual gearbox could be positioned below it. This allowed for more space in the cabin without the car having to be unacceptably long.

In an unusual move, Ferrari fitted just a single windscreen wiper to the Boxer. Using a pantograph arrangement, the windscreen was cleared surprisingly effectively at speed.

Although the engine was mounted behind the cabin, its radiator was positioned at the very front of the car. Pipes carried the coolant to the back of the car, while twin electric fans helped the radiator do its job.

The first Boxers featured a bodyshell that was partly glassfibre but mainly steel. The composite was used below the waistline to help in the fight against corrosion. This was all hung on a steel semi-monocoque.

Because the radiator and brake servo were positioned at the front of the car, there was nowhere left for the spare wheel to be put – thanks to the very low nose. The answer was a space-saver spare.

This is the third and final incarnation of the Boxer, with fuel injection and colour-coded front end. Previous models featured carburetted engines and a few more colour schemes with the lower half of the car entirely black.

Nobody likes being shown up by a major rival, so when Lamborghini unveiled its V12 mid-engined Miura in 1966, Ferrari must have smarted. Despite this, it took Ferrari another five years to come up with its own 12-cylinder mid-engined car. However, it may have taken half a decade to appear, but as soon as the

Boxer made its debut at the 1971 Turin motor show, the wait instantly seemed worthwhile. Here was a shape that was every bit as stunning as its deadly rival's, but there were some major differences to the engineering that meant it was no carbon-copy of its Lamborghini counterpart.

Flat-12 engine

One of the key differences with the Boxer was that its engine was a flat-12 rather than a V12. In theory the Boxer's engine was a V12, but with a 180-degree angle between the two banks of cylinders. But leaving the semantics to one side, the upshot of the design was that the powerplant's centre of gravity was significantly lower because the valve gear and cylinders were all below the level of the top of the crankcase. Ferrari's Formula One cars of the time were equipped with 12-cylinder boxer engines, with the benefits already proven. Transferring this technology to its road cars could only do the company enormous good thanks to the so-called 'halo-effect'.

Although the Boxer's engine was mounted longitudinally, the car's length could be kept to a minimum by mounting the gearbox underneath it. Of course this meant raising the height of the engine within its bay, which was hardly ideal because of the need to keep the centre of gravity as low as possible. But it did mean that the engine and transmission combination didn't eat into the cabin space too much.

Ferrari Boxer	
Years of production	1971–84
Displacement	4942cc (296.5ci)
Configuration	Mid-engined flat-12
Transmission	Five-speed manual
Power	251.6kW (340bhp) @ 6200rpm
Torque	446.8Nm (331lb ft) @ 4600rpm
Top speed	262.3km/h (163mph)
0–60mph (0–97km/h)	6.2sec
Power to weight ratio	161.3kW/ton (218bhp/ton)
Number built	2323

However, despite all this work, the engine still wasn't mounted entirely ahead of the rear axle line – the rear pair of cylinders were behind it.

The engine itself was a beautiful piece of engineering, although many of its components were carried over from the Daytona that preceded it. That's why the displacement was an identical 4.4 litres (267ci) – the pistons and con-rods were all re-used. However, the design was completely new, based as it was on the then-current Formula One practice. There were four camshafts actuating a pair of valves for each cylinder. The crankshaft was machined from a solid billet of steel and both the crankcase and the cylinder heads were made of aluminium. The result of all this was a power output of 266.4kW (360bhp) with a healthy 419.8Nm (311lb ft) of torque also being on offer.

Problems

While the Boxer featured one of the most beautiful bodies ever created, under the skin there were problems. With too much of the car's weight concentrated at the rear, the Boxer's handling left a lot to be desired while the car was still in prototype form. Tens of thousands of miles of testing had to take place, with constant fine-tuning, before the car was

ready to go on sale. Finally, in 1973, Ferrari was ready to deliver the first Boxers to their new owners.

Thanks to such thorough development, the Boxer was well received. But Ferrari could see that within three years of it going on sale it would need a larger engine if it wasn't to be outclassed in the American market, which demanded ever more stringent emissions regulations. The result was a bored and stroked engine being fitted from 1976 – the new capacity was 4942cc (296.5ci). The car got a new name at the same time – it was now the 512BB (Berlinetta Boxer) where it had previously been the 365BB. The new engine produced slightly less power (now 251.6kW / 340bhp) but there was more torque (446.8Nm / 331lb ft) which made the acceleration more linear. The biggest change came in 1981, however, when fuel injection replaced the four Weber carburettors. Power, torque and driveability were all increased, while the car retained its sensational looks. It was in 1984 that the looks were lost completely, which is when the Testarossa replaced the Boxer...

It's easy to see immediately that this is a Ferrari interior, with that chromed H-gate for the gearlever, two-tone leather seat trim and plenty of splindly chromed switchgear. It looked great, but it didn't necessarily last that well.

Lamborghini Countach

A car as dramatic as the Countach had to be fitted with an outrageous door design. Cue the arrival of beetle-wing doors – which have since become the norm on supercars.

The rear wheel arches were of a completely unconventional design, and in stark contrast to the more usual rounded arches at the front. The later bodykit would disguise the squared-off lines.

Although the original Countach featured a monocoque construction, the production car was fitted with a complex spaceframe. The bodyshell was made of aluminium, but with glassfibre floorpans.

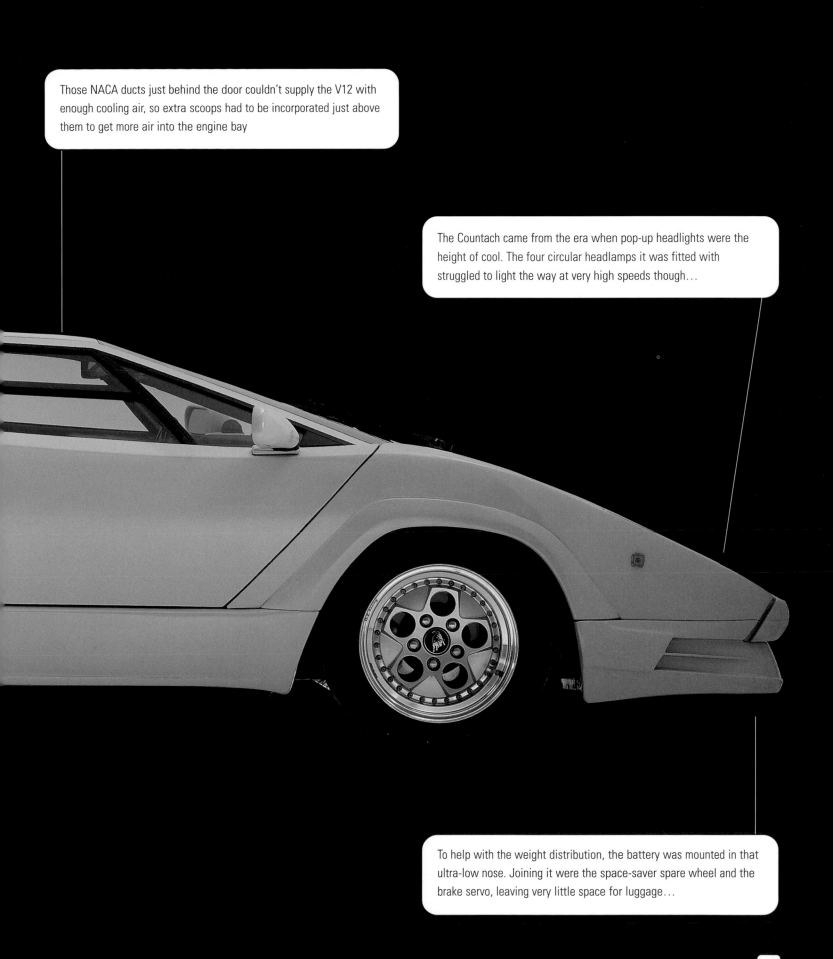

Those NACA ducts just behind the door couldn't supply the V12 with enough cooling air, so extra scoops had to be incorporated just above them to get more air into the engine bay

The Countach came from the era when pop-up headlights were the height of cool. The four circular headlamps it was fitted with struggled to light the way at very high speeds though…

To help with the weight distribution, the battery was mounted in that ultra-low nose. Joining it were the space-saver spare wheel and the brake servo, leaving very little space for luggage…

The name says it all – or at least it does if you're Piedmontese. But to anybody else the significance of the Countach's badge is lost. The very word 'Countach' is an exclamation, which has no direct translation, and when you've got a car as dramatic as this one, it's no understatement. When the Countach was first seen in prototype form, it carried the Project 122 tag. But as soon as designer Nuccio Bertone saw it he exclaimed 'Countach!' – and the name stuck.

The public had its first look at the Countach in 1971, when it was unveiled at the Geneva motor show in early prototype form. It was another creation from Marcello Gandini's pen, and where the Miura was aggressive and striking, the Countach was just plain brutal. But if the Countach really scored over its predecessor, it was in the driveability stakes. The Miura was twitchy on the limit, while the Countach would prove to be much more balanced. But that didn't mean it was easy to tame it…

First version

The first prototype was fitted with a 5-litre (303.5ci) engine, but this became a 4-litre (242.8ci) unit in the first production cars. Some of the design details also evolved, the most significant being the addition of extra scoops and ducts to help with cooling. Something that didn't change, though, was the fitting of beetle-wing doors – something that hadn't been seen before, but which became de rigueur on subsequent supercars.

Maybe the most significant development the Countach enjoyed over its predecessor was the engine and transmission design. The engine was mounted longitudinally, with the gearbox ahead of it. This was a more compact arrangement which gave better balance while also doing away with the Miura's shared lubrication. It also eliminated the troublesome gear linkage that had been an undesirable characteristic of the Miura.

In a bid to whet appetites, the Countach got another outing at the 1973 Geneva motor show, this time more or less in production form – but it would still be another year before the finished article was to be seen. When the production-ready car did emerge, it was badged LP400 Countach, denoting its 4-litre (244ci) V12 and the fact it was hung out the back (LP being short for Longitudinale Posteriore).

This first iteration of the Countach had a claimed 277.5kW (375bhp), which was supposedly enough to allow a top speed of over 305.7km/h (190mph) – but nobody ever verified it officially. Still, it certainly

This is one of the later derivatives of the Countach, the QV. The bodykit was standard (and necessary to cover those tyres), but the rear wing was optional – this car's owner must have saved his money for the petrol bills instead.

The beetle-wing doors that were a distinctive trademark of the Countach meant the car's sills were huge. That made access to the interior tricky, but once in it was a wonderful place to be, with its semi-reclining driving position.

looked the part and it went even better in 1978 when the LP400S arrived. With wider, stickier tyres and rejigged suspension the handling and roadholding were greatly improved – even if the car was no faster.

In a bid to stay one step ahead of Ferrari, there was an increase in the V12's capacity for 1982, when the

LP500S appeared. The engine grew to 4.8 litres (291.3ci) but the power remained at a quoted 277.5kW (375bhp) – it was the driveability that increased, instead.

The LP5005 QV

The launch of Ferrari's Testarossa in 1984 meant Lamborghini had to come up with something pretty special if it was to stay ahead – which is exactly what it did. New for the 1985 Geneva motor show was the Countach LP500S QV. The QV stood for Quattrovalvole, or four valves per cylinder. This allowed better breathing for the mighty V12 engine, which also grew to 5.2 litres (315.6ci) at the same time. The result of all this work was a power output of 336.7kW (455bhp) – enough to beat the Ferrari while also delivering a 0–60mph (0–97km/h) time of just 4.9 seconds. Tellingly, the top speed was just 286.4km/h (178mph) – which was significantly slower than the first Countach's official figure...

The final incarnation of the Countach appeared in 1988, with the rather overblown Anniversary edition. This tag was a reference to Lamborghini's 25th anniversary as a company, but the looks were something of a disappointment after the purity of the original concept. Gone were the clean lines, to be replaced by scoops, slats, ducts and spoilers galore, along with a tasteless bodykit. It was still pretty dramatic though!

Lamborghini Countach

Years of production	1974–90
Displacement	5167cc (310ci)
Configuration	Mid-mounted V12
Transmission	Five-speed manual, rear-wheel drive
Power	336.7kW (455bhp) @ 7000rpm
Torque	498.1Nm (369lb ft) @ 5200rpm
Top speed	286.4km/h (178mph)
0–60mph (0–97km/h)	4.9sec
Power to weight ratio	233.1kW/ton (315bhp/ton)
Number built	1997

Lancia Stratos

Immediately behind the cabin there was a hoop spoiler to generate downforce at high speed. This was in addition to the lip spoiler at the very back of the car.

Once the Stratos had been developed, Lancia was able to use the 2.4-litre (145.6ci) V6 engine, that was fitted to the Ferrari Dino. In the Lancia, however, the block was cast iron – power output was 140.6kW (190bhp).

To make the Stratos as agile as possible, the wheelbase was kept short; it was just 2172mm (85.5in). But that made it very twitchy, and in the wrong hands things could go bad!

The front and rear ends of the Stratos could be quickly removed for easy maintenance. The rear lifted off to remove the engine; the front section covered the radiator and brake servo.

There was a separate chassis, to which was attached a glassfibre bodyshell. The car's monocoque was built of sheet steel, which was made in the Bertone factory.

To rein in the speed there were disc brakes fitted all round. Suspension at the front was by wishbones while at the rear there were long-travel struts to cope with rough terrain.

Was there ever a rally car that looked as sensational as the Stratos? While it looked as though it was made for ultra-high speed cruising on the autostradas, it was actually developed for rally stages around the globe – something that it tackled with remarkable success throughout a career that spanned more than half a decade. Yet despite its jaw-dropping looks and sporting success, the Stratos wasn't that powerful – or even that fast.

Homologation special

The Stratos was one of the first homologation specials, which meant it was created specifically for rallying – with road cars being a necessary side-effect of the project. Indeed, as a road car the Stratos wasn't really very successful, but it was a force to be reckoned with on the rally circuits of the world. The car was conceived in the early 1970s, chiefly by Lancia's then competition director Cesare Fiorio. He needed to come up with a car that could replace the

They won't have helped the aerodynamics, but that stack of lights showed the Stratos meant business on the rally stages of the world. This is where it excelled, racking up one victory after another throughout the 1970s.

Lancia Stratos	
Years of production	1973–5
Displacement	2418cc (145.6ci)
Configuration	Mid-mounted V6
Transmission	Five-speed manual, rear-wheel drive
Power	140.6kW (190bhp) @ 7000rpm
Torque	224.1Nm (166lb ft) @ 5500rpm
Top speed	225.3km/h (140mph)
0–60mph (0–97km/h)	6.8 sec
Power to weight ratio	143.5kW/ton (194bhp/ton)
Number built	500 approx

ageing Fulvia which had already seen service for many years. But instead of creating a direct replacement for the Fulvia, he was asked to come up with something that would be successful in the GT category of Group 4. With this in mind, he knew that he had free rein in terms of the car's design, but it also meant that he had to create 500 examples of the car.

This figure included any race cars, but such a high number meant well over 400 road editions would have to find owners – a pretty tall order in the cash-strapped early 1970s.

Fiorio had a look around to see where the best starting-point was, and his eye was taken by the Stratos show car that had been shown by Bertone at the 1970 Turin motor show. Its incredibly futuristic wedge-shaped bodyshell was just what Fiorio wanted to boost Lancia's image – this would be a car that nobody could overlook. The problem was that the Stratos concept was completely impractical, with its one-piece hinged canopy for entry to the cabin. It was also powered by a relatively weedy Fulvia V4 engine – his rallying creation would need significantly more poke than that.

The Stratos HF

A potential answer surfaced in the form of Bertone's follow-up concept; the Stratos HF. This was shown at the 1971 Turin motor show, and with its Ferrari V6 powerplant it was much closer to what Fiorio reckoned he needed. Although its 2172mm (85.5in) wheelbase was the same as before, the new concept

It's when seen from this angle that the wedge shape of the Stratos is most apparent. These lines were fashionable at the time, with companies such as Triumph (TR7) and Lotus (Esprit) both jumping on the bandwagon.

was nearly 254mm (10in) taller, allowing for easier access to the cockpit. There were even proper doors and windows!

Lancia had been absorbed by the Fiat empire in 1969, after bankruptcy had threatened it with closure. Because Ferrari was already within the Fiat group, some of its technology would be available for Lancia's new rally star. Time was of the essence in getting the cars built and sold, so the Stratos could start its competition career as quickly as possible. To speed things up Bertone was enlisted to produce each of the 500 cars – Lancia didn't have the expertise to build such a specialized vehicle. Bertone started by creating a sheet steel centre section, into which Lancia's running gear would be put. The cars were then finished off by Bertone clothing the structure with glassfibre body panels.

By the end of 1974 the car had been homologated, which meant it was ready for entry on the official world rally stage. Despite this, the car scored its first victory while it was still a prototype; when it won the Spanish Firestone Rally in 1973. For the next six years the Stratos notched up one victory after another in every major rally around the world, except for the RAC and Safari. In total it could claim more than 80 international wins, with plenty more trophies gleaned from road races such as the Targa Florio. It may have had only 2.4 litres (145.6ci) and 140.6kW (190bhp), but it didn't seem to cause much of a problem!

Lotus Esprit

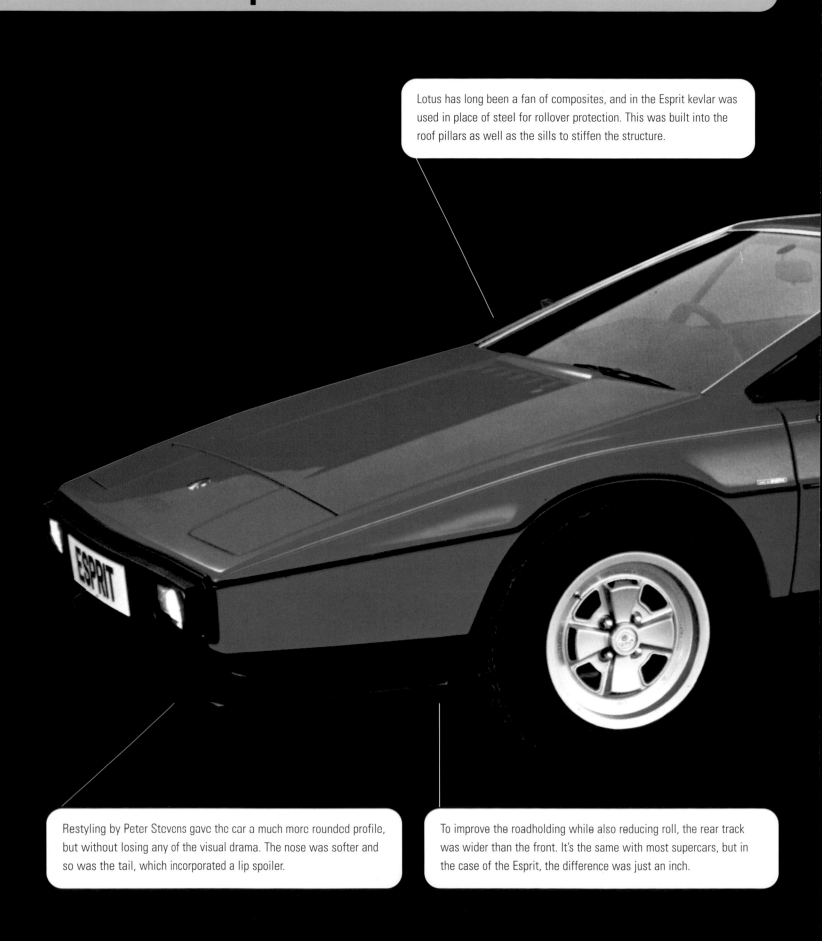

Lotus has long been a fan of composites, and in the Esprit kevlar was used in place of steel for rollover protection. This was built into the roof pillars as well as the sills to stiffen the structure.

Restyling by Peter Stevens gave the car a much more rounded profile, but without losing any of the visual drama. The nose was softer and so was the tail, which incorporated a lip spoiler.

To improve the roadholding while also reducing roll, the rear track was wider than the front. It's the same with most supercars, but in the case of the Esprit, the difference was just an inch.

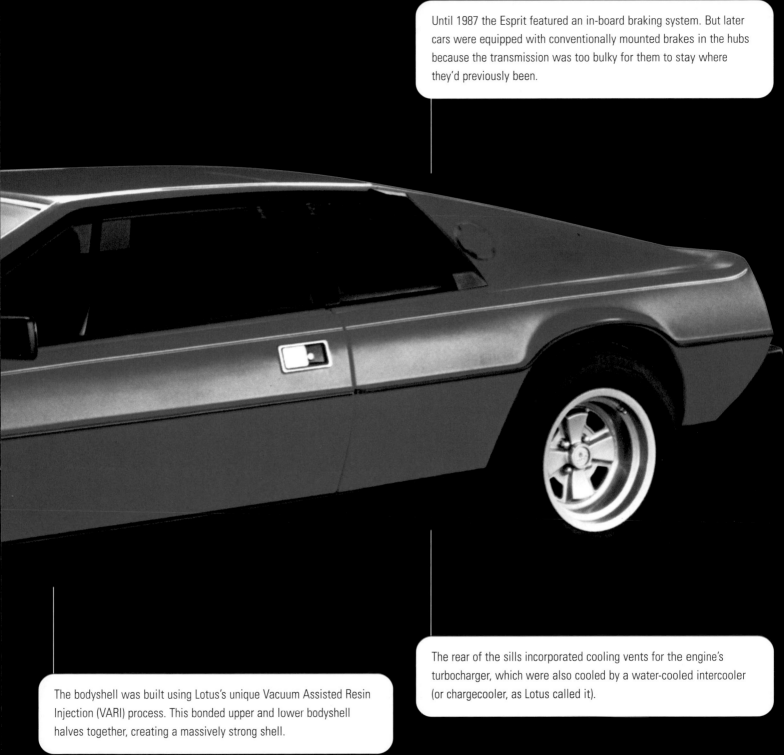

Until 1987 the Esprit featured an in-board braking system. But later cars were equipped with conventionally mounted brakes in the hubs because the transmission was too bulky for them to stay where they'd previously been.

The rear of the sills incorporated cooling vents for the engine's turbocharger, which were also cooled by a water-cooled intercooler (or chargecooler, as Lotus called it).

The bodyshell was built using Lotus's unique Vacuum Assisted Resin Injection (VARI) process. This bonded upper and lower bodyshell halves together, creating a massively strong shell.

It may have had a mere four cylinders, but when the Lotus Esprit hit the scene in the mid-1970s, it had the presence of cars that cost far more. Here was a car with a dramatic wedge profile that looked as though it could travel faster than anything to come out of Italy. Yet with a mere 118.4kW (160bhp) in its initial 2-litre (121.4ci) form, the car was barely capable of 193.1km/h (120mph). Even by the end of the 1970s, by which time the engine had been upgraded to a 2.2-litre (133.5ci) unit, the top speed was only 217.2km/h (135mph). It took the arrival of the brilliant Esprit Turbo, in 1980, to push the top speed beyond the magic 241.3km/h (150mph) mark. Then came a restyle in 1988, a V8 engine, and ever more power.

Wedge shape

The final Esprit, built in 2004, was a far cry from the first car seen over three decades earlier. Sharp-edged wedges were the order of the day in the 1970s, when Giorgetto Giugiaro's original Lotus Esprit styling

While the classic Giugaro-styled Esprit lasted for well over a decade, the Peter Stevens restyle that succeeded it was even better looking. This is one of the later derivatives, although it still featured a four-cylinder powerplant.

proposal was unveiled as the Silver Car concept at the Turin motor show in 1972. Giugiaro had approached Lotus at the 1971 Geneva motor show, suggesting that he create a supercar proposal based on a modified Europa twin-cam chassis. Lotus was keen on the idea and the first Esprit prototype was displayed at the 1973 Geneva salon.

It wasn't until 1975 that the Esprit was finally shown in production form, and it would be another year before the first customer cars were delivered. As was typical in the mid-1970s, customers were left to finish the car's development. The Esprit's predecessor, the Europa, had never been regarded as a particularly desirable car, with unattractive styling and poor interior packaging. The Esprit had to address these issues, and the fact that the concept still looks fresh today (if a little passé in execution) is a testament to the team which produced it.

Giugiaro had wanted to call the car Kiwi, but Lotus management were intent on a name beginning with the letter E, as is Lotus tradition. A trawl through the dictionary came up with Esprit, which they felt summed up the car's sprightliness. Even before the project had been properly initiated, the choice of powerplant was never in doubt, with Lotus having

In some ways the earlier cars have a more characterful interior and dashboard. But there's no denying that the later cars – such as this one – have a cabin that's far better made and much nicer to use.

recently completed development of its Type 907 twin-cam engine. Mounted ahead of the rear axle line, the unit has become one of the all-time greats.

Modifications and upgrades

The first Esprit was tagged the S1, with the S2, S2.2 and S3 following in time. While there were all sorts of modifications and upgrades along the way, the biggest thing to happen to the Esprit was a restyle by Peter Stevens in 1987. This much more rounded car retained the four-cylinder engine, but with a new Garrett T3 turbocharger. Whereas the old car had used a transaxle borrowed from the Citroën SM, the new one featured a Renault GTA unit, with slighter taller gearing to make the car more relaxed at speed. Because the transmission was bulkier, the rear brakes, which had previously been mounted in-board, were fitted conventionally on the wheel hubs.

Whereas the last of the previous-shape turbocharged Esprits peaked at 159.1kW (215bhp) (up from an earlier 155.4kW / 210bhp), by 1989 the new-shape car could claim to have 195.3kW (264bhp) on tap, thanks to the addition of an intercooler. There was also a move to fuel injection, in place of the previous Dellorto carburettors, which in turn allowed the

fitting of a catalytic converter. All this conspired to give a top speed of over 257.4km/h (160mph), along with a 0–60mph (0–97km/h) time of under five seconds. But of course the development continued apace, first with the Sport 300 of 1992 (with 222kW / 300bhp) then the V8 of 1996. This latter car replaced the S4 which had debuted in 1994, and with a twin-turbo 3.5-litre (212.4ci) engine there was as much power on offer as anyone was likely to need. By 1999 the last four-cylinder Esprit has been built – but it wasn't until 2004 that the model died altogether.

Lotus Esprit	
Years of production	1976–2004
Displacement	2174cc (130.4ci)
Configuration	Mid-mounted in-line four-cylinder
Transmission	Five-speed manual, rear-wheel drive
Power	195.3kW (264bhp) @ 6500rpm
Torque	352.3Nm (261lb ft) @ 3900rpm
Top speed	259km/h (161mph)
0–60mph (0–97km/h)	4.9sec
Power to weight ratio	162.8kW/ton (220bhp/ton)
Number built	10,575

Monteverdi Hai

The fuel tank was located in the car's nose, in a bid to help with the weight distribution. Once the fuel tank had been filled, the balance was surprisingly good at 46:54 front:rear.

The front suspension was by means of double wishbones, coil springs over Koni adjustable dampers and an adjustable anti-roll bar. At the back was a de Dion tube, Watts linkage and upper/lower trailing arms along with coil springs and Koni shock absorbers.

The Hai had an immensely strong chassis that was also torsionally stiff. Rather than try to come up with the lightest possible design, plenty of heavy-gauge steel was used.

Chrysler's legendary 426 Hemi engine was used. The car could reliably push out 333kW (450bhp) and 661.5Nm (490lb ft) of torque.

That curvy bodyshell looked fantastic, but there's some debate as to who designed it. Although Peter Monteverdi claims it was his, renowned stylist Trevor Fiore also claimed to have come up with it.

The rear brakes were mounted in-board, to reduce the unsprung weight. The front brakes were conventionally mounted, with the whole system using disc technology. There was also a servo fitted.

This staged shot shows just how close the engine was to the car's occupants. With the engine cover removed (along with the passenger seat), you can see why there was plenty of engine noise in the Hai's cockpit.

If you like your production cars to be on the exclusive side, the Monteverdi Hai is the one for you. Just three examples were built in a production run (if you can call it that) spanning two decades. The company claimed it could have sold far more, but the aim was to keep the car exclusive while also ensuring maximum publicity through it. This was the car that was meant to put Monteverdi in the spotlight. Despite this, you've probably never even heard of the company, never mind seen one of its cars.

Peter Monteverdi

Peter Monteverdi was born in 1934, and he was hooked on cars before he could even drive. His father ran a garage, and by the time Monteverdi was 17 he'd already built his first car, using the remains of an old Fiat. When his father died in 1956, the family repair business passed to him – in time it became more of a tuning outfit. He then started to race cars, notably Ferraris and Alfa Romeos. This in turn led to him becoming the Swiss Ferrari importer. But as with Ferruccio Lamborghini, Monteverdi fell out with Ferrari and so vowed to produce his own supercar.

Monteverdi had driven most of the contemporary supercars and knew what it took to produce something competitive. His first car was the 400SS, which used Chrysler's 440 V8 engine, but he was also keen to try the new mid-engined layout that Lamborghini had pioneered with its Miura. By early 1969 Monteverdi had formulated a plan for his mid-engined exotic beast – and he also came up with a name for it. It would be called 'Hai' which is the German word for shark.

The new car's chassis was built for exceptional rigidity rather than minimum weight, and the result was a frame constructed of heavy-gauge rectangular steel tubes. The suspension was much the same as the earlier Monteverdi cars, which meant that at the front there were double wishbones, coil springs over Koni adjustable dampers and an adjustable anti-roll bar. At the back was a de Dion tube, Watts linkage and upper/lower trailing arms along with coil springs and Koni shock absorbers. To balance out the weight distribution, the fuel tank was located ahead of the windscreen, while the major mechanical elements were behind the driver and passenger.

A premium GT

The Hai would be sold as a premium GT, which meant it had to be fitted with the best technology available. To that end, there were huge disc brakes at each corner, with servo assistance. The rear brakes were mounted in-board, to reduce unsprung weight. For this new car, Monteverdi asked Chrysler for its most powerful engine, the 426 Hemi. With a displacement of 6980cc (418.8ci) and when equipped with a pair of four-barrel Carter carburettors, there was a hefty 333kW (450bhp) on tap, along with 661.5Nm (490lb ft) of torque. Getting this power to the 381mm (15in) Borrani wire wheels was a five-speed ZF transaxle, and the result of all this power was a claimed 0–60mph (0–97km/h) time of just 4.8 seconds. This was never independently verified, but the car was tested at 281.6km/h (175mph) by a Swiss motoring magazine; the factory claimed it would do 289.6km/h (180mph).

A suitably spectacular design needed to be drawn up for the bodyshell, and when you look at the pictures you can see the goal was achieved. Both Trevor Fiore and Peter Monteverdi claim the credit for

Monteverdi Hai	
Years of production	1970–90
Displacement	6980cc (418.8ci)
Configuration	Mid-mounted V8
Transmission	Five-speed manual, rear-wheel drive
Power	333kW (450bhp) @ 5000rpm
Torque	661.5Nm (490lb ft) @ 4000rpm
Top speed	289.6km/h (180mph)
0–60mph (0–97km/h)	4.8sec
Power to weight ratio	258.2kW/ton (349bhp/ton)
Number built	3

the Hai's looks – the reality is that it was probably a collaboration between the two.

Monteverdi attempted to make a comeback in 1992, with the Hai 650. Based on his stillborn 1991 Formula 1 car, the car was powered by a 481kW (650bhp) Ford F1 engine. With an all-in weight of just 750kg (1653.7lb) (thanks to a carbon fibre bodyshell), the car was reputedly good for 0–125mph in just eight seconds. A maximum of 12 cars were set to be built, but there were no takers. It's unlikely there will be any more Monteverdis now; the company's founder died in 1998.

There's not much chance of ever seeing one of these – in any circumstances. Which is rather a shame because the Hai is one of the most beautiful supercar designs ever; there's no unnecessary clutter anywhere.

1980–1989

If the 1960s had been the decade when the supercar genre really got going, it was the 1980s that saw the breed truly blossom. With new materials and technology available like never before, supercars were suddenly more usable and more capable than ever before.

If the previous decade had been one of pessimism, the 1980s was quite the opposite. Towards the end of the decade the world's economy was in top form and it seemed that every other week there was a new supercar project being announced. Greed was good, and if there was a better symbol of that than an ultra-flash supercar, many were still to find it.

Companies such as Lamborghini, Aston Martin and Porsche flourished, while there was a new breed of supercar before the mid-point of the decade had been reached. This was the Group B rally car, each example of which had to have 200 road cars produced to be eligible to race in the formula. While these cars weren't about high top speeds, they were about massive power, equally massive acceleration, and transmissions that allowed them to exploit their power. The problem with the Group B cars was that

The RS200 was developed by Ford with just one aim in mind; to win the World Rally Championship. But by the time it was properly developed, the series for which it was born had already been scrapped. It made a cracking road car though...

they were made by mass-market companies such as Ford, Peugeot and Austin-Rover. While the cars may have been incredibly capable (the MG Metro 6R4 was the fastest car ever tested by *Autocar* magazine when it was put through its paces in 1985), they didn't have the cachet of one of the more exclusive marques more used to peddling mid-engined exotica. So even though these cars were ferociously quick, they languished in warehouses while customers spent their money on Porsches and Ferraris instead.

The 1980s was also the decade of high technology – the silicon chip ruled and new materials were coming out all the time. Carbon fibre and kevlar were the new wonder solutions, offering astonishing strength with incredible lightness – it really was the dawn of a new era in supercar production. Yet as the decade drew to a close it began to turn sour – in fact it was ending as it had begun.

While throughout the 1980s there had been no shortage of good times for any established maker of supercars, it all started to go wrong as the 1990s began to dawn and boom turned to bust.

Audi Sport quattro

Those proportions are a bit odd, and that short wheelbase made the car very twitchy on the limit. A whopping 317mm (12.5in) were removed from the standard car's wheelbase, so the axles were closer together than a Metro's.

That famous quattro transmission was as effective as ever, with a lockable centre diff to maintain stability in slippery conditions. The centre and rear diffs could both be locked if traction was a major problem.

Apart from the doors, which used Audi 80 items made from steel, the whole of the Sport was made of plastic and carbon composites. Even the air intakes and radiator cowling were of lightweight composites.

Although the 2.1-litre (127.4ci) five-cylinder engine shared the same basic specification as the standard quattro, the Sport's unit was made of alloy throughout. There was also a much bigger turbocharger to boost power to 226.4kW (306bhp).

Audi Sport quattro

To help boost power as much as possible, an intercooler was fitted to reduce the temperature of the air entering the engine. By reducing its temperature from 140°C (284°F) to just 60°C (140°F), it was much more dense.

The quattro Sport may have been utterly thrilling to drive, but the cabin didn't give much indication of that. It was all stock quattro, which meant great build quality and ergonomics, but little in the way of visual excitement.

carbon fibre and kevlar (with the sole exception of the doors), in place of the steel bodywork that adorned the standard road car. The cylinder head was different and so were the turbos – for this car to win rallies, it had to be seriously tweaked in the highly competitive world of Group B racing.

In the early 1980s, the quattro in standard production form was unlike anything else available at the time. Four-wheel drive was still for farmers, not road cars, and that turbocharged five-cylinder powerplant wasn't replicated anywhere else. In fact, the car formed the perfect basis for a highly developed supercar that could take on all comers.

Small and light

When you first clap eyes on the Sport, it looks diminutive – which isn't surprising when you consider that its wheelbase was an inch shorter than an Austin Metro's. But with those hefty 228x381mm (9x15in) wheels crammed under the arches, it certainly looked purposeful. With such a short wheelbase, it was no surprise that the car could get very twitchy when all the power was used – but at the same time the car was even more nimble than usual.

To keep weight down there were plenty of composites used throughout the Sport – the wings were constructed of kevlar-reinforced glassfibre, along with the roof and the front apron. Carbon fibre was also used to construct the air intakes and radiator cowling.

While the bodywork was relatively low-key (at least for road versions of the car), the mechanicals were anything but. Stuffed into the stubby nose was a five-cylinder powerplant that on paper was the same as the unit found in the standard car. However, in the Sport it was made of alloy throughout, cutting the weight down by 23kg (50.7lbs). There were four valves per cylinder and a pair of overhead camshafts, and it still displaced 2.1 litres (127.4ci). But the major difference was the turbocharger bolted to it – a massive KKK unit that ran at 17.4psi and produced some of the greatest lag ever known in a boosted car. The power was increased further (to 226.4kW / 306bhp for road versions) with the addition of an intercooler – but race cars were equipped with anything from 333kW (450bhp) upwards. With 348.5Nm (258lb ft) of torque at 3700rpm, and

At first glance, it's easy to dismiss the Sport quattro as merely a shortened version of the standard production car. But it was so much more than merely a standard quattro with the wheelbase chopped by 317mm (12.5in). Instead of a cast-iron engine there was an all-alloy unit up front. The bodywork was all lightweight

Audi Sport quattro	
Years of production	1984–5
Displacement	2134cc (128ci)
Configuration	Front-engined in-line five
Transmission	Five-speed manual, four-wheel drive
Power	226.4kW (306bhp) @ 6700rpm
Torque	348.5Nm (258lb ft) @ 3700rpm
Top speed	249.4km/h (155mph)
0–60mph (0–97km/h)	4.8sec
Power to weight ratio	177.6kW/ton (240bhp/ton)
Number built	214

relatively short gearing, the Sport could crack the 0–60mph (0–97km/h) sprint in just 4.8 seconds; faster than both the Porsche 911 Turbo and the Lamborghini Countach.

Adjustability

All four wheels were permanently driven, as was typical for any quattro-equipped car. But there was a lot of adjustability built into the system, with the driver being able to lock the centre and/or rear diffs if things got really slippery. There were five ratios to choose from in the manual gearbox and the specification was the same for the suspension at each end. That meant wishbones with coil springs and

While the regular quattro was all-conquering on the roads as well as rally stages, Audi moved up several gears with the introduction of the S1. With 333kw (450bhp) on tap, it made mincemeat of its rivals as it tackled Pike's Peak (a racing track in Colorado, USA).

dampers, along with an anti-roll bar. While the suspension wasn't adjustable by the driver, the braking system was. Anti-lock was fitted, but it could be switched off if the conditions warranted it. For example, if the car was being driven on gravel, it was sometimes better to lock the wheels and build up a wedge of stones under the wheels.

Although the quattro had dominated rallying in the early 1980s, the emergence of the Group B series meant the goalposts were moved significantly. Suddenly four-wheel drive, bespoke lightweight bodyshells and huge power outputs were par for the course. Audi no longer had things its own way, and during the 1986 rally season the success of the quattro (in Sport form) wasn't what Audi was used to. Before the car had really got into its stride, the series had been scrapped – so the car never achieved what Audi hoped it would. But it's still every bit as cracking as it ever was.

Chevrolet Corvette ZR-1

Since the first Corvette of 1953, all generations of America's best-known supercar have featured glassfibre bodyshells. For greater strength, the front and rear bumpers are of more sophisticated composites.

The ZR-1 was the first Corvette ever to be fitted with tyre pressure monitors. There was one on each wheel, and if the pressure fell at any corner, a warning light illuminated on the dash to say so.

Although the Americans like their cars to have an automatic gearbox, the Corvette was the world's first car to be fitted with a six-speed manual transmission. It had been optional the previous year on the standard car.

The 5.7-litre (345.9ci) V8 may sound like the engine fitted to the standard Corvette, but the ZR-1's was all-alloy and featured four valves per cylinder. It was also developed by Lotus, unlike that of the standard car.

TUNED PORT INJECTION

The suspension incorporated a system called selective ride control, which enabled the driver to adjust the softness of the dampers, so it was more or less sporty depending on how the car was being driven.

To rein in the prodigious power on tap, there were various electronic driver aids. Traction control helped put the power down while anti-lock brakes were also fitted as standard.

In 1953 Chevrolet decided to create a limited run of 300 sports cars. The car was called the Corvette – and it failed to sell. By the end of the first year a third of the cars built were still left sitting in showrooms, but rather than throw in the towel, Chevrolet decided to develop the car further, to make it more desirable. To that end a small-block V8 engine was installed, transforming the car and also its success rate.

The development continued apace, with a new body in 1956; at the same time a larger engine was fitted. An all-new design appeared in 1963 along with some major mechanical upgrades – this was also the first time that a coupé was offered, as until now all Corvettes were roadsters. For 1967 there was another major redesign, which lasted all the way through until 1984. It was this incarnation of the Corvette that was to provide the basis for the ZR-1, but that wouldn't appear until this fourth generation of Corvette had been in production for half a decade.

The latest Corvette continues in the same vein as its predecessors, with its glassfibre bodyshell and potent V8 engine mounted up front. The new model is faster and better built and handles sharper than ever into the bargain.

Six-speed gearbox

Therefore, the Corvette had already been in production for well over three decades before the first cutting-edge derivative was produced – until the ZR-1 arrived the Corvette had never been especially advanced. The new model's aim was to change all

Chevrolet Corvette ZR-1	
Years of production	1989–95
Displacement	5727cc (345.9ci)
Configuration	Front-mounted V8
Transmission	Six-speed manual, rear-wheel drive
Power	277.5kW (375bhp) @ 5800rpm
Torque	499.5Nm (370lb ft) @ 4800rpm
Top speed	275.1km/h (171mph)
0–60mph (0–97km/h)	5.6sec
Power to weight ratio	173.9kW/ton (235bhp/ton)
Number built	6939

that, with its more high-tech engine and six-speed manual gearbox; the first time anywhere in the world that such a transmission had been offered. And it wasn't just any six-speed gearbox; under certain conditions, to save fuel, a solenoid intervened to prevent second and third gears from being used under acceleration. That meant a driver had to go from first to fourth – although there was plenty of torque to facilitate this. It also featured more modern composites in some of its construction – although the Corvette's bodyshell had always been constructed of glassfibre.

During the 1960s, the Corvette could hold its own among the crop of current supercars – some of the wilder big-block cars of that decade offered pretty astonishing performance. But during the 1970s and early 1980s the model had gone off the boil; some of the more mundane sports cars could beat it at its own game. General Motors realized that something needed to be done before the Corvette lost its hard-won reputation altogether, so it enlisted the help of Lotus. This company was asked to design and develop a V8 engine that would allow the Corvette to take on any supercar from anywhere in the world, and beat it.

Lotus engine
The results of Lotus's labours was an all-alloy 5.7-litre (345.9ci) which featured four valves per cylinder and a pair of camshafts for each bank of cylinders.

Although the target power output for this unit had been 296kW (400bhp), the final tally of horses was 375 – which was still enough for the car to top 273.5km/h (170mph) while sprinting from a standing start to 60mph (97km/h) in a mere 5.6 seconds. Chevrolet's initial plan had been to retain the existing engine, but fit four-valve heads to it. That way the engine bay wouldn't need to be significantly re-engineered. But in the event the ZR-1 was developed as a wider version of the standard car, so that the powerplant could fit between the wheel arches. The powerplant was known as the LT5 unit, and it had to be created because had Chevrolet stuck to its original plan of developing its existing engine, the noise and emission regulations in force at the time wouldn't have been able to be met.

Despite the impressive performance on offer, the ZR-1 was no stripped-out racetrack special. It was fitted with all the luxury equipment demanded by America's drivers. The standard specification sheet included items such as air-conditioning, a solar glass roof panel, electric windows and central locking. All this pushed the car's kerb weight up to nearly 1573kg (1486lbs), which didn't help the car's agility, but it couldn't be denied that the car was impressively fast.

The third-generation Corvette was the most aggressively styled of all the derivatives. Current from 1968 until 1982, those rear haunches and dramatic front wings give the car an amazingly muscular look.

Ferrari 288 GTO

The three gills behind the rear wheel arches were there to let hot air escape – the brakes became very hot when the car was being driven hard. They were also a styling link with the original GTO.

It may look like a common-or-garden 308 GTB, but the 288 GTO was 63mm (2.5in) longer overall. It was also 101mm (4in) wider and the wheelbase was a significant 114mm (4.5in) longer.

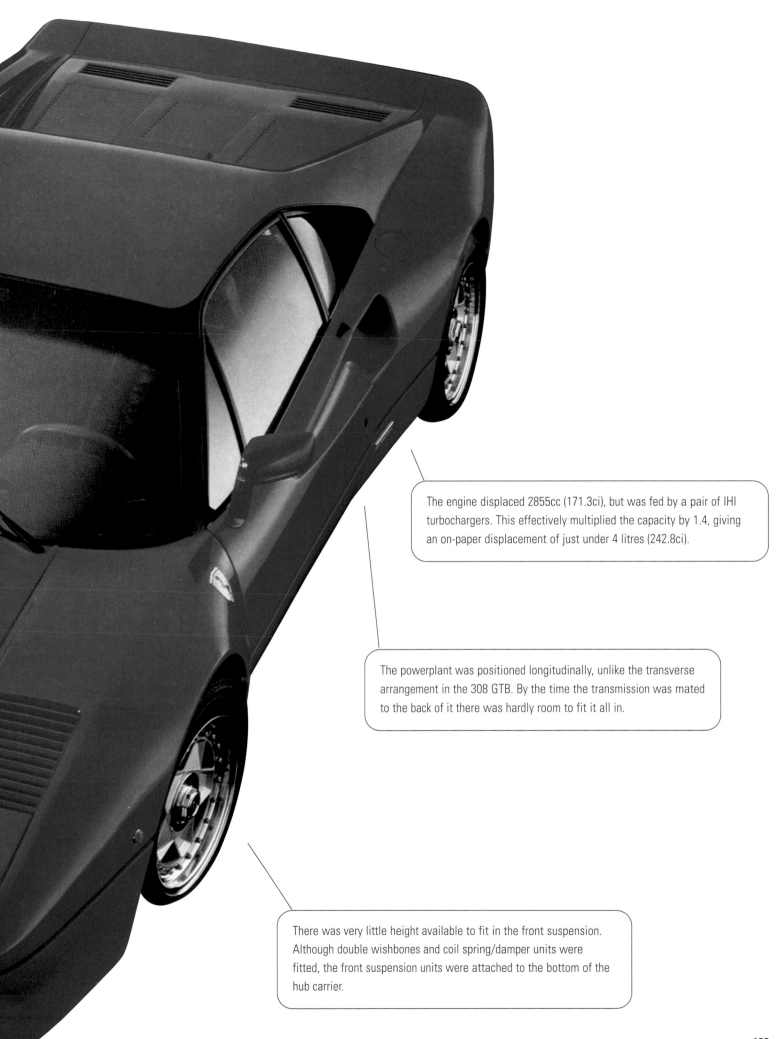

The engine displaced 2855cc (171.3ci), but was fed by a pair of IHI turbochargers. This effectively multiplied the capacity by 1.4, giving an on-paper displacement of just under 4 litres (242.8ci).

The powerplant was positioned longitudinally, unlike the transverse arrangement in the 308 GTB. By the time the transmission was mated to the back of it there was hardly room to fit it all in.

There was very little height available to fit in the front suspension. Although double wishbones and coil spring/damper units were fitted, the front suspension units were attached to the bottom of the hub carrier.

It would have been very easy to have included just about every car ever made by Ferrari in this book, but it wasn't possible. One of the cars that didn't quite manage to get in was the original Ferrari GTO – based on the 250 of 1960. Just 39 were built, and they've gone on to become some of the most valuable cars ever made. Ferrari decided to cash in on that heritage by introducing a new GTO model in the 1980s, based on the design of the entry-level 308 GTB. Bearing in mind that the 288 GTO cost twice as much as the 308 GTB, it was unfortunate that the two looked so similar – especially as there were very few parts which were interchangeable between the two (the doors and windscreen being the main ones). But put the two cars next to each other and the differences were immediately obvious, not least of all the much greater width of the GTO.

Gran Turismo Omologato

The GTO name has its roots in motorsport; it's short for Gran Turismo Omologato, which essentially means a homologation special – usually built in tiny

Although the 288 GTO was by far the most expensive Ferrari available at the time, its lines were based on those of the entry-level model, the 308 GTB. That made no difference though – the car was still an instant sell-out.

Ferrari 288 GTO	
Years of production	1984–7
Displacement	2855cc (171.3ci)
Configuration	Mid-mounted V8, twin-turbo
Transmission	Five-speed manual, rear-wheel drive
Power	296kW (400bhp) @ 7000rpm
Torque	494.1Nm (366lb ft) @ 3800rpm
Top speed	304.1km/h (189mph)
0–60 (0–97km/h)	4.8sec
Power to weight ratio	254.5kW/ton (344bhp/ton)
Number built	272

numbers. The first GTO (the 250) won Le Mans in 1962 as well as the 1962, 1963 and 1964 World Grand Touring Championships – so as a part of Ferrari's heritage, the badge is not to be underestimated. The 288 GTO was to be Ferrari's technological tour de force, built specially for the Group B racing formula. This was the same time that several other car makers were pulling out all the stops for their Group B cars, and Ferrari didn't want to be left behind. The new car

would use the most advanced technology to produce a lightweight bodyshell, while the mechanicals would have all the innovations thrown at it that Ferrari could muster.

The bodywork was built largely of reinforced plastics, with carbon fibre and kevlar in some key areas. The bonnet was made of a kevlar/glassfibre honeycomb composite, as was the bulkhead between the engine bay and cabin. Using the best Formula One technology available at the time, this construction offered massive rigidity with light weight.

If the GTO's exterior was impressive, its cabin was definitely a let-down. It essentially took the 308's cockpit and added very little – but the car was never supposed to be about luxury. What was there was good quality, with plenty of leather and chrome. But the GTO wasn't about long lists of standard equipment – that just weighed it down.

Engine

The powerplant was a development of the V8 that usually nestled transversely in the 308 GTB's engine bay. The Group B formula carried a displacement limit of 4 litres (242.8ci), which is why the GTO's engine was taken down to 2855cc (171.3ci). By adding a turbocharger (or two, in the case of the GTO), this had the effect of multiplying the capacity by 1.4, so the effective displacement for the engine became 3997cc (239.8ci). This was the first time that Ferrari

had turbocharged a production car, apart from the Italy-only tax-break special, the 208 GTB. But of course the powerplant wasn't just a blown GTB engine – it was much more than that. There was a pair of overhead camshafts for each bank of cylinders, with each combustion chamber having four valves. The crankshaft was machined from a solid billet of steel and there were two intercoolers that helped boost the available power to 296kW (400bhp) at 7000rpm. There was also 494.1Nm (366lb ft) of torque at 3800rpm – enough to take the car from a standstill to 60mph (97km/h) in just 4.8 seconds, before running out of steam at 304.1km/h (189mph).

The powerplant was positioned longitudinally, with the five-speed transaxle slung out behind it. Only the rear wheels were driven, while the suspension was exactly what anybody would have expected from Ferrari. That meant there were unequal-length wishbones at each corner, with coil springs, Koni dampers and anti-roll bars. Each front suspension unit connected with the lower portion of its hub carrier to feed loads into the body between the wishbone mounts, so that the overall height of the suspension could be kept to a minimum.

It was no coincidence that the leather-trimmed seats of the 288 GTO echoed those of its predecessor, the 250 GTO. For better ventilation the seats featured eyelets, while luxury equipment was kept to a minimum to keep weight down.

Ferrari F40

While the engine was at the back, the radiator was at the front. However, there were separate coolers for the engine and transmission oils; each of these coolers were mounted at the very back of the car, behind the four slats in the rear wings.

Underneath the composite bodywork was a relatively conventional steel monocoque. It was a very rigid structure that offered high crash resistance and increased body stiffness to improve handling.

Those slats in the rear window were there to allow as much heat out of the engine bay as possible. Slatted windows were popular in the 1970s, but the F40 updated the idea with transparent panels for better visibility.

The 3-litre (176.1ci) mid-mounted engine is an engineering tour de force, with four belt-driven overhead camshafts, eight cylinders, 32 valves and a pair of intercooled turbochargers. The result was 353.7kW (478bhp) at 7000rpm.

There were no fewer than 13 different NACA ducts on the F40's body. They were there to cool the brakes, engine and intercoolers, which between them generated huge amounts of heat.

When you've got the portfolio that Ferrari has, it's not easy to come up with a new car that's especially sensational. With so many ultra-fast and exclusive cars to its name, the Modena-based company had to pull out all the stops to come up with something special to celebrate its 40th anniversary. You only have to take a quick look at the F40 to see that Ferrari didn't hold back, though – few road cars have ever looked so extreme.

Despite its arresting looks, the F40 wasn't especially advanced under the skin. There was no four-wheel drive or even anti-lock brakes. Even the doors were opened by a piece of cord and the first cars didn't even have windows capable of being wound down. But generous specification levels was never what the F40 was meant to be about. Instead, it was built to show how hardcore a road car Ferrari could produce – this was to be a track car for the road with nothing held back.

40th anniversary model

The F40, launched in 1987 to commemorate four decades of Ferrari car production (hence the name), was directly descended from the 288 GTO of 1984.

If you're looking for luxury here, you've come to the wrong place. The F40 may have cost huge amounts of money, but that was directed at what was underneath the skin – not on gadgets to make the car comfier to drive.

That model began as a track car, although it was never raced by Ferrari or its customers. However, Ferrari found it so easy to sell every 288 GTO it could make that the decision was quickly made to produce a follow-up that would be even more extreme. Remarkably, once the decision had been made to produce this follow up, it took barely more than a year to have a production-ready vehicle available. The project was speeded up by basing the F40 on the 288 GTO Evoluzione, which as the name suggests was a development of the standard 288 GTO.

The two keys to the F40's astonishing performance were its low weight and huge power. To keep the weight down as much as possible, the bodyshell was built entirely from carbon fibre and kevlar. There was still a tubular chassis underneath the skin, but this was constructed from various steel alloys for maximum strength and lightness. By paying such attention to detail, the F40 tipped the scales at just

1102kg (2425lb). For a car with a massive 353.7kW (478bhp) on tap, that meant a barely credible 321.9kW/ton (435bhp/ton) was on offer.

The all-alloy V8 engine was a heavily reworked version of the GTO's, with a displacement of 2936cc (176.1ci). Boosted by a pair of IHI turbochargers, the maximum power was delivered at 7000rpm, along with 573.7Nm (425lb ft) of torque from 4000rpm. To aid breathing at high revs there were four valves per cylinder, driven by a quartet of overhead camshafts. All this power was sent to the rear wheels only via a five-speed manual gearbox.

Balance and stability

The F40 wasn't just about outright power and performance – there were also things such as balance and stability to be taken into account. That's why the weight distribution was as even as Ferrari could make it while great attention to detail had been paid where the aerodynamics were concerned. When Pininfarina had been given the brief to come up with an extreme road car to commemorate Ferrari's 40th birthday, it also had to come up with a shape that had a drag co-efficient of just 0.34. This was achieved partly by smoothing the underpan as much as possible.

The suspension was classic race car, with double wishbones and coil springs and adjustable Koni damper units. There was also height adjustment built into the system, with a standard setting and a lower one for high-speed cruising, with the car sitting 20mm (0.7in) closer to the ground. The final setting was for urban use, where the car could be raised to 20mm

Most mid-engined cars featured a cover over the powerplant that hid it from view. Ferrari turned that on its head by fitting a clear plastic cover that showed the engine off to the world.

(0.7in) above standard. Cast-iron brake discs measuring 330mm (12.9in) across were fitted at each corner, with no ABS or servo assistance. The rear wheels were 431mm (17in) wide, while the front wheels were 331mm (13in) across.

Taking all this into account, it was hard to see how Ferrari could ever top the F40 in terms of looks, performance or engineering. But when the F50 arrived a decade later, it did exactly that.

Ferrari F40	
Years of production	1987–92
Displacement	2936cc (176.1ci)
Configuration	Mid-engined V8, twin-turbo
Transmission	Five-speed manual, rear-wheel drive
Power	353.7kW (478bhp) @ 7000rpm
Torque	573.7Nm (425lb ft) @ 4000rpm
Top speed	323.4km/h (201mph)
0–60mph (0–97km/h)	4.5sec
Power to weight ratio	321.9kW/ton (435bhp/ton)
Number built	1315

Ferrari Testarossa

Air conditioning had to be fitted as standard because of the huge windscreen, which allowed the cabin to warm up in hot weather. The glass area was larger than usual because of its shallow angle.

Although the radiators were positioned behind those side strakes, there was still a prominent air intake in the car's nose. This was to feed the air conditioning system as well as the front brakes.

The mechanical layout of the Testarossa was much like its predecessor's, the Boxer. The 12-cylinder boxer engine sat behind the cabin, with the gearbox beneath it. This kept the car's length down.

One of the most controversial aspects of the Testarossa's design was the series of slats down each side of the car. These slats were echoed in the rear light design, with the lenses hidden behind metal grilles.

The rear track was a massive 152mm (6in) wider than the front, making it very easy to kerb the rear wheels when manoeuvring. The track was wide because of the need to house the flat-12 powerplant.

The 1980s was the decade for being big and brash, and Ferrari took this to extremes with the Testarossa. After the lithe shapes penned by Pininfarina for the Modenese company, the Testarossa was a rude shock.

It may have been fast, expensive and very exclusive, but nobody was quite prepared for the Testarossa when it first broke cover at the 1984 Paris motor show. After decades of lithe designs, this brutally aggressive car from the Prancing Horse stable was not what Ferrari's customers had become used to. Following in the tyre tracks of the beautiful Boxer, the impossibly wide Testarossa was rather ungainly in the eyes of many – but that didn't stop Ferrari from selling every example it could build.

Design
The Boxer was well over a decade old when the Testarossa came along. It still looked great, but it was outdated dynamically – what was needed was a clean-sheet redesign. Although the engine and gearbox were carried over from the Boxer in their most basic form, everything else was new. The core specification of the car didn't change, however, with double wishbone suspension at each corner and ventilated disc brakes all round – although these weren't the same parts that had been fitted to the previous car.

Iconic car makers were already starting to trade on their heritage in the early 1980s, which is why Ferrari dipped into its archives and borrowed the name of one of its 1950s racers. The Testarossa badge was a reference to that car's red cam covers (the name means 'red head'), and when the new model's covers were painted the same colour, the classic name was bestowed upon the new arrival.

It wasn't the name that caused a stir though – it was the exterior design. This was the result of a decision having been made to move the engine's radiators from the nose to the sides of the car. Whereas Pininfarina could have tried to hide the scoops necessary to allow

Ferrari Testarossa	
Years of production	1984–1995
Displacement	4942cc (296.5ci)
Configuration	Mid-engined flat-12
Transmission	Five-speed manual, rear-wheel drive
Power	288.6kW (390bhp) @ 6300rpm
Torque	488.7Nm (362lb ft) @ 4500rpm
Top speed	275.1km/h (171mph)
0–60mph (0–97km/h)	5.2sec
Power to weight ratio	173.1kW/ton (234bhp/ton)
Number built	N/A

the requisite amount of air to the radiators, it was instead decided to turn them into a feature. As a consequence, those huge side strakes made their first (but not their last) appearance in the Ferrari range. The rear track was also incredibly wide, giving the car a rather fat-hipped look. The track was wide to prevent the car from rolling too much on the corners – something it would have been prone to with the weight of that flat-12 powerplant out the back.

Engine

The flat-12 was essentially the same as the Boxer's, although there were four valves for each cylinder in place of the previous two. This move meant Ferrari was able to sell the car in America – the Boxer's engine was too dirty to pass the strict emissions laws. Not being able to sell a car such as the Testarossa in the world's biggest supercar market didn't make much sense, which is why the engine had to be developed whether Ferrari liked it or not. Other developments included improved intake and exhaust systems while the fuel injection also evolved from the mechanical K-Jetronic to the much more advanced electronically controlled KE Jetronic. With a Magnetti-Marelli electronic control unit for the whole engine, the upshot was a powerplant capable of producing 37kW (50bhp) more while consuming less fuel.

To allow for easier servicing of the engine, it was mounted on a subframe which could be removed from the car in its entirety. This also gave access to the rear suspension, which comprised of double wishbones and coil spring/damper units, just like at the front. But because of the weight of that massive flat-12 over the rear wheels there were twin spring/damper units at each rear corner.

The Testarossa evolved into the 512TR in 1992, the brief being to make it faster, handle better and give it more grip. Visual changes were slight; 457mm (18in) wheels, a less fussy nose and a simpler engine cover were the main adjustments. Engine changes increased power to 312.2kW (422bhp) while the gearbox was beefed up and the bodyshell stiffened.

The final derivative was the F512M, which appeared in 1994. Lighter and more powerful (with 325.6kW / 440bhp) than the 512TR, those distinctive pop-up headlamps were replaced by faired-in units. Top speed jumped to around 321.8km/h (200mph) while it was all done in more comfort than ever. But it didn't half look old-fashioned when the 550M arrived in 1996…

For a supercar, the Testarossa was amazingly comfortable and practical. The seats were supportive, the ergonomics were excellent and the whole interior was well laid out – which was quite unusual for a Ferrari.

Ford RS200

The first design proposals didn't include that large rear spoiler, but it soon became clear that it was essential to create the downforce necessary to keep the wheels on the ground.

Mounted ahead of the rear axle was the 1.8-litre (109.2ci) Ford BDT (Belt-Driven Turbo) engine. With 16 valves, two overhead camshafts and four cylinders, in standard turbocharged form it developed 185kW (250bhp).

On competition versions there was an intercooler fitted at the top of the rear window. Wind tunnel tests showed this to be the ideal location for getting the most cool air to the turbocharger.

The RS200 wasn't built down to a price. Its bodyshell was constructed from carbon fibre composites and aluminium honeycomb sections for maximum strength and minimum weight.

There was plenty of suspension travel, as the car was designed to be thrown about at high speed on rally stages. For greater toughness, the suspension featured twin coil/damper units at each corner.

Ford reckoned you could keep your wall-to-wall leather trim, preferring to swathe the RS200's cockpit with plastic. There was also plenty of parts-bin switchgear, which conspired to make the cabin feel downmarket.

You might wonder what a car powered by a 1.8-litre (109.2ci) four-cylinder engine is doing in this book. After all, at least double the capacity and twice the number of cylinders is par for the course where any supercar is concerned. But ultimately it's all about power, and that's where the RS200 had no trouble trying to compete. While the road cars produced a fairly modest 185kW (250bhp), the competition cars could be tuned to generate rather more than 444kW (600bhp) – beating most of the other cars featured in these pages. It was also no slouch as a result; equipped with the full 600 horses, the RS200 could sprint from a standing start to 60mph (97km/h) in just 3.6 seconds, with 100mph (160km/h) arriving in a mere 8.1 seconds. By the time 13.6 seconds had been clocked up, the car would be back to a standing start, so 1.8 litres or not, the RS200 was not a slow car!

A new approach

The RS200 project started in 1983, when Stuart Turner returned to Ford as competitions manager – a post he'd previously held in the 1970s. Ford's rally car strategy was in disarray and Turner needed to get a competitive rally car developed and built as quickly as possible. His predecessor, Karl Ludvigsen, had initiated the RS1700T, based on the Mk3 Escort. But Turner felt it needed an entirely new approach, which would be safer and easier to maintain. The new car had to be fitted with four-wheel drive, and its shape had to be unique so that it wouldn't be obsolete as soon as it was introduced. Unfortunately for Ford, the

Ford RS200

Years of production	1984–6
Displacement	1803cc (108.1ci)
Configuration	Mid-engined, in-line four
Transmission	Five-speed manual, four-wheel drive
Power	185kW (250bhp) @ 6000rpm
Torque	290.2Nm (215lb ft) @ 4000rpm
Top speed	225.3km/h (140mph)
0–60mph (0–97km/h)	6.1sec
Power to weight ratio	156.1kW (211bhp/ton)
Number built	200

RS200 was built to compete in the Group B class, and by the time it was ready to compete, that class would have been axed because of its poor safety record. So while the shape may not have been obsolete, the class in which the car was meant to compete would no longer exist…

The basis for the RS200 was established pretty quickly; an incredibly rigid chassis constructed from honeycombed aluminium, steel and composites. Over this was draped a composite bodyshell and powering the lot would be Ford's 16-valve BDT twin-cam engine. A redundant Reliant factory was chosen to assemble the 200 cars necessary to pass the Group B homologation requirements and by March 1984 the first prototype had been built. Three more cars quickly followed and by November 1984 the RS200 was ready to make its world debut at the Turin motor show.

The end of Group ß

It wasn't until October 1985 that the first production cars rolled off the lines; by then the RS200 had already won its first works outing, the Lindisfarne Rally. It won a few more rallies at the start of 1986 but the writing was on the wall after a series of horrific fatal crashes involving Group B cars. The final production cars were made in January 1986, but by the time they were delivered to their new owners at the end of that year, the RS200's competition career was over.

Because of the cancellation of the Group B series, some potential owners decided they no longer wanted their cars. As a result Ford decided to strip down 50 of the cars already built and resell them, but with the option of extra equipment. By the end of 1988 they'd all been sold once more, but it wasn't until 1990 that the final cars were delivered; by this stage some of them were fitted with equipment such as air-conditioning and tuned engines.

Despite the advanced engineering incorporated in the RS200's design, it was surprising that there was no servo assistance for the brakes, never mind ABS. It was also pretty unrefined and the clutch was impossibly sharp for many drivers. The interior was also a bit of a parts-bin special, with components from elsewhere within the Ford empire very much in evidence. But in the right hands, a 444kW (600bhp) example is so spectacular, who cares where the indicator stalks originally came from?

The roadgoing version of the RS200 was amazingly understated, with very little in the way of aerodynamic aids. The full-on racing versions were quite the opposite, however, with plenty of spoilers and skirts.

MG Metro 6R4

To enable the car to be serviced quickly, and also to facilitate fast engine changes, the whole of the rear of the 6R4 was accessible by lifting the one-piece top-hinged tailgate.

The 3-litre (182.1ci) V6 engine featured a pair of camshafts for each bank of cylinders, with four valves per cylinder for better breathing. Once tuned, 518kW (700bhp) could reliably be extracted from it.

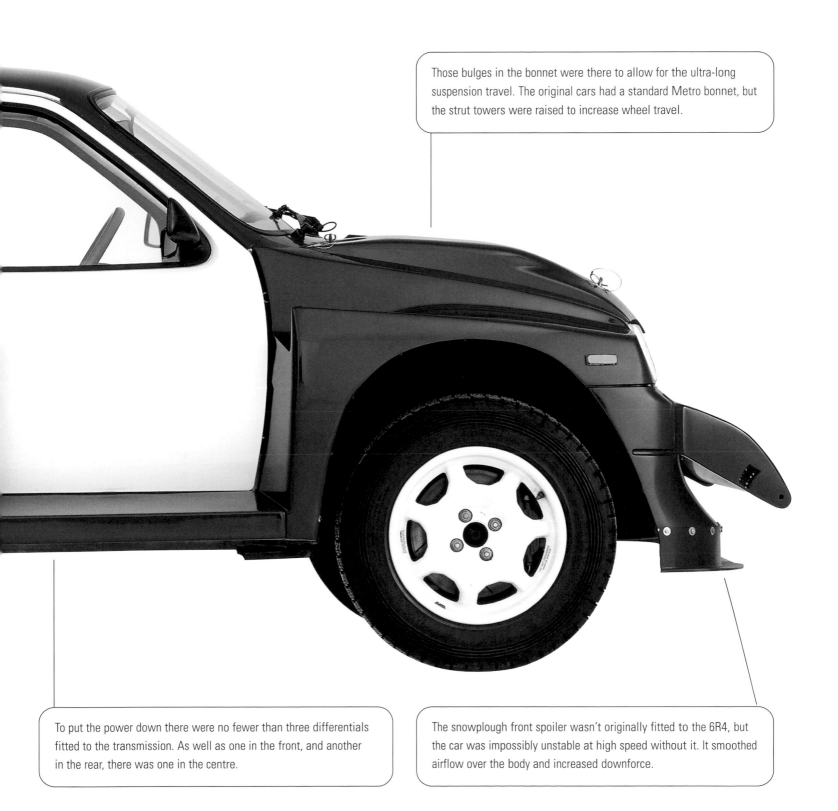

Those bulges in the bonnet were there to allow for the ultra-long suspension travel. The original cars had a standard Metro bonnet, but the strut towers were raised to increase wheel travel.

To put the power down there were no fewer than three differentials fitted to the transmission. As well as one in the front, and another in the rear, there was one in the centre.

The snowplough front spoiler wasn't originally fitted to the 6R4, but the car was impossibly unstable at high speed without it. It smoothed airflow over the body and increased downforce.

An MG Metro in a book about supercars – surely not? Well this is no ordinary Metro, because not many cars came out of the MG factory which were capable of despatching the 0–60mph (0–97km/h) sprint in little more than three seconds – but the 6R4 was one of them. In fact when *Autocar* magazine tested the 6R4 upon its introduction, the car took the record for logging the quickest 0–60mph (0–97km/h) sprint ever seen by the publication – which it held for several years after.

Purpose-built rally car

The 6R4 came about from British Leyland's need to develop a bespoke rally car for the 1980s. During the 1970s the company had relied on modified versions of its road cars, such as the Dolomite and TR7, but if it was to be competitive it needed something purpose-built for rallying. Because the new Group B formula had been launched in 1982, it made sense to build something that was eligible for this new super-class. Only 200 cars needed to be built, including any road cars, and the sky was the limit in terms of the car's technical specification. A recent rule change had meant four-wheel drive was now allowed, and the arrival of Audi's quattro showed how effective such a powertrain could be.

One of the key things decided before the 6R4 even got as far as the drawing board was that the car wouldn't be developed in-house, even though it would carry MG badges. Austin-Rover didn't have the resources to develop a car as complex as the 6R4, but it made little sense to create such a car and not get some sort of marketing benefit as a result. That's why although the car's silhouette could have been anything Austin-Rover wanted, it made sense to give it the basic outline of one of the company's existing models – so the Metro was chosen.

The man behind the project was Austin-Rover's motorsport director John Davenport, who teamed up with Patrick Head from Williams Grand Prix Engineering. Their aim was to make the car as light and compact as possible, to give it the best power to weight ratio they could as well as to keep it very nimble. It didn't take long to decide that the engine needed to go behind the seats, and that its power should be permanently directed to all four wheels.

Work got underway on the project in 1981 and the first prototype was finished by the end of 1982. It was powered by a cut-down version of the Rover V8, sporting six cylinders, but it wasn't shown to anybody publicly until the spring of 1984. It didn't take long for the car to start winning rallies, but this first

It may have been badged a Metro, and may have looked basically like one, but this shows that the 6R4 owed nothing to the city car of the same name. It was good for the standard car's image though.

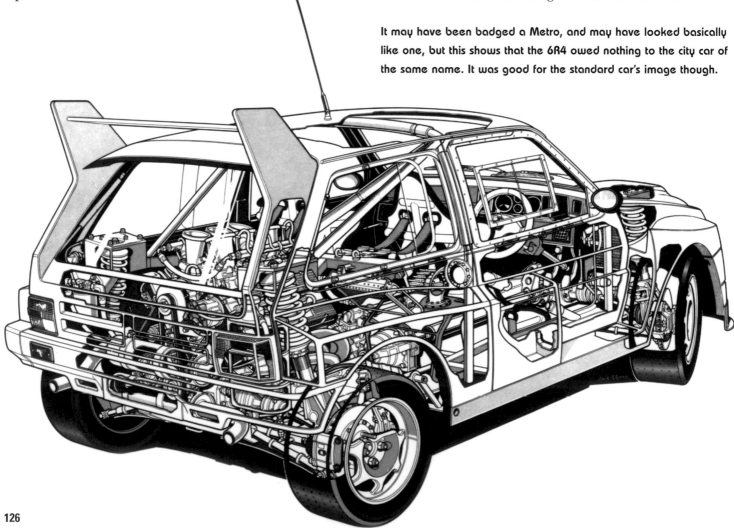

The 6R4's official competition career got off to a great start, with Tony Pond achieving great things on the 1985 RAC Rally. But things turned sour the following year with the car outclassed already – then the series was scrapped.

prototype was fitted with an engine that wasn't fully developed. The aim was to create a V6 powerplant that was unique to the 6R4, and by the start of 1985 this had been produced and was ready to run.

Sales problems

With everything now set for production, a corner of the firm's Longbridge plant was put to one side, and the cars were assembled there. Transmissions were shipped in from FF Developments while body panels were provided by external suppliers. As a result it didn't take long to put them all together – what took a lot longer was getting customers to buy them.

The car's official competition debut was a phenomenal success, with Tony Pond setting fastest stage no fewer than nine times in the 1985 RAC Rally. But by 1986 it was clear that the normally aspirated 3-litre (182.1ci) V6 engine was outclassed by the turbocharged cars which were gaining in popularity. With only 303.4kW (410bhp) on tap, there simply

wasn't enough power available to beat the opposition. But 1986 was the year in which Group B was cancelled anyway, after a series of fatal accidents. As a result, Austin-Rover decided to cut its losses and sell off the cars, choosing to walk away from the whole exercise. A tragic end to what could have been a rather more successful story.

MG Metro 6R4	
Years of production	1985
Displacement	2991cc (179.4ci)
Configuration	Mid-mounted V6
Transmission	Five-speed manual, four-wheel drive
Power	185kW (250bhp) @ 7000rpm
Torque	303.7Nm (225lb ft) @ 6500rpm
Top speed	225.3km/h (140mph)
0–60mph (0–97km/h)	4.5sec
Power to weight ratio	179.8kW/ton (243bhp/ton)
Number built	220

Nissan Mid 4

The front suspension was straightforward, with double wishbones and coil spring/damper units. But at the back there was a complex multi-link arrangement which ensured maximum control of the wheels at all times.

The brakes were the most advanced specification available at the time. While the ventilated discs weren't anything particularly cutting-edge, the four-channel anti-lock system was.

The interior was designed in true Japanese fashion – which meant it was much more about usability than visual excitement. Although there was leather trim, there was also plenty of plastic and parts-bin switchgear.

The V6 engine was mounted behind the cabin, with its power being fed to all four wheels. With a capacity of 3 litres (182.1ci), it could generate 244.2kW (330bhp) at 6800rpm along with 380.7Nm (282lb ft) of torque at 3200rpm.

A twin-plate clutch was at the heart of the five-speed manual gearbox, which transmitted the torque to all four wheels. The transmission also incorporated a centre differential with a viscous coupling.

While it may look very understated now, the Mid 4 was a very racy design when first shown. Japan wasn't known for its mid-engined supercars (and still isn't); this car could have improved Nissan's image no end.

When it comes to selling supercars, image is as important as ability. Take the Honda NSX or Renault A610 for example – both extremely capable cars, but held back by badges that didn't say the right things about their owners. At least the Renault came from Europe though – any supercar hailing from anywhere else has its work cut out trying to earn respect no matter how able it is. So it was with Nissan's Mid 4, which was as technologically advanced as the best European cars when it was unveiled in 1985. And being Japanese, such technology could be assumed to remain reliable for years – unlike that in many European vehicles...

Cutting-edge technology

The first of three generations of Mid 4 was unveiled at the 1985 Frankfurt motor show, with a declaration from Nissan that the car would be on sale in the autumn of 1986. With its angular styling and unfussy lines its design wasn't especially original, but it was a very tidy first effort.

Motive power was provided by a 2960cc (177.6ci) V6, which was usually to be found in the 300ZX. With four overhead camshafts and a quartet of valves for each cylinder, the engine fitted to the first prototype was also equipped with computer and hydraulically controlled variable valve timing along with a twin-plenum variable induction system; this was no mere backyard special. But the best bit was that even though this cutting-edge technology wasn't to be found anywhere else, it was all intended to be part of the production car's standard spec sheet.

The result of all this technology was a maximum power of 170.2kW (230bhp), delivered at 6000rpm. While that wasn't an especially large number of horses on tap, the rest of the car's chassis made such power easy to exploit. The drivetrain included a planetary gear-type central differential and viscous coupling for optimum torque distribution between the front and rear wheels. However, at this stage things were still fairly crude because while the torque split ratio could be altered, it couldn't be done while the car was on the move.

Perhaps the most advanced part of the car was its rear suspension. At the front there were MacPherson struts, but at the back there was a modified Chapman strut which incorporated Nissan's HICAS (High Capacity Actively Controlled Suspension) technology. This was a form of four-wheel steering, whereby the suspension subframe was steered by a pair of hydraulic pumps, which were controlled by a

Nissan Mid 4	
Years of production	1987
Displacement	2960cc (177.6ci)
Configuration	Mid-mounted V6, twin-turbo
Transmission	Five-speed manual, four-wheel drive
Power	244.2kW (330bhp) @ 6800rpm
Torque	380.7Nm (282lb ft) @ 3200rpm
Top speed	270.3km/h (168mph)
0–60mph (0–97km/h)	5.0sec
Power to weight ratio	173.9kW/ton (235bhp/ton)
Number built	N/A

computer that took its cues from the front wheel steering. The reasoning behind this was that in high-speed manoeuvring, if the rear wheels steered in the same direction as the front ones, the car would be much more stable.

Developments

The Mid 4 was developed into a Mk2 version, which was first shown at the end of 1987. On paper very little had changed; the car had been restyled, but it was still powered by a 3-litre (182.1ci) V6, albeit with 244.2kW (330bhp) now on offer. There was still a five-speed manual gearbox along with four-wheel drive via viscous couplings. The suspension still incorporated Nissan's HICAS four-wheel steering system but this time round there was more aluminium used in the car's construction, to keep the weight down. The car was also much wider, in a bid to soften the damping rates without destroying the car's cornering abilities.

The best was saved for last, with a third-generation car that was revealed to the world's media in the autumn of 1990. Nissan had again redeveloped the car, with the designs suggesting that it was closer to a Honda NSX than anything else. This time round

The interior is where the Mid 4 starts to go wrong. It may work well – and keep working well – but if there's one area in which the Japanese have traditionally faltered, it's eye-catching interior design.

though there was no prototype to show – merely a series of sketches which showed Nissan's intent. While Nissan was serious about launching an assault on the supercar market, it knew the car would have to be extremely capable – and cheap – to prise people out of their Porsches. There was talk of an all-alloy quad-cam 4.5-litre (273.1ci) V8, with the car being launched wearing Infiniti badges (Nissan's upmarket division). But when boom turned to bust at the start of the 1990s, the Mid 4 disappeared into obscurity.

Nissan's second attempt at a Mid 4 looked far better resolved than the first effort, shown on the left. Not only was the car more rounded, but details such as the side-mounted scoops were far more neatly integrated as well.

Panther Solo

The motive power was supplied by the same 2-litre (121.4ci) four-cylinder engine that was fitted to the Sierra RS Cosworth. With the aid of a turbocharger it generated 150.9kW (204bhp) at 6000rpm.

Those huge intakes just ahead of the rear wheel were there to allow cooling air to the radiator, which was mounted alongside the engine. There were other cooling ducts in the engine bay cover.

Panther pulled out all the stops to come up with a lightweight bodyshell for the Solo. The basic structure was constructed of steel and alloy honeycomb, which was then surrounded by kevlar and glassfibre panels.

In a different twist on headlamp design, the front lights revolved open when needed. Whereas everyone else was fitting fixed or pop-up units, Panther reckoned it could borrow the Opel GT's system for individuality.

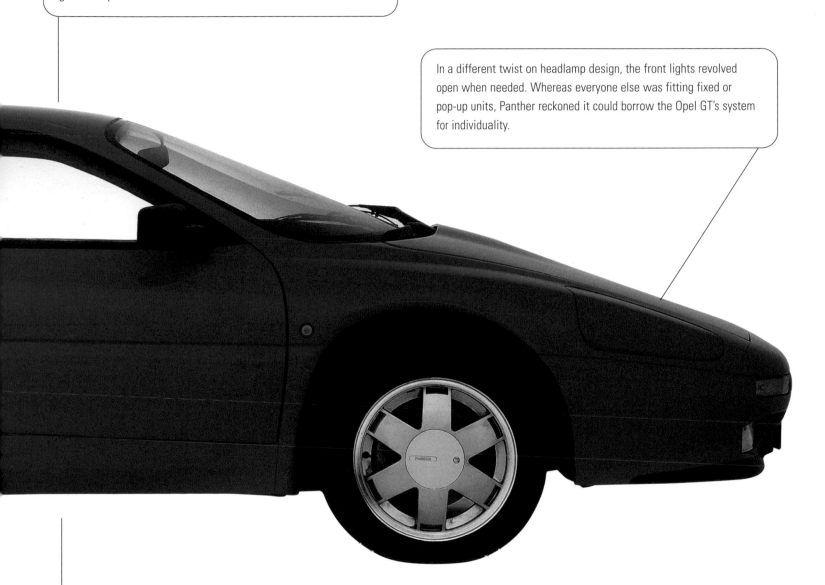

Despite the tiny production numbers involved, Panther managed to include anti-lock brakes in the Solo's standard specification. It was essentially the same system that was fitted to the Ford Granada.

Had the Panther Solo stuck to its original development course, it would never have made it into this book. And despite the car reaching the marketplace, it still only just scraped in because when the project became much more ambitious than originally envisaged, it nearly failed altogether.

The bigger the company, the easier it is to absorb production costs for cars that don't do too well. If you spend over £10 million developing a car and sell just a dozen, it's a pretty expensive mistake to make. But when you're a company the size of Panther, it's devastating. Things could have been so different if it hadn't been for the launch of the Toyota MR2. Panther was aiming to introduce a 1.6-litre (97.1ci) affordable sports car using Ford's XR3i engine. Slung out the back, the 77.7kW (105bhp) powerplant would drive the rear wheels only and the whole shooting-match would be priced at a very affordable level – forecasts were for up to 2000 cars each year to roll out of the Byfleet factory.

Price escalation

But it wasn't to be – as soon as Toyota reinvented the cheap sportster, the Solo project was stopped dead in its tracks. The MR2 was built to typical Japanese standards and was a hoot to drive, all while selling at only two-thirds of what Panther planned to charge for the Solo – competing would be madness. The decision was taken to move the project upmarket, and that meant starting all over again, making the

Panther Solo	
Years of production	1989–90
Displacement	1993cc (119.5ci)
Configuration	Mid-mounted in-line four, turbocharged
Transmission	Five-speed manual, four-wheel drive
Power	150.9kW (204bhp) @ 6000rpm
Torque	267.3Nm (198lb ft) @ 4500rpm
Top speed	228.5km/h (142mph)
0–60mph (0–97km/h)	7.0sec
Power to weight ratio	122.1kW/ton (165bhp/ton)
Number built	12 approx

gestation period a long, drawn-out affair. As the car got more complicated, the technical hurdles were bigger and increasingly pricey to overcome. By the time the Solo 2 was launched at the end of the 1980s, the price had trebled and power had gone up to 150.9kW (204bhp), courtesy of a Ford/Cosworth turbocharged 2-litre (121.4ci) engine. By this stage,

This cutaway drawing shows why the Solo was so expensive to produce, crippling its maker in the process. The composite bodyshell was horrifically expensive to build, while the four-wheel drive transmission was also very costly.

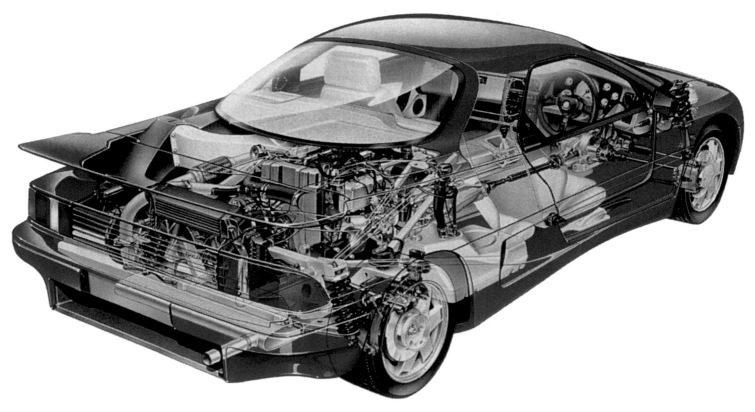

not only had the cost of developing the Solo 2 spiralled out of control but Panther was also losing a fortune on each car.

As soon as you get into the Solo 2 you can see why the project went belly-up – the fit and finish of the interior isn't in keeping with the price, just like some of the exterior. With Ford bits all over the place it's little better than a kit car in many respects, and although there are 204 horses behind you, the car's weight hides the fact very well. Although it's not lethargic, there's no rush as the turbo cuts in and when you think that for less money it was possible to buy a Lotus Esprit or Jaguar XJ-S, it was no surprise that most people shunned the Solo.

Engine problems

The four-cylinder engine could easily have been tuned to offer huge amounts of extra power, but it wasn't nearly smooth enough for such an expensive car, even in standard form. Squeezing more power out of it wouldn't have made it any smoother – what was really needed was a V6 or V8 engine to compete with its key rivals. The powerplant was supplied straight from Ford, with whom Panther had an excellent relationship. An in-line four, the engine featured a cast-iron block and a pair of overhead camshafts, with four valves for each cylinder. The pistons and cylinder head were made of alloy, and to ensure the crankshaft was strong enough to cope it was a forged steel item with five main bearings.

A four-wheel drive transmission ensured the power was transmitted faithfully to the road, but the gearchange for the five-speed gearbox was unacceptably notchy – shifting ratios in a hurry was pretty much impossible some of the time.

By the time the Solo was launched, 80 per cent of Panther had been bought by Korean company Ssangyong. Although it went ahead and launched the Solo in 1989, it had bigger fish to fry. Then when it was discovered that each Solo cost around double to build what it was selling for, the car's fate was sealed.

The Solo's cockpit was basically well laid out, but the build quality was nothing short of dire. It was every bit as bad as a poorly executed kit car, with Ford switchgear shoehorned in wherever it would fit.

Peugeot 205 T16

Unlike the production 205s, there was no monocoque construction. Instead there was a tubular steel spaceframe onto which the panels were hung. This allowed for easy access to the mechanicals.

At each corner there were unequal-length double wishbones and coil springs with dampers. But instead of the springs and dampers being mounted within the wishbones, they were mounted above the top wishbones.

588 EPA 75

The whole of the rear end was top-hinged, to allow easy access to the engine. This was essential in rallying, when the whole engine may have to be replaced during competition.

The twin-cam four-cylinder engine was related to the unit used in Peugeot's production cars. With turbocharging, the road cars developed 148kW (200bhp), but the competition cars could generate more than double that.

A state-of-the-art transmission was essential to get the power down. As well as four-wheel drive there were three differentials and a viscous coupling, which allowed the torque split to be adjusted front to rear.

Of all the Group B cars, the Peugeot 205 Turbo 16 must rate as the best looking – with the possible exception of the Porsche 959. With those rounded looks and compact dimensions, there wasn't a superfluous detail on the car anywhere, and even more than two decades after the car went out of production, it still looks great from every angle.

As with all the other Group B cars, the 205 T16 project began in the early 1980s. It was the brainchild of Jean Todt, the man in charge of Peugeot-Talbot's rallying programme at the time. His aim was to create a four-wheel drive supercar that was identifiable as a Peugeot, and the decision was made to base the exterior design of the new model on the compact 205. The Group B rules stated that there would have to be 200 cars made; any of those 200 that weren't built for racing would have to be produced as road vehicles.

Transverse-mounted engine

Although the T16 looked much like a regular 205 GTi from the outside, the reality was that very little was carried over. The car was not only 127mm (5in) longer, but it was also 101mm (4in) wider. The construction was also all-new, with a pressed-steel central tub along with steel crossmembers and box sections at the front. Behind the occupants was a tubular chassis which was detachable from the main

Although the T16 looked like a pumped-up version of the standard 205, it was actually longer and wider. This gave it a more purposeful stance, although the handling wasn't helped by the way the engine was mounted to one side.

monocoque. To allow for easy access to the engine and transmission, the whole of the rear of the car could be hinged upwards, or even removed altogether. It was also made of lightweight composite, just like the rest of the panelwork, although the roof was made of steel for maximum strength in case of a roll over.

The engine was Peugeot's new XU unit, as seen in the Talbot Horizon diesel. In the T16 it was in 1755cc (106.5ci) form, with four valves per cylinder and a pair of overhead camshafts. With Bosch fuel injection and a single KKK turbocharger, there was 148kW (200bhp) available at 6750rpm as far as the road cars were concerned. But competition cars had around 259kW (350bhp) on tap – and by increasing the turbo boost this could easily be raised to around 370kW (500bhp) or so.

Unusually, the engine and transmission were positioned transversely, which led to some very odd handling characteristics. Although Peugeot's engineers had tried to even out the weight distribution by positioning fuel tanks strategically, it wasn't enough. If the throttle was snapped shut just before the T16 took off over a bump, it would rotate around its crankshaft, causing loss of control. A fix was attempted, which focused on moving the oil coolers and gearbox to improve the weight bias. It helped, but it didn't solve the problem completely.

Transmission and brakes

While the engine's position was a fundamental flaw, the transmission was as advanced as transmissions came at the time. All four wheels were driven, of course, with a total of three differentials keeping the car moving. A central differential incorporated a viscous coupling that allowed the torque split to be adjusted to anywhere between 25:75 and 45:55 front:rear. The central and rear differentials were also limited-slip items, to ensure the wheels didn't spin all the power away on loose surfaces. The gearbox was a five-speed manual unit while the suspension was independent all round thanks to the use of double wishbones at each corner.

The braking system wasn't especially complex, with ventilated discs fitted all round. There were four calipers at each corner to give huge stopping power, but there was no ABS, as being able to lock the wheels is often a distinct advantage during rallying.

There wasn't much to give away the origins of the T16, looking at its interior. The dash was new, as was the transmission and seating – once those were removed from the equation there wasn't much left!

Peugeot's key driver in the Group B series was initially Ari Vatanen, who raced with some success – but the car's engineering was flawed. When the E2 models appeared with their improved weight bias and also extra power, the car instantly became more successful in the hands of Vatanen, Timo Salonen and Juha Kankkunen. But it ultimately made very little difference, because the Group B series was soon to be scrapped, this was following the unfortunate death of Henri Toivonen at the wheel of his Lancia Delta S4.

Peugeot 205 T16

Years of production	1984–6
Displacement	1775cc (106.5ci)
Configuration	Mid-mounted in-line four, turbocharged
Transmission	Five-speed manual, four-wheel drive
Power	148kW (200bhp) @ 6750rpm
Torque	253.6Nm (188lb ft) @ 4000rpm
Top speed	205.9km/h (128mph)
0–60mph (0–97km/h)	7.8sec
Power to weight ratio	133.9kW/ton (181bhp/ton)
Number built	200

Porsche 959

There were scoops and ducts all over the bodyshell, with turbo vents at the rear corners, engine cooling ducts behind the doors and grilles at the front to cool the oil and water.

In keeping with 911 tradition, the engine is located at the back of the car. But unlike the iconic Porsche, the 959 featured water cooling for the cylinder heads.

All four wheels were driven through a six-speed manual gearbox. The front pair was driven by a torque tube that rigidly connected the gearbox with the front differential.

Variable ride height meant the ground clearance could be increased if the car was driven over rough ground. Standard setting was 120mm (4.7in), but this could increase to 180mm (7in) when necessary.

The nosecone was made of elastic polyurethane, in a bid to reduce weight as well as crash repair bills. It was the same at the back, while the floors were reinforced with nomex.

Each corner of the car was fitted with two telescopic dampers and two coil springs. Not only did this help to spread the suspension's load in tough conditions, but it also allowed the car's adjustable ride height control to work properly.

When it was launched, the 959 looked quite unlike the 911 of the day – the car on which it was effectively based. But that nose gave a good idea of how the 911 would evolve, a couple of generations later.

When the 1983 Frankfurt motor show opened its doors, nobody realized what an impact it would have on the supercar world. It's not often a supercar appears that redefines the breed, but the Gruppe B concept did just that; it was the most technologically advanced car that money could buy. Although the Gruppe B was faithful to the 911 concept, whose centre section it retained, it was as though Porsche had ripped up the rulebook to start again.

Gruppe B

Gone were the familiar front and rear ends, to be replaced by all-new panelwork designed to cut lift as well as drag. The end result was a car that could top 305.7km/h (190mph) – not that many people would ever get to experience the sensation. That was partly due to its incredibly high price but also because Porsche planned to build just 200 roadgoing examples.

The Gruppe B (Group B) name gave some indication of Porsche's plans for its new car – to enter top-level rallying. With its electronically controlled four-wheel drive, race-style double wishbone suspension all round and six-speed gearbox, the car could have beaten all comers. But it wasn't to be, because the car was so complicated that it took much longer to develop than Porsche had anticipated. By the time the car was ready for competition the Group B series had been axed, after a succession of serious accidents.

Before the Group B formula had been cancelled, Porsche had already demonstrated its intention to put the car into limited production for the road by giving it the name 959. The competition version would be known as the 961 and development work continued apace to get those first roadgoing cars delivered to customers – all of whom had to be existing Porsche owners. To make the car more reliable there were more cooling vents than on the original prototype. The wheels also grew in diameter and to minimize the risk of a loss of control due to tyre deflation, there were warning sensors on each wheel to report on any loss of pressure.

Porsche 959

Porsche 959	
Years of production	1987–8
Displacement	2851cc (171ci)
Configuration	Flat-six, rear-engined
Transmission	Six-speed manual, four-wheel drive
Power	333kW (450bhp) @ 6500rpm
Torque	499.5Nm (370lb ft) @ 5500rpm
Top speed	317km/h (197mph)
0–60mph (0–97km/h)	3.6sec
Power to weight ratio	229.4kW/ton (310bhp/ton)
Number built	283

The powerplant was a development of the classic Porsche flat-6, still mounted at the rear but this time with a capacity of 2.8 litres (169.9ci). This was a smaller capacity than the standard production car, but a pair of turbochargers boosted power to 333kW (450bhp), with a peak torque figure of 499.5Nm (370lb ft) – enough to despatch the 0–60mph (0–97km/h) sprint in just 3.6 seconds before going on to a top speed of 305.7km/h (190mph). In keeping with Porsche's ethos, there was plenty of high-tech engineering in the 959's engine such as titanium con-rods and sodium-filled valves for more efficient cooling. Four chain-driven camshafts controlled 24

valves between them and Bosch Motronic fuel injection squeezed every last bit of power from each gallon of petrol.

Variants

The whole production run was sold out before the first car was even built, although things took a lot longer to get going than Porsche had planned. Development problems and a series of strikes within the motor industry meant the first cars weren't delivered until 1987. When the car was ready for sale there were two variants on offer. The first was the Comfort, complete with air-conditioning, electric windows, leather trim and central locking. For more hardcore drivers there was the option of a Sport derivative, which dispensed with all these creature comforts – as well as the back seat and the adjustable ride height that the standard car featured.

By the time those first cars were delivered, the 959's competition career was already over. A trio of 911s equipped with some 959 parts had competed in the 1984 Paris–Dakar Rally, which Porsche went on to win. But this wasn't the 959 proper – and even the following year the cars entered weren't examples of the final car. At least the 1985 Pharaohs' Rally and 1986 Paris–Dakar were won by 959s, but time was about to be called on the Group B formula.

The 959 was the most technologically advanced car of its time, featuring far more electronic gadgetry than any of its rivals. The four-wheel drive transmission and suspension were also cutting-edge.

Venturi Atlantique

Hung on the monocoque were composite panels, which were lighter than steel and also corrosion resistant. They were also cheaper to produce, helping to keep the manufacturing costs down.

At the heart of the Atlantique is a sheet steel monocoque, which offers huge levels of torsional stiffness. This made it safe in a crash and also improved the handling by not allowing the car to flex on corners.

Later cars had the option of a convertible roof arrangement that also offered a targa setting. This was because the roof was split into two sections, which could be raised or stowed independently of each other.

The PRV V6 engine had been around since the mid-1970s, developed in a partnership between Peugeot, Renault and Volvo. Venturi extracted 192.4kW (260bhp) from it, to give a claimed 270.3km/h (168mph) top speed.

The rear suspension was intelligently designed, with passive rear-wheel steering built in from the outset. The suspension bushes were designed to give slightly, so that if a driver lifted off mid-corner, the car didn't spin.

The 400GT was the ultimate incarnation of the Venturi formula, before the whole project finally imploded. It was all a great tragedy, as the cars were well engineered, well built and good to drive. Ultimately, it all came down to brand — or lack of it.

There's an unwritten rule which applies to the world of manufacturing supercars. It dictates that frequent management changes and regular bankruptcies are essential, to maintain a certain mystique. Think Lotus, Lamborghini or Bugatti and you won't be far off the mark. But roll the trials and tribulations of all three companies together and you're still not even close to the sad, sorry saga of MVS, which was later to become Venturi.

Manufactures des Voitures de Sport

It all started in 1984, when MVS (Manufactures des Voitures de Sport) showed its first prototype at that year's Paris Salon. The brainchild of Gérard Godfroy (previously with French coachbuilder Heuliez) and Claude Poiraud (ex-Alpine engineer), the car went down a storm. Of course nobody expected this Golf GTi-powered projectile to see production, but the prototype appeared to be nicely built and beautifully designed. At that stage it wore Ventury badges, later to become Venturi in reference to the aerodynamic term.

With the car having been so well received, it didn't take long for somebody to put their hand in their pocket and try to get involved. That someone was Hervé Boulan, a wealthy financier and car enthusiast,

The interior was every bit as good to look at as the exterior, with lashings of high-quality materials and a great driving position.

who became the first chairman of MVS from summer 1985. It wasn't long before he was joined by Hervé Le Jeune, who left Citroën to lend a hand at MVS. Unfortunately, soon after this happened the partnership between Poiraud and Godfroy went sour, with the latter walking out. At this point Jean Rondeau then appeared, offering money and a factory. He'd won Le Mans in 1980 and his involvement gave the project a big credibility boost. But when he was killed a few months later it seemed that the project was doomed once more.

Things progressed despite the various setbacks, and at the 1986 Paris Salon a revised car was shown, with PRV (Peugeot/Renault/Volvo) V6 power. Developing 192.4kW (260bhp), the car was finally ready for production in 1987. By the end of the year, 52 examples had been delivered — but the company wasn't in the clear yet. For MVS to break even, at

least 200 cars needed to be sold each year. With the Atlantique more expensive than Alpine's A610 (its nearest rival), and with no heritage as such, things looked pretty tough.

The Atlantique 300

The company had yet another new chief by 1989, with Xavier de la Chapelle dropping the MVS name and badging the cars Venturis. This didn't really help, and neither did a foray into Formula One in 1992. A year later the twin-turbo 400GT materialized, with Ferrari F40-inspired lines and 301.9kW (408bhp). It was a fantastic car, but far too exclusive. The answer seemed to be to build a more affordable car, so the previous Venturi 260 was reworked to become the Atlantique 300. It was more rounded than its predecessor and offered 207.9kW (281bhp) from its 2975cc (178.5ci) V6. But it was all too little, too late. By 1995 the company had filed for bankruptcy, but it didn't take long for a saviour to turn up in the shape of Thai group Nakarin Benz.

From 1998 a twin-turbo version of the 300 was offered, but the project had suffered so many false starts that nobody really had any faith in the product any more. The twentieth century was barely over and Venturi's assets were being sold off at a knock-down

Venturi Atlantique	
Years of production	1987–95
Displacement	2849cc (170.9ci)
Configuration	Mid-engined V6
Transmission	Five-speed manual, rear-wheel drive
Power	192.4kW (260bhp) @ 5500rpm
Torque	429.3Nm (318lb ft) @ 2000rpm
Top speed	270.3km/h (168mph)
0–60mph (0–97km/h)	5.3sec
Power to weight ratio	148kW/ton (200bhp/ton)
Number built	600 approx

price. Although production rights were taken over (by Monaco-based property investor Gildo Pallance-Pastor), the Atlantique seems to have disappeared altogether.

However, this wasn't the end of the Venturi marque. At the 2002 Geneva Salon a small roadster was shown which sported Venturi badges. Called the Fétish, it was similar in concept to the Lotus Elise. But the similarities to the British roadster start and end there as it was powered by electricity and cost around half a million euros. So the chances of Venturi cars continuing to be made are more or less nil. If only the company's management had kept their feet on the ground, things could have been so very different…

The Transcup cabriolet featured an electrically operated folding roof, which worked brilliantly. But the car took twice as long to build as a coupé, and Venturi didn't have the resources to produce many open cars – so they're incredibly rare.

1990–1999

After the 'greed is good' decade that was the 1980s, the 1990s proved to be a difficult time for supercar makers around the globe. But for the few buyers who could afford to spend large sums of money on a fast toy, this was a great period. Never before had there been so many massively capable – and relatively affordable – supercars.

With the world's economy in reverse, the early 1990s was not a good time to be a supercar maker. Few people could afford to buy an impractical hypercar that cost a fortune to run and while years of growth had raised expectations at many of the world's supercar builders, they were in for a shock with the dawn of a new decade. Projects such as the Bugatti EB110 and Cizeta V16T foundered, and more established rivals such as Ferrari had to cut back its production knowing that there simply wasn't the necessary number of buyers available. It was the same story for the Jaguar XJ220 – like the Bugatti and Cizeta, the vehicle had been conceived in a better economic climate, when the more outrageous a supercar was, the more people there were queuing up to buy it. Even at this stage, the number of cars that could exceed 321.8km/h (200mph) were few and far between, so it seemed the XJ220 and V16T were

After years of instability, Lamborghini finally began to find its feet with the launch of the Diablo. But just as the company began to raise its game, rivals from around the globe also moved up a gear. This was the best time for supercar buyers yet.

guaranteed to succeed with their massive power and 321.8+km/h (200+mph) top speeds. Developing such cars is not the work of a few weeks and by the time the cars were available, the buyers had disappeared.

The 1990s was also a decade of consolidation. Aston Martin had passed into Ford's ownership in the late 1980s, bringing with it the greatest stability the company had ever enjoyed. In the 1990s it was Lamborghini's turn; the Italian marque was snapped up by Audi, along with Bugatti. While such long-lived supercar builders were busy trying to get onto an even keel, there were rival companies setting up shop to take them on at their own game. Cizeta, Panoz and Yamaha were all attempting to put hypercars into production – and of those just one is still trading.

Elsewhere, Honda was trying to boost its image by introducing its own supercar, the NSX. Very capable, it was held back by its badge – just as the equally capable (but less technically impressive) Renault A610 was. All this paled into insignificance alongside what must rank as the most profound supercar ever made – the McLaren F1. It's still the hypercar that all other supercar builders aspire to.

Aston Martin DB7 Vantage

The 457mm (18in) multi-spoke alloy wheels were designed especially for the DB7 Vantage; 229mm (9in) wide at the back and 203mm (8in) wide at the front, they were wrapped in Bridgestone SO2 rubber.

A serious braking system was fitted, which was engineered by Brembo. Incorporating ventilated and cross-drilled discs all round, there was also a Teves four-channel anti-lock braking system as standard.

Trying to improve on a shape as beautiful as the DB7's wasn't an easy task, so it was just beefed up in key areas; the sills were made chunkier while the front spoiler received larger grilles.

For the first time ever in a production Aston Martin, the DB7 Vantage was fitted with a 12-cylinder engine. The all-alloy unit featured four overhead camshafts and 48 valves to produce 310.8kW (420bhp).

V12 AML

While a close-ratio six-speed manual gearbox was standard, buyers could also specify a ZF five-speed automatic transmission if they preferred. Only the rear wheels were driven, via a limited-slip differential.

For years, Aston Martin had been out in the wilderness. Production levels had gone through the floor at various times in the company's existence, and the purchase of the company by Ford in 1987 wasn't necessarily a good thing. After all, how could a company used to building cars by the million relate to a company that spent a week just constructing an engine? While some sort of financial stability could only be a good thing, enthusiasts were more concerned that Ford's management wasn't capable of understanding such a traditional approach to building cars. But their fears weren't realized – Ford's ownership of the company, and the subsequent introduction of the DB7, brought the best ever years for Aston Martin.

12-cylinder engine

The DB7 had been introduced in 1994, and while it was fundamentally based on the ancient Jaguar XJS platform, it was an instant hit. It didn't take long to become the biggest-selling Aston ever – helped in no small way by the production processes used as well as its relative affordability. With its supercharged six-cylinder powerplant, there was 247.9kW (335bhp) on tap, along with a top speed of 265.5km/h (165mph).

Going back to the glory days of the 1960s, those faired-in headlamps echo those of the DB5 and DB6. The ploy clearly worked, because the DB7 went on to become by far the biggest selling Aston Martin ever.

So the DB7 was no slouch, but it was left behind compared with the exotica being churned out by the Italians and Germans. What was needed was something quick, with a more exotic powerplant.

At the 1999 Geneva motor show, the DB7 Vantage was unveiled – the car that was to catapult the DB7 into the true supercar league. From the outset there were coupé and convertible (Volante) versions available, with the first cars being delivered in summer 2000.

While the Vantage wasn't merely a standard DB7 with a bigger engine shoehorned in, it was the powerplant that was the big news. This was the first time a 12-cylinder engine had been fitted to a production Aston Martin, with the all-alloy unit having a capacity of 5935cc (365.1ci). Maximum power was 310.8kW (420bhp) while the torque peaked at 540Nm (400lb ft) – giving the coupé a top speed of 297.7km/h (185mph). Aston wimped out with the Volante though, and instead of leaving it unrestricted, there was a speed limiter fitted which stopped the fun at 265.5km/h (165mph) – but as both versions could sprint to 100km/h (62mph) in just 5.0 seconds, it wasn't all bad news...

Safety

Although the DB7 Vantage was a true supercar, it also made an excellent grand tourer. That meant it had to be available with an automatic gearbox, for effortless cruising as well as urban and back-road driving. Alongside the six-speed manual transmission there was the option of having a five-speed automatic gearbox fitted. These options, along with the fitting of the V12 engine, meant the car's underside had to be redesigned so that everything could be shoehorned in. This created the perfect opportunity to increase the car's torsional stiffness at the same time, helping to improve the handling while also making the car safer in the event of a crash.

Beefier brakes allowed the stopping distances to be cut. The system was engineered by Brembo, and it featured ventilated and cross-drilled discs at each end. The front items were 355mm (13.9in) across while those at the back measured 330mm (12.9in). This was backed up by a four-channel anti-lock system and the whole lot sat behind purposeful 457mm (18in) alloy wheels designed and made

It wouldn't be an Aston Martin without wood and leather all over the cabin. However, with that centre console it looks Jaguar-inspired, which is no coincidence as the DB7 was based on an XJS platform.

Aston Martin DB7 Vantage	
Years of production	1999–2004
Displacement	5935cc (365.1ci)
Configuration	Front-mounted V12
Transmission	Six-speed manual or five-speed auto, rear-wheel drive
Power	310.8kW (420bhp) @ 6000rpm
Torque	540Nm (400lb ft) @ 5000rpm
Top speed	297.7km/h (185mph); 265.5km/h (165mph) Volante
0–62mph (0–100km/h)	5.0sec
Power to weight ratio	174.6kW/ton (236bhp/ton)
Number built	7000 approx (all DB7 derivatives)

specially for the Vantage. These were shod with ZR-rated Bridgestone SO2 tyres, with 265/35 items at the back and 245/40 at the front. To help get the power down there was a limited-slip differential fitted as well as a traction control system. This latter feature used the anti-lock braking sensors to detect wheel spin, and within 64 milliseconds of it starting, the rear brakes would be applied to prevent the power from being spun away.

There were few external changes to the car; a more aggressive front end and restyled sills that were more prominent.

Aston Martin Vantage 600

In place of the usual six-spoke alloy wheels were these gorgeous 457mm (18in) magnesium Dymag items. These weighed 5.8kg (13lb) less, thanks to their hollow spokes which shared their air with the tyres.

The gearbox was borrowed from the Chevrolet Corvette ZR-1. It was therefore a six-speed manual item initially, but Aston Martin blanked off top gear and adjusted the final drive ratio.

The exterior colour scheme was chosen by the customer, with the sky being the limit. Once the paint colour had been chosen, there was also an infinite number of interior colour schemes to choose from.

The engine was the reason for upgrading to a V600. The twin-supercharged unit was treated to a pair of extra intercoolers. These increased the cooling capacity four-fold, allowing the boost pressure to be increased.

AMV 8

For some people, too much is not enough. There are those who reckon that it's not possible to have too much power – and the Aston Martin Vantage V600 was built for just that type of person. After all, the standard Aston V8 Vantage offered 407kW (550bhp), and could already claim to be the world's most powerful 2+2 coupé. What sort of person would find that standard car lacking in any way? Luckily for Aston Martin, there were enough well-heeled people wanting to buy this over-egged leviathan to make production worthwhile – although it was never going to be anything but exclusive.

Last coachbuilt car

The Vantage V600 was an extremely significant car for Aston Martin, because in Le Mans form it marked the end of coachbuilt cars from the company. This model was the swan-song for the V8-based cars before Aston Martin focused exclusively on the DB7, much of which was formed by machine rather than craftsmen.

The V600 made its debut at the 1998 British motor show, with the car being based on a standard V8 Vantage. Customers wanting to buy a V600 had to first purchase a standard car then take it to the Works Prepared division of Aston Martin (in the same building as the factory) to have the car converted. Bearing in mind that the modifications cost £43,000 (taking the total to £233,700), it wasn't a question of just replacing the chip in the engine's ECU.

The first job was to upgrade the braking system, by fitting AP Racing six-pot calipers, along with larger brake pads all round plus grooved and ventilated discs. At the back there were four-pot calipers, and anti-lock brakes were also fitted as standard.

The next job was to tweak the suspension and steering, so the driver didn't have heart failure as 321.8km/h (200mph) approached. Adjustable shock absorbers allowed the stiffness of the suspension to be altered to suit the conditions, with spring and damper rates typically being around 10 per cent stiffer. A beefier anti-roll bar was then slotted in, both at the front as well as the rear.

Although the regular Vantage's wheels weren't lacking, they were still upgraded to Dymag 457mm (18in) units for the V600. Made of magnesium alloy, they were 5.8kg (13lb) lighter than the usual wheels and they also featured hollow spokes which shared their air with the tyres. It was a novel approach to improving the ride and it worked.

Engine

However, all the aforementioned was mere window-dressing compared with what Works Prepared did with the engine. While it managed to get a relatively small 10 per cent increase over the standard unit, that did mean a handy 37kW (50bhp) and 67.5Nm (50lb ft) of torque extra – meaning 444kW (600bhp) and 810Nm (600lb ft) of torque. This increase was achieved by adding a pair of extra intercoolers, which increased the cooling capacity four-fold, thus reducing

In an attempt to make the V600 appear rather more modern, there was plenty of brushed aluminium detailing around the cabin, instead of the wood that usually swathed everything.

the intake charge temperature to a maximum of 35 degrees, allowing the boost pressure to be increased. To all this was added a stainless steel big-bore exhaust system that allowed the engine to throw out the exhaust gases a bit more efficiently – while also sounding more purposeful.

All this torque was sent to the rear wheel via a five-speed manual gearbox, which started out as a six-speed unit from the Chevrolet Corvette ZR-1. The sixth gear was blanked off and by adjusting the final drive ratio the car could cruise at a very relaxed 54.7km/h (34mph) per 1000rpm. From the outside there were few clues as to the V600's status, aside from those wheels, a piece of chrome trim in the grille and some discreet 'Works Prepared' badges on the front and rear. Discretion was the word.

The final incarnation of the V600 was the Le Mans special edition, limited to just 40 examples and introduced at the 1999 British motor show. Not all Le Mans cars were V600s, as the standard 407kW (550bhp) car was also available in Le Mans spec.

The number plate says it all. With 600 horses under the bonnet, the Vantage V600 was a phenonomenal machine that was far more agile – and faster – than its massive proportions suggested.

Aston Martin Vantage 600

Years of production	1998–
Displacement	5340cc (320.4ci)
Configuration	Front-mounted V8, twin superchargers
Transmission	Five-speed manual, rear-wheel drive
Power	444kW (600bhp) @ 6200rpm
Torque	810Nm (600lb ft) @ 4400rpm
Top speed	321.8km/h (200mph)
0–60mph (0–97km/h)	3.9sec
Power to weight ratio	23.4kW/ton (302bhp/ton)
Number built	50 approx

Bugatti EB110

With such a huge amount of power available, the only way of launching the car off the line without spinning all the power away was to fit four-wheel drive. The torque split was 27:63 front:rear.

The only Bugatti reference design-wise was the tiny grille in the car's nose. Behind this sat the radiator, despite the fact that the engine was mounted on the other side of the passenger cell.

The 3.5-litre (212.4ci) all-alloy V12 engine was mounted behind the car's two occupants. It was capable of revving all the way to 8200rpm, developing a massive 414.4kW (560bhp) along the way. It also featured four turbos and five valves per cylinder.

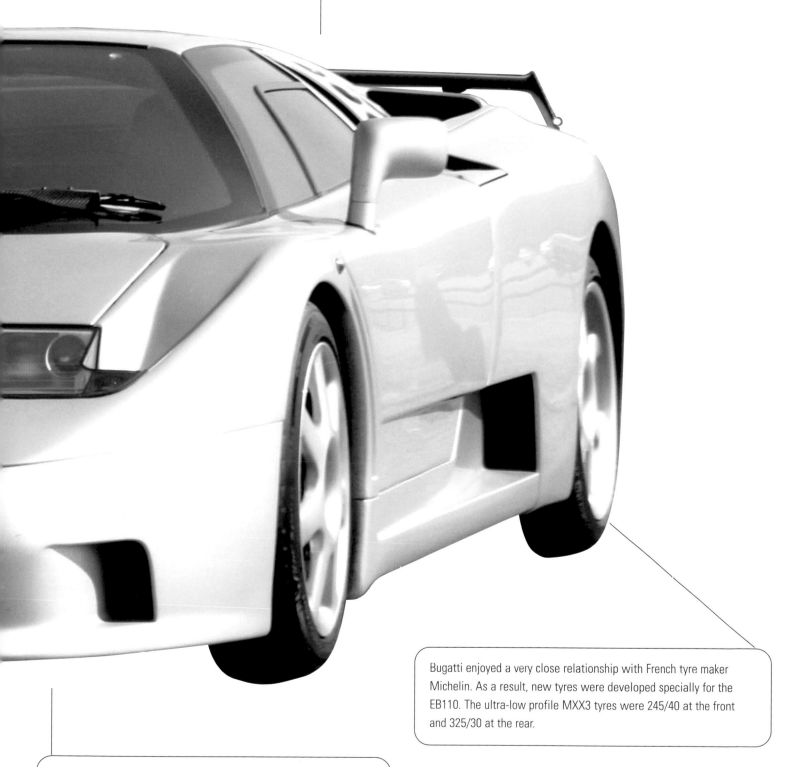

Bugatti enjoyed a very close relationship with French tyre maker Michelin. As a result, new tyres were developed specially for the EB110. The ultra-low profile MXX3 tyres were 245/40 at the front and 325/30 at the rear.

Aside from aerodynamics, the key factor to stunning performance is a monster power to weight ratio. To keep the EB110 as light as possible, its bodyshell was made of aluminium alloy.

The EB110's interior was very understated, unlike its successor, the Veyron. It also wasn't especially well put together, feeling much like a kit car. At least the fitted luggage that went behind the seats was nice.

In the world of the supercar, the stories behind the cars are often more interesting than the cars themselves. While that's not meant to sound as though the EB110 is uninteresting, the reincarnation of the Bugatti marque took such a convoluted route that it's almost like something out of a story book.

The Bugatti revival

The Bugatti revival started in the mid-1980s, when Ferruccio Lamborghini started talking to Lamborghini enthusiast Jean-Marc Borel. The former no longer had anything to do with the company which bore his name, while the latter reckoned it was time to start up a new supercar maker. In time wealthy financier Romano Artioli got involved. It was his idea to resurrect the Bugatti name, but it wasn't straightforward as the name was owned by the French government — and it didn't want to let it go.

After two years of trying to buy the name, the deal was done and a factory was set up in Modena — the traditional home of the supercar. At this point the decision had already been made that the world's most

usable supercar would be developed, and to facilitate this the cream of Italy's supercar engineers and designers were drafted in to complete the project. The whole thing was bankrolled by Artioli, despite the fact that there was never any prospect of him really ever getting his money back. The development costs were far too high for any real chance of that.

If Bugatti wanted to beat all the other supercar makers at their own game, it needed to come up with something pretty special. Sticking to road car technology didn't really allow this, so the decision was made to use aerospace technology, in partnership with French company Aerospatiale. This collaboration led to the production of a lightweight carbon fibre tub that was incredibly light while also being massively strong. A partnership was also set up with Michelin, to produce a tyre capable of running at 321.8km/h (200mph); it also incorporated pressure sensors to indicate if air was being lost. The final collaboration was with oil company Elf, with the brief to develop a new generation of oil capable of working under the most extreme conditions imaginable.

Although two engine suppliers were approached with a view to developing an all-new engine, in the end it was decided to produce the EB110's amazing powerplant in-house. With a capacity of 3.5 litres

(212.4ci), the quad-turbo V12 was able to generate 414.4kW (560bhp), which was transmitted to the road via a four-wheel drive transmission. By building a car that was both lighter and smaller than its rivals, Bugatti reckoned a top speed of around 337.9km/h (210mph) was achievable.

Design

All this technology was in vain if the car didn't look spectacular, but the first attempts to produce something fitting weren't very successful. The man signed up to do the job was none other than Marcello Gandini, well known for his jaw-dropping designs for Lamborghini. The problem was that his first efforts looked too much like a Diablo – something more distinctive was needed. In the end the EB110 was a committee design, which is why although it's distinctive, it looks awkward from some angles.

By 1992 the first cars were being delivered to their owners; in the previous year an EB110 GT was clocked at 334.3km/h (214mph) to clinch a new world record. The project was going brilliantly – until the world's richest countries went into recession, taking the supercar market with it. Sales virtually stopped,

Bugatti EB110	
Years of production	1992–5
Displacement	3500cc (212.4ci)
Configuration	Mid-mounted V12, quad-turbo
Transmission	Six-speed manual, four-wheel drive
Power	414.4kW (560bhp) @ 8000rpm
Torque	608.8Nm (451lb ft) @ 3750rpm
Top speed	334.3km/h (214mph)
0–60mph (0–97km/h)	3.4sec
Power to weight ratio	255.3kW (345bhp/ton)
Number built	115

after just 85 standard cars had been made. On top of these another 30 Supersports were produced, each producing 66.6kW (90bhp) more than the standard car while also weighing a handy 200kg (441lb) less. A few unfinished examples were later bought by German tuning outfit Dauer, which were then turned into roadgoing examples. Another 20 tubs were acquired by B Engineering as the basis for the Edonis, which surfaced in 2000. If there was a car that made the EB110 look tame, that was it…

Although the EB110's design is far from understated, the car has often been overlooked because it wasn't as flash as some of its contemporaries. The Bugatti grille stuck in the nose didn't help.

Cizeta V16T

Supercars are renowned for being wide, in a bid to increase their cornering limits. But the Cizeta outdid them all thanks to its transversely mounted V16 engine. It was nearly 2130mm (7ft) wide as a result.

The V16 engine was quite an animal, with a capacity of 5995cc (359.7ci) and no fewer than 64 valves which were actuated via four camshafts (two per bank). Then there were the four distributors feeding 16 spark plugs…

The five-speed manual gearbox transmitted the power to the rear wheels only. But it wasn't mounted to one side of the engine – instead it took the power from the middle of the engine which was effectively two V8s.

The bodyshell didn't make use of composite technology. Instead it featured hand-beaten aluminium panels. The whole thing was based around a steel tube chassis, which was more 1960s than 1990s.

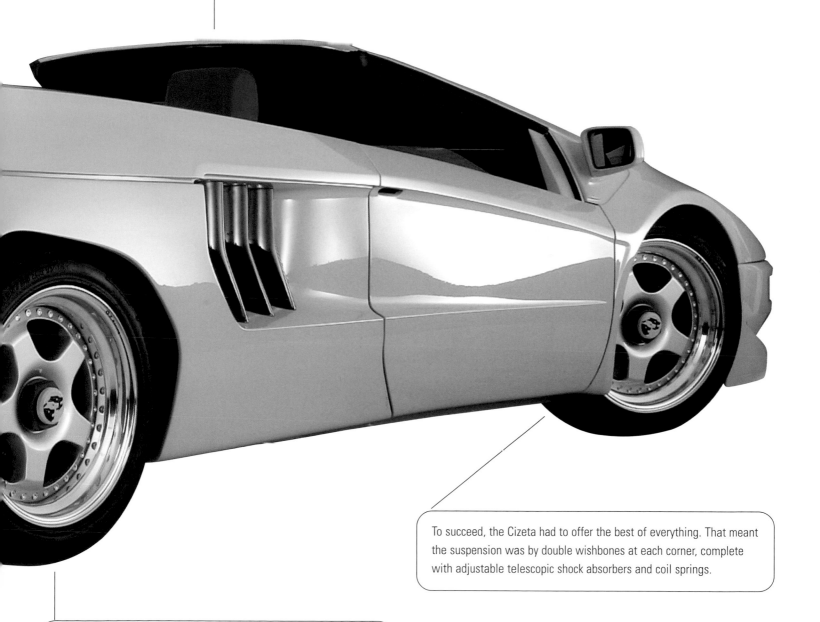

To succeed, the Cizeta had to offer the best of everything. That meant the suspension was by double wishbones at each corner, complete with adjustable telescopic shock absorbers and coil springs.

Unsurprisingly, ventilated disc brakes were fitted at both the front and the rear. But there was no anti-lock braking system to keep the driver out of trouble if he/she got caught out by the car's huge power.

The Cizeta was made in tiny numbers, with attention being lavished on the building of each example. Despite this, the interiors of the early coupés looked poorly finished – unlike this later Roadster.

If supercars are about extremes, welcome to what must be the ultimate supercar in this book. While it may be largely forgotten, the Cizeta V16T is the only car in these pages to feature a 16-cylinder engine. Not only that, but it's located behind the driver – and quite incredibly is transversely mounted. Think about that for a minute; a V16 engine across the width of a car. Armed with that one fact, you can now see why the Cizeta is so monstrously wide – it had to accommodate eight cylinders across its girth.

The outrageous Cizeta came about thanks to the supercar boom of the late 1980s. Ferrari couldn't make enough cars, and vehicles such as the Porsche 959 were an instant sell-out. Even Lamborghini was doing relatively well, so perhaps there was room in the marketplace for another supercar that was even

more extreme than anything from any of these established makers. That was the thought of Claudio Zampolli, a wealthy businessman who sold and serviced Italian exotica in Los Angeles. He got talking to music composer and car enthusiast Giorgio Moroder, who also happened to have huge amounts of money available. It was through this partnership that the car took its title, for its full name was Cizeta-Moroder V16T. Cizeta, pronounced 'chee-zeta', is the Italian way of saying the initials CZ, for Claudio Zampolli. The V16T was short for a V16-engined car with a T-drive, which is how the drive was taken from the powerplant.

Engine

With a capacity of 5995cc (359.7ci), the claimed power output of that amazing engine was 414.4kW (560bhp) at a dizzying 8000rpm – although its redline was set at an astonishing 9000rpm. At full chat the noise was awe-inspiring, with two overhead

Just when everyone thought the Cizeta project was dead, Claudio Zampolli unveiled a Roadster version of the car. Produced in his California-based workshops, total production numbers would be as tiny as for the coupé.

camshafts per bank spinning away and 64 valves doing their stuff. The engine was no less than 1524mm (5ft) wide, which is why there was no alternative to taking the drive from its middle. In effect, the powerplant was effectively a pair of V8s mated to each other, with the power taken from the middle via a T-shaped transmission. This offered five manually selected gears, which then transitted the power to the rear wheels.

With so much power and torque available, it was no surprise that Cizeta claimed some pretty amazing performance figures. The company said its V16T was capable of 328.2km/h (204mph) as well as 0–60mph (0–97km/h) in just 4.4 seconds. But nobody ever officially tested the car, so whether or not it was really capable of such feats will forever remain open to conjecture.

Design

The V16T was yet another creation of Marcello Gandini, the man who must have designed more supercars than anyone else. Besides the Bugatti EB110 and Lancia Stratos, he also designed numerous Lamborghinis such as the Countach and Diablo. Look at these cars and you can see his mark in all of them; the extreme cab-forward stance, the cut-off rear wheel arch and the plunging side windows at the front – and the V16T was no different. After the excesses of the exterior, the cabin was rather tame – perhaps even something of a let-down. It was well put together, but

didn't look any better than some of the better kit cars that were being produced at the time.

Despite the prototype having first been shown in 1989, it was another three years before the first cars were ready to be delivered to their owners. In the meantime Giorgio Moroder had lost interest and walked away, taking his money with him. With funding now a serious issue, and the Lamborghini Diablo having been launched at half the price, it was only a matter of time before the company called it a day, although it lingered on until 1995.

However, that's not the end of the story. In 2005 Zampolli unveiled a roadster version of the V16T, with the promise of up to another four to follow. So while the Cizeta will never become a common sight, its final production tally could grow by around half by the time the final car is delivered.

Cizeta V16T	
Years of production	1991–4
Displacement	5995cc (359.7ci)
Configuration	Mid-mounted V16
Transmission	Five-speed manual, rear-wheel drive
Power	414.4kW (560bhp) @ 8000rpm
Torque	633.1Nm (469lb ft) @ 6000rpm
Top speed	328.2km/h (204mph) (claimed)
0–60mph (0–97km/h)	4.4sec (claimed)
Power to weight ratio	243.4kW/ton (329bhp/ton)
Number built	9

Dodge Viper

Although the wheels didn't look especially complicated, they weren't as simple as they seemed. The main section was cast alloy while the rim was made of spun alloy. The two parts were then welded together.

The V10 engine was very straightforward with the technology it employed; there was just one camshaft, two valves per cylinder and there were overhead valves. But with 8 litres, 296kW (400bhp) was easy to achieve.

The bodyshell was free of unnecessary design features – there were very few scoops, slats, ducts or spoilers. The main feature was the massive vents ahead of the doors, which allowed hot air to escape from the engine bay.

Under the skin there was a massively strong chassis, constructed from square-section tube and box sections. To help stiffen things even further, there was a substantial roll bar immediately behind the cabin.

In true hot-rod fashion, the exhausts exited from the sills of the car rather than from the rear. But only North American cars could be built this way — export models had to have the pipes coming out the back.

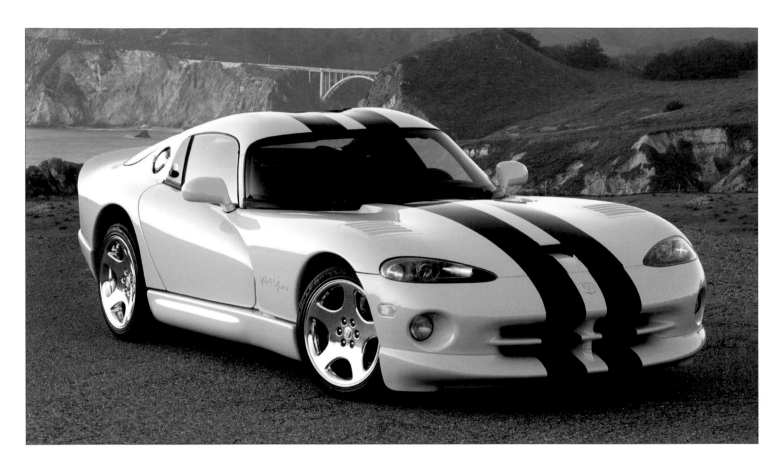

Although the original Viper was shown as a convertible only, the GTS coupé was a welcome addition to the family. This 2002 car offered a stiffer bodyshell than the open car, in turn giving it much better handling.

When the Dodge Viper RT/10 was first shown at the 1989 Detroit motor show, everyone went wild. There was no way the Chrysler Corporation was going to build anything as outrageous as this 8-litre (410ci) V10 monster. With 296kW (400bhp) and 607.5Nm (450lb ft) of torque on offer, it was just too mad to ever go into production. Except it did, because by 1992 the car was available to buy, by 1996 a closed coupé version had been launched and more than a decade after the original concept was shown, a new Viper was in the showrooms.

A challenging car

Although the first Viper RT/10 concept was just a non-running mock-up, by the time the car made its motor show debut it was made of steel and featured the V10 engine that had been developed for light truck use. The concept came about because nobody was still building raw, powerful cars in the same vein as the original AC Cobra. That car was the raw sports car of the 1960s – huge power and little in the way of comfort or refinement. Driver aids were also notably absent, although of course at that time, few cars were

what you'd now call sophisticated. Carroll Shelby was the man responsible for the Cobra so it was only natural that his help was enlisted to get the Viper project off the ground. Sports cars had become too comfortable, too sanitized and too sensible, whereas the team at Chrysler reckoned there was still a niche for something altogether more challenging, and the Viper RT/10 was their answer. The car also acted as a tool for Chrysler to demonstrate that they hadn't given up on cars for the enthusiast altogether. The company

Dodge Viper	
Years of production	1992–
Displacement	7997cc (479.8ci)
Configuration	Front-mounted V10
Transmission	Six-speed manual, rear-wheel drive
Power	296kW (400bhp) @ 4600rpm
Torque	607.5Nm (450lb ft) @ 3200rpm
Top speed	255.8km/h (159mph)
0–60mph (0–97km/h)	4.6sec
Power to weight ratio	203.5kW/ton (275bhp/ton)
Number built	N/A

had recently moved over to front-wheel drive exclusively, and no true enthusiast likes anything other than rear-wheel drive – with which the Viper RT/10 was equipped.

Although the Viper RT/10 used modern equipment such as disc brakes at the front and rear along with independent rear suspension, there wasn't much else to keep the driver out of trouble. Four-wheel drive, traction control and anti-lock brakes were all rejected because they diluted the driving experience too much. The truck-based engine was mechanically very simple, with overhead valves and a complete reliance on size rather than technology to provide those huge levels of power and torque. When revealed, the Viper RT/10 was touted as the purist's alternative to technological tours de force such as the Porsche 959 and Jaguar XJ220, which were crammed with technology to make them go faster, yet weren't that involving to drive.

No luxuries

Comfort also wasn't very high on the list of priorities, as air-conditioning, electric windows and central locking were all left off the equipment list – anything that added weight unnecessarily was omitted. To that end the interior was very simply laid out, with just a few bits of switchgear and basic instrumentation.

There was also no roof, although a simple, tensioned piece of fabric to offer basic protection from the elements wouldn't take much to engineer.

All this weight loss and power overload would have been in vain if the car's looks hadn't been anything other than jaw-droppingly dramatic – and the Viper RT/10 was more than happy to rise to the challenge. In true hot-rod style there were side-exit exhausts while there was also a massive bonnet to hide the V10 engine. Huge scallops ahead of the doors allowed hot air to exit from the engine bay and the huge wheels and tyres showed that the Viper RT/10 meant business. There wasn't a straight line on the whole car – every surface was curved in at least one plane – while there was also the minimum of decoration both inside and out.

If the original Viper looked amazingly aggressive, Chrysler managed to repeat the feat in 2003, with the arrival of an all-new Viper. Instantly recognizable as the V10-powered muscle car, everything was new – including the 8.3-litre (503.8ci) V10 that offered 370kW (500bhp) and 675Nm (500lb ft) of torque.

The Viper was never intended to be a luxury car, and as a result the interior was pretty basic. However, to reduce weight even further the GTS/R dispensed with trim and equipment to maximise the power to weight ratio.

Ferrari 550 and 575

Ferrari saved money in developing the 550, by basing it on the 456GT four-seater already in the Ferrari range. Although the 65-degree V12 engine shared the 456GT's block and displacement, everything else was new.

It was nearly a quarter of a century since Ferrari had given up on front-engined two-seaters, in favour of mid-engined cars. But the 550M marked a return to the supercar with the powerplant positioned in the nose.

The steering rack was a speed-sensitive power-assisted Servotronic item, which required just 2.2 turns from lock to lock. The steering also incorporated new geometry to reduce nervousness at high speeds.

The ASR traction control system was unique in that it allowed the driver to select the level of assistance given. This was done via a switch on the dashboard, and it also altered the damper rates at the same time.

To reduce unsprung weight the brakes discs were drilled, while the stub axles and brake calipers were constructed of lightweight aluminium alloy. The wheels were made of magnesium alloy — they were 25 per cent lighter than normal.

As if the standard 550 wasn't exclusive enough, a special edition Barchetta was produced. Just 448 were delivered, each one featuring a cut-down windscreen and nothing more than very basic weather protection.

When the Ferrari 550 was launched in 1996, it put the cat among the pigeons. Here was a two-seater from the greatest name in supercars – with the engine at the front. Had Ferrari learned nothing from more than two decades of building uncompromising supercars? Well, yes it had. It had learned that owners don't always want a complete lack of compromises – sometimes they want practicality too. And while Ferraris were never supposed to be about practicality, it didn't necessarily follow that by putting the engine in the front, handling would automatically be destroyed. Compared with its predecessor (the F512M), the 550 Maranello was capable of lapping Ferrari's Fiorano test circuit significantly quicker. What's more, the car could be used for long-distance touring, with decent amounts of luggage being taken along for the ride.

Front-mounted engine

Although the 550 carried its engine at the front, Ferrari didn't turn its back on mid-engined cars altogether. Instead, such a layout was reserved for the entry-level cars (such as the F355 and F360/F430) as well as the much more expensive ones (F50, Enzo). The change of heart came about thanks to Ferrari's

new head, Luca di Montezemolo, who felt that Ferrari owners should use their cars more. They weren't helped to do that if they couldn't go anywhere without sending their luggage separately. He also felt that Ferraris should be far better made considering their price tags, which is why the 550 Maranello ushered in a new era in build-quality from the Prancing Horse.

When the 550 Maranello was launched, it wasn't the only front-engined V12 car in the Ferrari stable. Alongside it was the 456GT, which was Ferrari's slow-

Ferrari 550 and 575	
Years of production	1996–2002
Displacement	5474cc (328.4ci)
Configuration	Front-mounted V12
Transmission	Six-speed manual, rear-wheel drive
Power	354.4kW (479bhp) @ 7000rpm
Torque	565.6Nm (419lb ft) @ 5000rpm
Top speed	320.2km/h (199mph)
0–60mph (0–97km/h)	4.6sec
Power to weight ratio	212.3kW/ton (287bhp/ton)
Number built	N/A

selling four-seater offering. The 550 took the 456's 65-degree alloy cylinder block, but all the internals were new – there were lightweight pistons and titanium con-rods which allowed a rev limit of 7600rpm. Maximum power of 354.4kW (479bhp) was developed at 7000rpm – an increase of 31.8kW (43bhp) over the 456GT. There were also variable-volume intake and exhaust systems designed to increase low-end torque without sacrificing top-end power – helping to flatten out the torque curve along the way. Although other cars in the Ferrari range were fitted with five valves per cylinder, the 550 made do with just four because it simply didn't need any more.

Suspension

If there was a potential problem, it was that there wasn't much weight over the driven (rear) wheels – instead, the 235kg (518lb) of V12 engine sat in the car's nose. This reduced the levels of grip available at the back, which is why the suspension design was crucial. Ferrari performed its usual trick of fitting pressed-steel unequal-length double wishbones, with a wider track at the rear than the front, to aid turn in. There was also independent suspension at the back, complete with electronic damping, which allowed the roll of the outside damper to be controlled during cornering, reducing the amount of roll. Thrown into the mix were anti-dive and squat geometry, which helped to retain equal contact patches during

acceleration and braking. This also allowed for a Sport setting that stiffened everything while allowing for a bit more slippage in the traction control system if wanted. For the true hooligans the traction control could be switched off altogether…

In a bid to keep up with the competition, Ferrari replaced the 550M with the 575M in 2002. Capable of 325km/h (202mph), its top speed was on a par with the F50 and F40 thanks to an increase in capacity by 274cc (16.4ci) – taking the V12 engine to 5748cc (344.8ci). This increased the available power to 375.9kW (508bhp) at 7250rpm, while peak torque climbed to 585.9Nm (434lb ft) at 5250rpm – an increase of 20.2Nm (15lb ft). To help transmit this power as efficiently as possible to the rear wheels, a paddle-shift automated gearbox was fitted as standard – which Ferrari claimed could shift ratios more quickly than anybody could manage with a conventional manual system.

There were few changes visually, the main one being a redesigned grille – although there was also a reprofiled central bonnet vent. More importantly, there was also a new adaptive damping system, with drivers being able to choose between Sport and Comfort modes.

The 575 was phenomenally fast, but it wasn't a patch on the 575 GTC. The white arrows on the back point to the rings that allow the boot to be opened without touching the impressive paintwork.

Ferrari F50

The suspension was based heavily on that of Ferrari's Formula One cars, with fully rose-jointed double wishbones, which acted on specially developed Bilstein dampers. This allowed for softer springs and a wider damper range.

There were few concessions to luxury, as even the windows were wind-up items. There was no sound system (or even provision for one to be fitted), although air-conditioning was standard because of markets such as Japan and the US.

There was a removable roof panel supplied with each F50, but it couldn't be stowed anywhere in the car. It took around 30 minutes to swap between open and closed modes, so spur-of-the-moment topless driving was out!

The mid-mounted V12 engine was closely related to the 3.5-litre (212.4ci) Formula One unit campaigned during the 1992 and 1993 seasons. In the F50 it displaced 4.7 litres (281.8ci) and generated 354.8kW (520bhp).

There were no ceramic brakes for the F50 — instead the ventilated discs were made of cast iron. Engineered by Brembo, the discs measured 355mm (13.9in) in diameter at the front and 335mm (13.1in) across at the back.

When you've got a car like the F40 in your portfolio, how do you set about creating an encore? Trying to produce something with as much visual drama, which is also capable of even higher top speeds and greater acceleration takes some doing. But that's just what Ferrari managed with the F50, which was first unveiled at the end of 1995.

Formula One performance

The rationale behind the F50 was that it should offer a driving experience that was closer to a Formula One car than had ever been available in a road car before. To that end, the F50's powerplant was derived from the 65-degree 3.5-litre (212.4ci) unit that Ferrari had used during the 1992 and 1993 seasons. For the F50, however, the capacity was increased to 4.7 litres (285.2ci), to generate the necessary levels of torque. In the early development phases, Ferrari was experimenting with 4.2-litre (254.9ci) units, but it was clear another half a litre was necessary if the required levels of reliability were going to be reached.

That wedge-shaped nose has overtones of the F40 when seen in profile – a car which was an incredibly tough act to follow. But Ferrari pulled it off with the F50, which was even more spectacular than its predecessor.

As was to be expected, Ferrari didn't want to resort to turbocharging to get the massive power required to deliver a top speed beyond 321.8km/h (200mph). Instead, it threw all the technology it had into getting 82.1kW (111bhp) per litre from the normally-aspirated V12 that sat behind the cockpit. Delivered at an astronomical 8500rpm was the peak power of 354.8kW (520bhp), but the F50 wasn't about being the fastest car on the road. The McLaren F1 had the F50 well and truly licked; the target with the F50 was have a higher top speed than the F40 and to lap Ferrari's test circuit (Fiorano) in less time than the F40. The end result was a car that could get round Fiorano a massive four seconds quicker.

The F50 was to be proof that Ferrari could produce the most cutting-edge road racer available anywhere, which is why it was hoped there would be a sequential manual gearbox, operated by paddle shifts on the steering wheel. But the system couldn't be engineered in time, which was why there was a conventional six-speed manual unit fitted instead.

Weight

Ferrari also failed to meet its target weight of 975kg (2150lb), although at first it claimed the F50 would still weigh below a ton. However, by the time the car

Ferrari F50

Years of production	1995–7
Displacement	4698cc (281.8ci)
Configuration	Mid-mounted V12
Transmission	Six-speed manual
Power	354.8kW (520bhp) @ 8000rpm
Torque	468.4Nm (347lb ft) @ 6500rpm
Top speed	325km/h (202mph)
0–60mph (0–97km/h)	3.7sec
Power to weight ratio	308.5kW/ton (417bhp/ton)
Number built	349

car the suspension, engine and gearbox attachment points were provided by light alloy inserts, bonded to the chassis. It had been done on single-seaters before, but never on a road car. Helping keep the weight down was a lack of standard equipment; there was virtually no carpeting and gadgetry was kept to a minimum. There was no provision for a hi-fi, while electric windows and seats were also absent. The only luxury fitted was air-conditioning – something that was anything but a luxury for certain markets, where it was absolutely essential for the car to be usable.

The suspension was also derived from the Formula One car, with rose-jointed wishbones and pushrods acting on specially developed electronically-controlled Bilstein shock absorbers. These allowed the ride to be reasonably comfortable, but could stiffen up automatically as soon as the car was being driven hard. Helping rein in the speed were massive cast-iron ventilated brake discs, without servo-assistance or anti-lock. These were bolted to titanium hubs, in a bid to reduce weight further – just like the magnesium Speedline wheels which helped to cut another 25 per cent off the unsprung weight at each corner. This may sound like something that would be impossible to top; Ferrari did so when the Enzo was unveiled in 2002.

was unveiled it was a relatively portly 1230kg (2712lb)– but it didn't matter at all because with a power to weight ratio of 308.5kW/ton (417bhp/ton) it was hardly a slouch. Not only could the car top 321.8km/h (200mph) but it could also sprint to 97km/h (60mph) from standstill in just 3.7 seconds.

The F50's low weight was due to the use of composites just about everywhere. Even the gearknob and gearlever were carbon fibre, while the monocoque and panels were made of carbon fibre, kevlar and Nomex honeycomb for maximum strength with minimum lightness. For the first time ever in a road

Ferrari didn't hold back when engineering the F50, with all the stops pulled out to create the lightest, most powerful and fastest roadgoing car ever seen from the company. Even the clip-on roof panel was lightweight.

Honda NSX

There was plenty of glass in the NSX; while visibility is usually a nightmare from mid-engined cars, the NSX pilot enjoyed a 312-degree field of view from the driving seat.

To keep the weight down, the bodyshell of the NSX was made entirely of aluminium. This is far lighter than steel, and clever use of different types of alloy maintained the car's strength.

To optimize grip while keeping the steering as precise as possible, smaller, narrower tyres and wheels were fitted at the front (205/50 ZR 15) compared with the rear (where 225/50 ZR 16s were fitted).

Although the radiator was conventionally sited at the front of the car, the ducts behind the doors fed cooling air to the mid-mounted V6. The powerplant's position gave the car a 42:58 weight bias to the rear.

Even the wheels were forged instead of cast, so they were lighter (by 6kg (13.2lb). This kept overall weight down, as well as the unsprung mass — which helped improve the handling.

Unusually for a supercar, there was the choice of an automatic transmission in place of the standard five-speed manual unit (six-speed from 1997). The self-shifting gearbox was dubbed the F-Matic.

Until the point when the NSX first went into production, there was an assumption that a true supercar had to be temperamental, and a bit of a pig to drive if you wanted to get the best out of it. But in typical Japanese fashion, the engineers at Honda created a car that was exhilarating to drive but didn't compromise when it came to usability and reliability.

The Honda supercar project had started as early as 1984, although it wasn't until the 1989 Geneva motor show that anybody saw the fruits of Honda's labours. The project started out as the New Sportscar - eXperimental, which was shortened to NSX in time; a name which stuck.

Aluminium construction

Head of the NSX's development was Nobuhiko Kawamoto, a brilliant engineer who went on to become President of Honda. His task was to produce a supercar which was extremely fast, but which was tractable around town. It had to be compact and light, which ruled out complexities such as four-wheel drive or four-wheel steering, to give it the best possible power to weight ratio. By building the car out of aluminium instead of steel, around 40 per cent could be slashed from the car's weight. Even the double-wishbone suspension was made of alloy, just like the subframes on which it was mounted.

During the development of the NSX, Honda was a

In an attempt to broaden the appeal of the NSX, Honda started to offer a targa-topped derivative from 1995. Called the NSX-T, the removable roof panel was stored behind the car's two occupants.

Usability was the key to the NSX, with family hatch levels of practicality and ergonomics. While to most drivers these traits would only be viewed as a good thing, the press complained that the NSX was lacking in character.

key player in Formula One, in terms of engine supply. While it would have been easy to have fitted a V10, a 3-litre (182.1ci) V6 was soon settled upon – again for low weight. There was also no turbocharging allowed – Kawamoto wanted a linear power delivery with a really sharp throttle response. To allow the V6 to breathe as freely as possible, there were four valves for each cylinder. There was also variable valve

timing (or VTEC in Honda parlance), which was the key to low-end torque while also offering plenty of top-end power.

One of the benefits of opting for a V6 in place of the V8s and V12s that were often seen elsewhere, was that the NSX's engine could be installed transversely. This enabled the car to have a shorter wheelbase than usual, which Honda claimed led to it being more nimble than its rivals. But in theory the only true rival was the Porsche 911 when it came to practicality, performance and reliability – and nobody had ever complained of a lack of agility or durability where Porsche's evergreen icon was concerned!

Variants

Although there was just one model available when the NSX was launched, in time the family expanded. Honda produced a very limited number of NSX Type Rs in 1992 for the Japanese market only. Major changes included stiffer suspension and a weight reduction to 1230kg (2712lb) from the normal weight of 1350kg (2976lb). The model was track-oriented as it lacked sound deadening, audio, electric windows, and air-conditioning in an effort to reduce weight.

By 1995 the NSX-T had arrived, complete with T-bar targa top. At the same time there was also the option of an automatic gearbox, with that model dubbed the F-Matic. Two years later the 3.0-litre (182.1ci) V6 was

It was to be more than a decade after the NSX first went on sale before there would be any major cosmetic changes. These appeared in 2002, when faired-in headlamps replaced the pop-up items and the rear lighting went full-width.

Honda NSX	
Years of production	1990–2005
Displacement	2977cc (178.6ci)
Configuration	Mid-engined V6
Transmission	Five-speed manual, rear-wheel drive
Power	202.7kW (274bhp) @ 7000rpm
Torque	283.5Nm (210lb ft) @ 5300rpm
Top speed	260.7km/h (162mph)
0–60mph (0–97km/h)	5.2 sec
Power to weight ratio	148kW/ton (200bhp/ton)
Number built	N/A

superseded by a 3.2-litre (194.2ci) unit to give a bit more power as well as a useful increase in torque. At the same time, the Japanese market received the Type S and NSX Type S Zero, weighing in at 1320kg (2910lb) and 1280kg (2822lb) respectively, and both with stiffer suspension than the normal NSX. The biggest change for the NSX came in 2002, when it received a face-lift with fixed headlights. In the same year, a second iteration of the Type-R, dubbed NSX-R, was released in 2002, again exclusively for Japan.

While the NSX was always a supremely capable car, it never really lifted the brand's image. By 2005 time was called on the car, and while the sensational-looking HSC concept car was hoped to be the NSX's replacement, sadly it wasn't to be.

Jaguar XJ220

Reducing weight as far as possible was the key to achieving as high a top speed as possible. This was done by building the body from alloy panels in the main, although plastic composites were also employed.

The radiators were mounted in the nose of the XJ220, although the engine was located at the back of the car. This was because the engine bay was too crowded for them, with its two turbochargers and intercoolers.

It's the Jaguar with an MG Metro engine! The quad-cam V6 that powered the XJ220 was related to the unit seen in the Metro 6R4. The original XJ220 prototype had featured a V12 powerplant though.

The underbody of the XJ220 was revolutionary for a road car at the time, especially the rear area. None of its contemporaries could claim to feature venturis designed to suck the car onto the road.

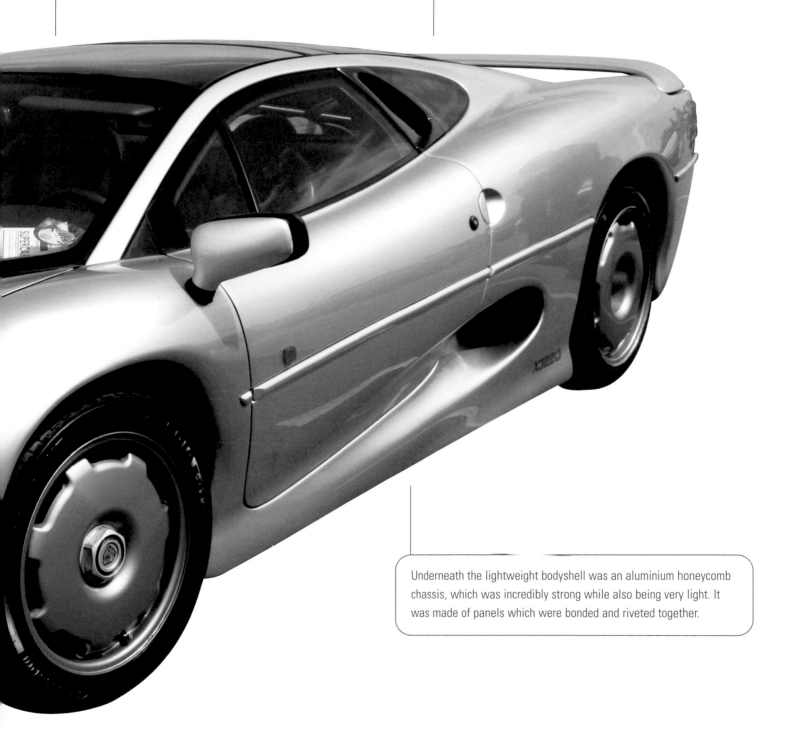

Underneath the lightweight bodyshell was an aluminium honeycomb chassis, which was incredibly strong while also being very light. It was made of panels which were bonded and riveted together.

Just like achieving the perfect comedy routine, the key to building a successful supercar is all in the timing. Unfortunately for Jaguar, the timing of its XJ220 was all wrong, with the entire project descending into chaos and litigation. But it could have been so very different…

The XJ220 story started – as far as the public was concerned – with the last-minute appearance of a concept on the Jaguar stand at the 1988 British motor show. It had been cobbled together by Jaguar workers in their spare time, the project having been led by Jim Randle, who was head of product development at the time. The aim was to show that Britain could lead the world when it came to both performance and design.

Concept

When the wraps were taken off that first concept, there was talk that the car could potentially be offered for production. As the car was displayed, it featured a V12 engine, four-wheel drive and anti-lock brakes.

Although the XJ220's cabin didn't feel particularly special, it wasn't a bad place to sit while travelling at 321km/h (200mph). There was plenty of headroom and it was nicely finished – but not worth the vast amount that Jaguar charged for it.

Jaguar XJ220	
Years of production	1992–5
Displacement	3498cc (209.8ci)
Configuration	Mid-mounted V6, twin-turbo
Transmission	Five-speed manual, rear-wheel drive
Power	401kW (542bhp) @ 7000rpm
Torque	641.2Nm (475lb ft) @ 4500rpm
Top speed	339.5km/h (211mph)
0–60mph (0–97km/h)	3.6sec
Power to weight ratio	273kW/ton (369bhp/ton)
Number built	280

There was also the possibility of traction control, adaptive suspension and four-wheel steering, but what made potential buyers excited was that the powerplant was a detuned version of the Le Mans-winning XJR-12 V12 unit, in detuned form but with four valves per cylinder.

The car had such an overwhelmingly positive reaction that Jaguar decided to look into developing the car for production. A feasibility study declared that if the car was to profitable, it would have to be far less complex than originally intended. In place of the V12 engine there would have to be a twin-turbo V6, while only the rear wheels would be driven instead of all four as initially stated. Into the bargain, the production car would also have to be both lighter and shorter, but at least there was no reason for the essential design elements of the concept to be discarded. It may have been a poor relation to the concept, but the proposed production XJ220 was still going to be capable of extremely high speeds and would look as outrageous as that first show car.

On offer was a 3.5-litre (212.4ci) twin-turbo V6 mated to a five-speed manual gearbox. There were double wishbones and ventilated discs at each corner, but the key selling point was that gorgeous shape. If buyers felt their car was on the slow side, they could always go to Tom Walkinshaw Racing, which produced a variant called the XJ220 S. While the standard car had a mere 401kW (542bhp) on tap, the tweaked version offered 503.2kW (680bhp) – enough to take it to 388.5km/h (229mph) in place of the standard car's 339.5km/h (211mph). With all this up for grabs, what could possibly go wrong? Plenty, sadly.

Problems

The first hiccup was the acquisition of Jaguar by Ford, which put the brakes on the project until it received a thumbs-up. Once this was given, development work continued apace, with the announcement in December 1989 that up to 350 examples of the car would be available. The company was overwhelmed with deposits from people wanting to buy an XJ220, but many of these were only purchasing in the hope of making a quick profit. At this point, supercars were hot property which commanded huge prices if they were rare and desirable. The Jaguar's rarity was guaranteed and desirability was assumed – but when boom turned to bust very shortly after, the supercar market went into meltdown. Buyers tried to wriggle out of their contracts, saying the car wasn't worth the asking price – Jaguar retaliated by threatening to sue, and it took until 1995 before the dispute was finally resolved.

Despite the final production tally numbering just 250 or so, the last cars weren't sold until 1999. With an official price tag of over £400,000, potential buyers couldn't justify such expenditure in the certain knowledge that the car would be worth a fraction of that price as soon as the car had turned a wheel. A sad end to what should have been one of the most exciting supercars ever.

This was part of the XJ220's problem, as far as potential owners were concerned. The initial concept car had packed a V12 punch, but the six-cylinder unit fitted to production cars was based on the MG Metro 6R4's.

Lamborghini Diablo

The small ducts at the base of the windscreen were there to feed cool air to the Diablo's cabin, which became very hot thanks to that huge windscreen. That was why air-conditioning was fitted as standard.

Although the Countach featured a spare wheel under the bonnet, the Diablo had luggage space instead – and no spare wheel. Lamborghini said its customers weren't likely to change wheels by the side of the road...

The final version of the Countach had introduced the concept of a Lamborghini on three-piece alloy wheels. The Diablo continued this, with 432mm (17in) items all round; 203mm (8in) wide at the front and 330mm (13in) at the rear.

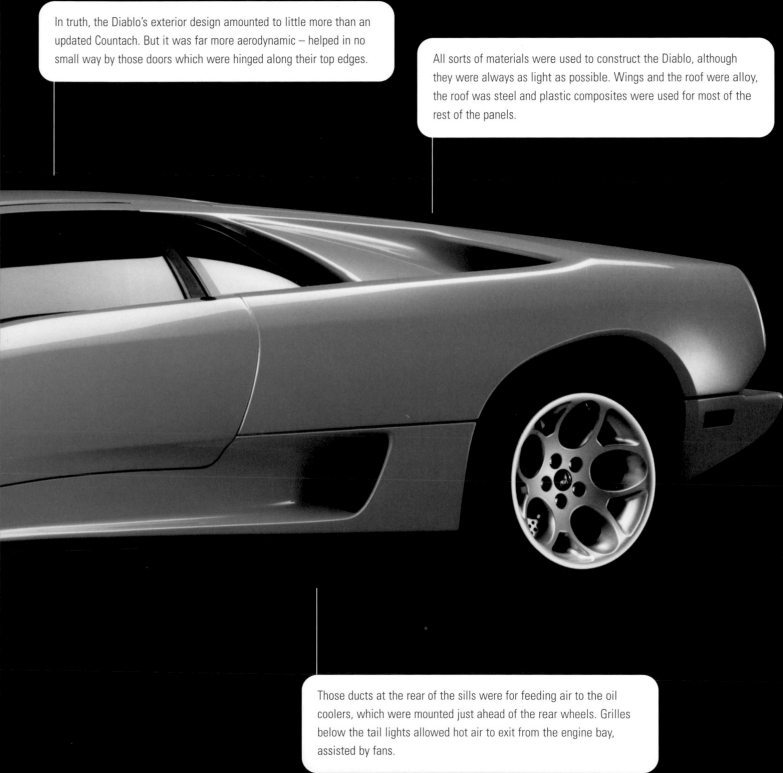

In truth, the Diablo's exterior design amounted to little more than an updated Countach. But it was far more aerodynamic – helped in no small way by those doors which were hinged along their top edges.

All sorts of materials were used to construct the Diablo, although they were always as light as possible. Wings and the roof were alloy, the roof was steel and plastic composites were used for most of the rest of the panels.

Those ducts at the rear of the sills were for feeding air to the oil coolers, which were mounted just ahead of the rear wheels. Grilles below the tail lights allowed hot air to exit from the engine bay, assisted by fans.

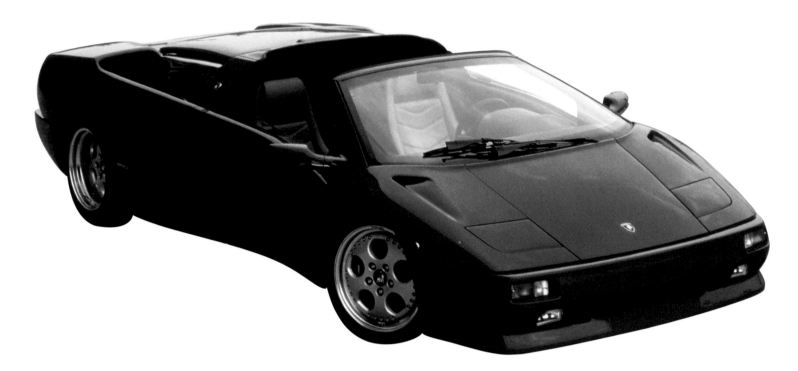

If you liked the wind in your toupée at 329.9km/h (205mph), the Diablo was the car for you – if you couldn't quite run to a Ferrari F50. Because it was the same as the standard car under the skin, it was ferociously quick – and expensive.

When you've a car as dramatic as the Countach, just how do you go about designing an encore? With great difficulty, as Chrysler found out after its acquisition of Lamborghini in 1987. By that stage the Countach was getting rather long in the tooth, and a clean-sheet redesign was needed. Not only would the bodyshell need to be all-new, but the engine required a major overhaul. The mechanical layout would also need a thorough rethink – after all, it was 17 years between the arrival of the Countach and the debut of its successor. In that time the supercar landscape had changed radically, and if Lamborghini was to retain its crown it needed to come up with something very special.

Successor to the Countach

The Diablo was the first Lamborghini to be developed by Luigi Marmaroli, who had joined the company after leaving Alfa Romeo's unsuccessful Formula One team. He changed companies in January 1985 and had one key brief; to develop a successor to the Countach. The services of Marcello Gandini were once again called upon to come up with a jaw-dropping design and by 1989 a running prototype had been developed. But despite an upgraded Countach engine being used in a completely new bodyshell that was far more slippery, the car wasn't fast enough. The answer was

to develop the powerplant even further while also making the car even more aerodynamic. The result was a bodyshell with a substantially redesigned rear end, with the engine having grown to 5729cc (343.7ci). This pushed out 364kW (492bhp) – nearly 29.6kW (40bhp) more than the Countach had managed – which was enough to take the Diablo to over 321.8km/h (200mph), despatching the 0–60mph (0–97km/h) sprint in 4.5 seconds along the way.

The powerplant retained its longitudinal layout, with only one version produced for all the markets around the world. That meant it had to be extremely clean, so a three-way catalytic converter was standard, along with Weber-Marelli fuel injection. The gearbox was still a five-speed manual unit, and at first only the rear wheels were driven – although when the VT (Viscous Transmission) model appeared in 1992, it brought with it a four-wheel drive transmission. Although power-assisted steering wasn't initially available, it became standard equipment from 1992.

Variants

The VT was the second derivative of the Diablo to arrive – with many more variants still to come before the car's demise in 2001. This four-wheel drive model featured a differential in the nose, which was fed power by a viscous coupling via a propshaft from the front of the gearbox. In normal driving conditions only the rear wheels were driven, but if these started to lose traction, up to 25 per cent of the available power would be fed to the front. While the associated technology added to the Diablo's weight, there were no extra transmission losses in normal running, which is why Lamborghini claimed identical top speeds of 325km/h (202mph) for both the VT and the standard car. Another feature of the VT was electronically controlled damping, which firmed up the suspension as speeds rose. Until 128.7km/h (80mph) the ride was fairly soft, but between this speed and 193.1km/h (120mph) things firmed up; at 249.4km/h (155mph) the ride became really stiff to keep the handling taut.

The next Diablo introduction was the SE30, introduced in 1993 to celebrate 30 years of Lamborghini. With 384.8kW (520bhp), its claimed top speed was 329.9km/h (205mph), but this was eclipsed by the SE Jota which came next, with its claimed 444kW (600bhp). According to the factory, this car could crack 333.1km/h (207mph), although Lamborghini's technicians reckoned it was capable of 354km/h (220mph). Next up was the Roadster, which arrived in 1995. This was mechanically the same as the standard Diablo, but featured a removable targa top which could be stored above the engine. The

Once you'd opened the Diablo's scissor-action door you more or less fell into the car. There was no way of getting in or out gracefully with those wide sills, and once you were strapped in it wasn't a place you wanted to leave in a hurry.

Lamborghini Diablo

Years of production	1990–2001
Displacement	5729cc (343.7ci)
Configuration	Mid-mounted V12
Transmission	Five-speed manual, rear-wheel drive/ four-wheel drive
Power	364kW (492bhp) @ 7000rpm
Torque	577.8Nm (428lb ft) @ 5200rpm
Top speed	329.9km/h (205mph)
0–60mph (0–97km/h)	4.2sec
Power to weight ratio	230.8kW/ton (312bhp/ton)
Number built	2884

Diablo SV of 1995 offered 370kW (500bhp), with a few Roadster versions also being built. From 2000 the Diablo's engine was taken up to 5992cc (359.5ci), marking the start of Audi's ownership of the company – which is what sparked the arrival of a new car to replace the Diablo. This was the Murcielago, which first went on sale in 2001.

Lotus Carlton

The straight-six mounted at the sharp end delivered more power than most fully fledged supercars. With 278.9kW (377bhp) available, the car could do 284.8km/h (177mph) and 0–60mph (0–97km/h) in just 5.1 seconds.

Those wheels were unusually large for the time – at least where saloon cars were concerned. They were 432mm (17in) in diameter and were 216mm (8.5in) wide at the front and 25.4mm (1in) wider at the back.

Although there was no shortage of torque available (565.6Nm / 419lb ft), there was a six-speed gearbox fitted. While the first three ratios were conventional, the top gear was set up for relaxed motorway cruising.

Despite the astonishing performance available, the Carlton's interior was lavishly trimmed – this was no track-day special. There was wood trim and leather seating, air-conditioning, central locking and electric windows.

The Carlton could stop every bit as well as it could go. There were massive ventilated discs at each corner, measuring 330mm (12.9in) across at the front and 300mm (11.8in) across at the rear. Anti-lock brakes were also fitted.

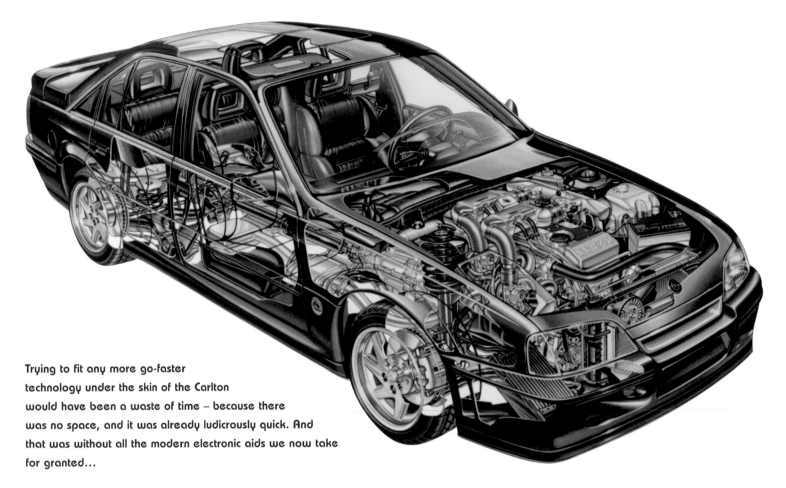

Trying to fit any more go-faster
technology under the skin of the Carlton
would have been a waste of time – because there
was no space, and it was already ludicrously quick. And
that was without all the modern electronic aids we now take
for granted...

In an age where you can take your pick from family saloons (and even estates) that can give impractical supercars a run for their money, it's hard to comprehend the significance of the Lotus Carlton. When it was launched in 1993, there was nothing else like it. A family saloon that could do nearly 289.6km/h (180mph)? Surely the stuff of dreams?

When the Lotus Carlton was introduced in 1990, Vauxhall's image needed a boost. This was the company of dependable but dull cars such as the Cavalier, Astra and Nova (as well as the Carlton itself); some excitement was desperately needed. While it may have been irrelevant for just about everyone, the car certainly grabbed headlines, generating much-needed publicity. Everyone was asking why the world needed a saloon car that could crack 281.6km/h (175mph), but nobody questioned the need for any of the Italian supercars – or British ones.

Speed

Perhaps it was because the Lotus Carlton was faster than all of them, with the notable exception of the Lamborghini Diablo. The Ferrari Testarossa was left trailing in its wake on everything except top speed – the Lotus Carlton was seriously quick. When *Autocar* magazine tested it, the Carlton racked up some of the most impressive performance figures ever recorded by the magazine. In fact it was so fast that land speed record holder Richard Noble was called in to do the testing. Not only was the car capable of 0–200km/h (0–124mph) in just 24 seconds, but it could dismiss the 0–160km/h (0–100mph) sprint in just 11.1 seconds. The quarter-mile was despatched in 13.5 seconds and incredibly it was also the first time that

Lotus Carlton	
Years of production	1990–3
Displacement	3615cc (218.5ci)
Configuration	Front-mounted straight-six
Transmission	Six-speed manual, rear-wheel drive
Power	278.9kW (377bhp) @ 5200rpm
Torque	565.6Nm (419lb ft) @ 4200rpm
Top speed	284.8km/h (177mph)
0–60mph (0–97km/h)	5.1sec
Power to weight ratio	168.7kW/ton (228bhp/ton)
Number built	1100

the magazine had ever attempted a fifth gear 225–257km/h (140–160mph) time, with 14.2 seconds recorded. No slouch then…

Although the Lotus-tuned Carlton was stupendously quick, the car it was based on wasn't especially slow to start with. The donor vehicle was the 3-litre (182.1ci) Carlton GSi, which was good for 239.7km/h (149mph) even in standard trim. However, adding nearly 48.2km/h (30mph) onto this, while also making the car handle, stop and corner sharply was quite a feat. To make it handle better, the suspension was beefed up with extra wheel travel and uprated bushes; otherwise, the MacPherson struts and multi-link/semi-trailing arm arrangement was carried over more or less intact.

Engine

While the chassis was undeniably special, it was the engine that claimed most of the glory. The idea of slotting the Corvette ZR-1's V8 powerplant into the engine bay was suggested, but it would fit – which is why the existing unit was breathed upon (heavily) instead. As well as being taken out to 3.6 litres (218.5ci), a pair of Garret T25 turbochargers were bolted on, along with a water-cooled intercooler. There was also distributorless ignition and the whole shooting match was controlled by an advanced

Sitting here you could be at the wheel of the same type of Carlton that ploughed up and down British motorways or German autobahns day in day out. That was until you turned the key and stamped on the throttle…

computer which kept tabs on functions such as coolant temperature, throttle position, engine speed and boost pressure. The upshot of all this jiggery-pokery was a maximum power output of 278.9kW (377bhp) at 5200rpm while torque peaked at 565.6Nm (419lb ft) at 4200rpm. Even at 2000rpm there was 405Nm (300lb ft) of torque available.

Transmitting the power to the rear wheels was the same ZF six-speed manual gearbox that usually resided in the Corvette ZR-1. The wheels themselves were 432mm (17in) in diameter – such a size was essential so that the massive brake discs could be housed behind them. Shod with 235/45 rubber at the front and 265/40 at the back, such sizes may be commonplace now, but they weren't back in 1990…

It would have been a waste to have done all this work then to cover it all up in a bland bodyshell. While Lotus didn't go overboard with the styling, the car was definitely beefed up where it counted. The rear wing and front spoiler helped cut lift at high speeds, while the extra air inlets in the front helped the oil coolers to do their job. Bland this car was not!

McLaren F1

At the heart of the F1 was a BMW Motorsport-sourced V12 engine. Displacing 6064cc (363.8ci), this unit could generate 463.9kW (627bhp) and 646.6Nm (479lb ft) of torque, with its four chain-driven overhead camshafts and variable inlet valve timing.

As you'd expect, the brakes were pretty special. At the rear there was an aerofoil that rose under heavy braking, forcing the back of the car down onto the road. Ventilated discs were fitted at each corner, but there was no servo.

The windscreen glass was plasma-coated to reduce heat build-up in the cabin. It also provided a degree of tinting to reduce glare while speeding up the demisting and defrosting process in the winter.

One of the main differences between the F1 and its supercar rivals was the seating position. There were three seats in the cabin, with the driver's being in the middle. The other two were either side and slightly behind.

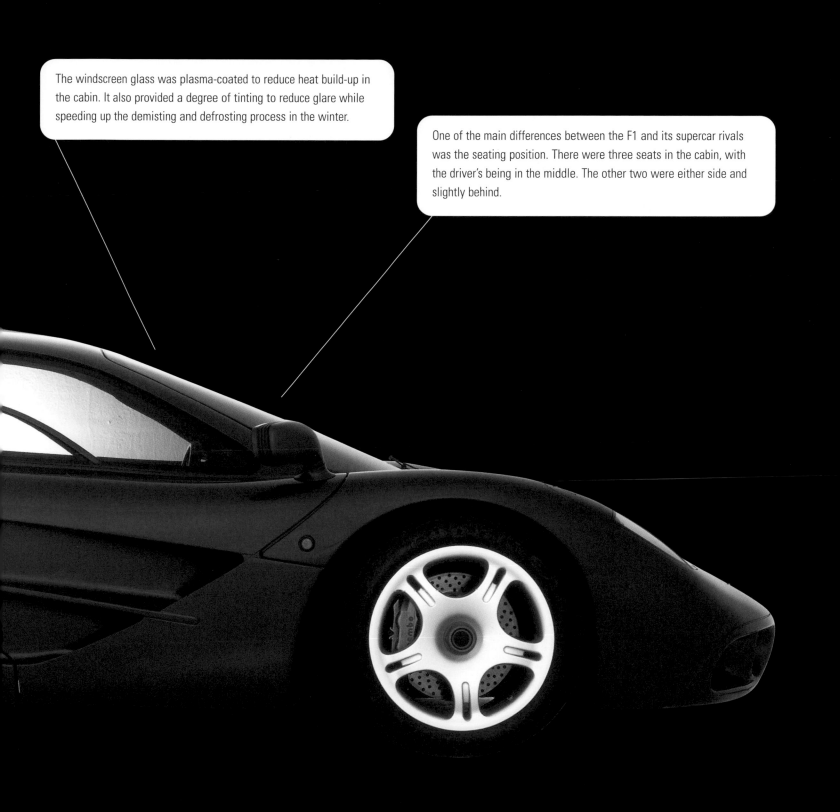

Stop 100 car enthusiasts in the street to ask them what the ultimate supercar of all time is, and the chances are that most of them will volunteer the McLaren F1. During the supercar glut of the 1980s and 1990s, the McLaren was the most outrageous, most powerful and also most intelligently designed supercar of the lot. It was also one of the lightest and most practical, but with production now finished, it's unfortunately become one of the most exclusive.

Radical design

The project got underway immediately after the 1988 Italian Grand Prix. The TAG-McLaren directors (Ron Dennis, Mansour Ojjeh, Creighton Brown) were waiting for a plane with chief engineer Gordon Murray, when the subject of road cars came up. It was felt that the time was right to expand beyond motorsport, so the subject of building the ultimate road car was raised. Although everybody knew it would be an incredibly tough project, that only added to the appeal.

When McLaren engineered the F1, it didn't care for convention. Even the doors featured a mechanism which hadn't been seen before, although the Ferrari Enzo went on to use the same arrangement.

The new McLaren road car would have the best possible packaging while also being incredibly fast and stable. To that end, Murray had to come up with something radical – which is what designer Peter Stevens did. While the F1's bodyshell looks relatively free of extraneous details, there's a lot going on to keep the centre of pressure as constant as possible. This gives the car stability at high speeds, it was aided by devices such as the adjustable aerofoil at the rear of the car (deployed under braking), the fixed headlamps and small aerofoil below the windscreen.

The body itself was made entirely of carbon composites, in keeping with its 'most advanced road car ever' tag. The monocoque incorporated the rear wings and front bulkheads, while there were double skins at strategic points to offer greater strength. The main strength, however, came from a pair of beams that ran down the centre of the floorpan, along with the central cell in which the occupants sat. It was this monocoque which accounted for the greatest part of the car's build costs.

The positioning of the engine was a given – it had to be positioned ahead of the rear axle but behind the passenger cell. Bought in from BMW Motorsport, the 6064cc (363.8ci) all-alloy V12 powerplant weighed

Continuing its unorthodox approach, the F1 was a three-seater, with the driver sitting in the centre. The passengers then sat either side, slightly behind, which was more space-efficient.

McLaren F1

Years of production	1993–6
Displacement	6064cc (363.8ci)
Configuration	Mid-mounted V12
Transmission	Six-speed manual, rear-wheel drive
Power	463.9kW (627bhp) @ 7000rpm
Torque	646.6Nm (479lb ft) @ 4000rpm
Top speed	386.2km/h (240mph)
0–60mph (0–97km/h)	3.6sec
Power to weight ratio	455.8kW/ton (616bhp/ton)
Number built	107

just 260kg (573lb). With 48 valves operated by four chain-driven camshafts, there was also variable valve timing to increase low-end torque without sacrificing top-end power. With TAG's own engine management system and fuel injection, the result was a scarcely-believable 463.9kW (627bhp) at 7000rpm.

Gears

Following Formula One practice, there was a small carbon clutch and aluminium flywheel for an ultra-fast engine response. A five-speed gearbox offered ratios spaced for the fastest possible acceleration to 257.4km/h (160mph), with the top gear set for comfortable cruising at speeds of 321.8km/h (200mph) or more. Even the gearchange times were analyzed; Murray stipulated that it had to be possible to shift ratios in only a quarter of a second. This was about half the normal time, and barely slower than a Formula One car could achieve. But Traction Products, which developed the gearbox, came up with the goods thanks to a new synchromesh system.

There was no power assistance for the steering or servo assistance for the brakes – the F1 was to offer driving in its purest form. The wheels measured 432mm (17in) across while the brakes were ventilated discs all round, cooled under heavy braking by adjustable ducts in the bodywork. Suspension was by unequal-length double wishbones all round and there was no four-wheel drive or traction control – that just added weight and complexity.

All this attention to detail guaranteed the car would become a record-holder – it also meant the car's place in the history of the supercar was assured. But while McLaren had intended to make 300 examples before finishing production, barely a third of that were built before the car went out of production in 1996.

Mercedes CLK GTR

The engine was mounted directly to the back of the GTR's carbon fibre monocoque, along with the six-speed sequential manual transmission. This fed power to the rear wheels only.

A 6.9-litre (413.8ci) V12 engine was mounted in the middle of the car; it was essentially the same unit found in other models in the Mercedes range. But until this point, its largest capacity anywhere else was a mere 6 litres (364.2ci).

Safety was an important factor in the GTR's design – which was no surprise as Mercedes has always been at the forefront of safety developments. Airbags were fitted along with an incredibly rigid safety cell.

Those twin circular headlamps gave the GTR the look of a CLK, but there was very little carried over from the road car to the racer. In fact, apart from the dashboard, everything was built specially for the GTR.

Aluminium alloy wheels were fitted at front and rear, and they measured 457mm (18in) across. They were wrapped in Bridgestone 345/35 ZR18 rubber at the back and 295/35 ZR18 at the front.

Any car that costs £1.1 million has to be pretty special. When the CLK GTR was announced, for that money you could have bought nearly a pair of McLaren F1s, seven Diablos – or no fewer than 30 regular CLK 320s. This had to be a special car indeed to command such sums. Yet the series was virtually sold out before even the first car had been built – helped by a production run of just 25 units.

Mercedes CLK GTR	
Years of production	1998–9
Displacement	6898cc (413.8ci)
Configuration	Mid-mounted V12
Transmission	Six-speed manual, rear-wheel drive
Power	452.8kW (612bhp) @ 6800rpm
Torque	772.2Nm (572lb ft) @ 5250rpm
Top speed	320.2km/h (199mph)
0–62mph (0–100km/h)	3.8sec
Power to weight ratio	307.8kW/ton (416bhp/ton)
Number built	25

It's that door arrangement again; once McLaren had used it for the F1, everybody wanted their supercar to have it. While the GTR was a fantastic-looking machine, in reality it was little more than a caricature of the regular CLK.

The CLK GTR came about because of Mercedes' desire to win at Le Mans – which meant building a car that featured the best of everything. It had to have lightweight bodywork, a massively powerful engine, and reliability that would allow it to run flat out for 24 hours, without a hitch. In the event, it wouldn't be the car's reliability that would prove the problem – it was the aerodynamics. This led to the car flipping at high speed, which did little for the car's placings in endurance racing…

The Silver Arrow

The CLK GTR was intended to be the spiritual successor to the legendary 300 SLR, while the project was dubbed the Silver Arrow by insiders; a reference to the glory days of the 1930s and mid-1950s. it was created to take on rivals from Porsche (GT1), McLaren (F1 GTR) and Nissan (R390), and while there was a passing resemblance to the production CLK, there was virtually nothing carried over. Apart from the dashboard, a CLK owner would have recognized very little – either on the outside, or underneath the kevlar skin. However, the GTR would be as safe as the regular production car as well as clean – which is why there were airbags fitted along with four-way catalytic converters. However, there was no anti-lock braking system, because the regulations which forced the production of the GTR also banned anti-lock technology from being used in racing.

The GTR was the work of Mercedes' in-house tuning division, AMG. This department was responsible for developing Mercedes' engines to get the maximum power out of them, and with the GTR is certainly had its work cut out. The obvious choice was the 6-litre (364.2ci) V12 unit normally found in cars such as the S600 and SL600. This 90-degree 48-valve unit was strong and relatively easy to develop – and easy to increase in capacity. The first job was to stroke the powerplant to 6898cc (413.8ci) then the internals were completely reworked to give maximum power and torque without the need for ultimate tractability or refinement. But because the car was to be sold in road trim, it would still have to run cleanly enough to pass emissions regulations – and it did still have to be usable to a degree.

There was no four-wheel drive in the GTR, as modern electronics could help harness the power with rear-wheel drive only. Taking the power to the back of the car was a six-speed manual gearbox. At both the front and rear there were rose-jointed double-wishbone suspension, which also featured adjustable dampers. The wheels were lightweight alloy, with a diameter of 457mm (18in) all round – it wouldn't be long before these were seen as a little on the small side as wheels became larger and larger.

Roadster version

Just when it seemed that the CLK GTR had disappeared into the history books, the man behind its development announced a roadster version. Hans-Werner Aufrescht was one of the co-founders of AMG, which by this stage had been swallowed up by Mercedes. In 2002 he revealed a drop-top car available in similar numbers to the original – and at a similar price. In place of the previous fixed roof was a pair of flying buttresses which incorporated cooling ducts for the engine and roll bars in case the driver's enthusiasm was greater than his/her skill. Mechanically the car was the same as its predecessor, with the same V12 engine pushing out 452.8kW (612bhp). With left-hand drive only, it was hoped to build around the same number of roadsters as coupés – although the price of the open car was little more than half that of the closed one.

It may have carried the CLK tag, but this V12-powered supercar didn't share much with the standard production car of the same name. It was very safe and clean, however, with airbags and cata}yltic converters aplenty.

Nissan R390

As you can imagine, there wasn't much luggage space in the R390, as practicality wasn't high on the list of priorities for Nissan's engineers. But there were small cubby-holes above each rear light.

Those air scoops positioned just behind each door were there to feed the V8's twin intercoolers. There were also discreet scoops just behind each rear wheel. This was to allow hot air to escape from the brakes.

With overtones of the Jaguar XJR-15 and even the Spectra R42, that swoopy bodywork was designed by Ian Callum, of Aston Martin fame. It had all the usual supercar cues; cab-forward stance, low bonnet line and a narrow central canopy.

There weren't as many differences between the race and road-spec R390s as you might imagine. One of the key ones was the amount of ground clearance; the suspension was raised for the road car so it didn't constantly ground.

Anti-lock brakes were fitted as standard and helping to haul the car down from huge speeds there were 355mm (14in) ventilated discs at each corner. The system was engineered by AP Racing.

At the end of the twentieth century and the beginning of the twenty-first, diversification was becoming the name of the game. Companies such as Mercedes and BMW were starting to develop smaller, cheaper models to break into fresh markets. Volkswagen was trying to do the opposite by going upmarket. But Nissan must have taken the biscuit for offering products at opposite ends of the scale – at one end of which was the Micra, while at the other there was the R390. Okay, so the latter was hardly a regular production model; in fact the company was compelled to make just one example under the GT racing rules. But it was still one hell of a job for a salesman somewhere, to sell a supercar from one corner of the showroom while also trying to peddle wares such as the Almera or Micra.

Le Mans

The R390 came about because Nissan was desperately keen to win the Le Mans 24-Hour race. When the project first got underway, only one Japanese car maker had ever managed to win there; Mazda's first victory in 1991 was also its last. Designed by Ian Callum (who also designed the Aston Martin DB7 along with a string of Jaguars), the R390 was engineered by Tom Walkinshaw Racing and Nissan Motorsport International, with durability and speed the two key ingredients. However, despite the Nissan

The R390's cockpit didn't share much with its more mundane siblings such as the Primera and Almera. If they'd featured a sequential manual gearchange and a 398.8kW (539bhp) V8 engine they may have been a bit more exciting.

setting the fastest time in pre-qualifying for the 1997 race, all three cars suffered from overheating gearboxes, with only one car finishing – in 12th place.

Nissan learned a lot from its experiences at the 1997 Le Mans, which is why when it had to be build a

Nissan R390

Years of production	1998
Displacement	3500cc (210ci)
Configuration	Mid-mounted V8, twin-turbo
Transmission	Six-speed sequential manual, rear-wheel drive
Power	398.8kW (539bhp) @ 6800rpm
Torque	634.5Nm (470lb ft) @ 4400rpm
Top speed	281.6km/h (175mph)
0–60mph (0–97km/h)	3.9sec
Power to weight ratio	321.9kW/ton (435bhp/ton)
Number built	1

single example of the road car, it incorporated a few developments. The main change was an increase in length by 120mm (4.7in) to 4720mm (185.5in), for various reasons. The main ones were to increase downforce and decrease drag, but it also allowed some extra luggage space to be incorporated above the rear lights.

Design

While the road car had to be essentially the same as the racers, there were some conflicts between what was demanded on the circuit and what was allowed (or was practicable) for the road. Ground clearance was a key example; while minimal clearance was desirable on the billiard-table smooth surfaces of Le Mans, a road car needed to be able to deal with potholes and speed bumps. Correspondingly, the suspension was raised by 80mm (3.1in) at the front and 100mm (3.9in) at the rear.

Power was provided by a 3500cc (210ci) V8 engine, mounted behind the passenger cell. With a pair of turbochargers the unit was capable of developing a massive 398.8kW (539bhp) – and when this was combined with a kerb weight of 1240kg (2734lb), it gave a healthy power to weight ratio of 321.9kW/ton (435bhp/ton). Maximum power was delivered at 6800rpm – lower down the scale, at 4400rpm, the torque peaked at 634.5Nm (470lb ft).

All this power and torque was channelled to the rear wheels via a six-speed sequential manual gearbox, although there were no paddle shifts. While the road car was restricted to 281.6km/h (175mph), the racer was capable of cracking 321.8km/h (200mph) – for hours on end. It could stop as well as it went though, with huge 355mm (14in) ventilated discs fitted to each wheel. Although anti-lock technology was banned on the track, the road car featured it as standard – if there is such a thing as standard when you have to build just one example. The system was developed by AP Racing, to give fade-free braking for lap after lap. With such a no-compromise car it was no surprise that double-wishbone suspension was fitted at each end. Attached to this there were alloy wheels that measured 457mm (18in) at the front and 482mm (19in) at the rear – wrapped around them were Bridgestone ZR-rated tyres.

Of course it was important that the R390 was engineered without compromise, because Nissan was deadly serious about winning at Le Mans. But as far as the road car project was concerned, the details didn't matter when it came to the specification. After all, when you're charging £1 million for a car, its specification hardly matters if it wears Nissan badges. Because nobody is going to buy it.

The fastest and most expensive Nissan road car ever developed was created to comply with the Le Mans GT1 Class regulations which required manufacturers to build at least one street-legal version of the race car.

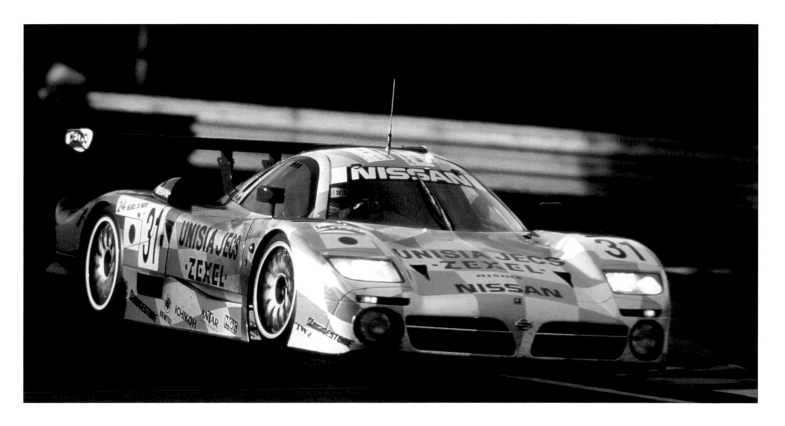

Panoz Roadster

Although most Americans wanted a laid-back driving experience from their sports cars, the Roadster was fitted with a five-speed manual gearbox, which drove the rear wheels only.

That retro-look bodyshell was made by hand, and was crafted completely from aluminium. While the open-heeled Roadster was clearly inspired by the Lotus Seven in concept, there were elements of the AC Cobra in there as well.

By using a Ford quad-cam V8 up front, the Roadster could be sold and maintained by Ford dealers throughout the US. Displacing 4.6 litres (279.3ci), the engine could generate 225.7kW (305bhp) and 405Nm (300lb ft) of torque.

There was independent suspension all round, with double wishbones, coil spring and damper units and an anti-roll bar at each end. With minimal overhangs at each end, the car could be positioned easily during press-on driving.

Despite the prodigious power on offer, the Panoz Roadster was a compact car, with little in the way of interior space. Still, that just meant it was easier to stay in your seat as you hurtled round bends at break-neck speeds.

While there was very little in the production Panoz Roadster that didn't hail from the USA, its roots actually lay in a project that was started by Frank Costin, in Great Britain. Costin (who left his mark thanks to a successful career with Lotus), had designed the Roadster's chassis, which was snapped up by Danny Panoz in the late 1980s. He then got Freeman Thomas to create a new retro-look bodyshell to adorn the chassis – Thomas was one of the key designers responsible for the look of the New Beetle that surfaced as the Concept One at the 1994 Detroit motor show.

Aluminium Intensive Vehicle

By 1989, Panoz Auto Development had been founded, but it wasn't until the following year that the company's first car became available. This was a very limited production version of the Roadster, which trickled out of the factory in tiny numbers until 1996, when Panoz invested in a new production unit that could build the Roadster in greater numbers – even though it was hardly what you could call a mass-produced car. It was

at this point that the car became the AIV Roadster – for Aluminium Intensive Vehicle. This was on account of 65 per cent of the vehicle's weight being accounted for by alloy panelling. The exterior was formed by using an aerospace process called SPF, or Super Plastic Forming. This used pressurized air to mould heated sheets of aluminium alloy in dies, the result being stress-free panels of uniform thickness. The chassis, which was essentially a boxy spaceframe, was made from

Panoz Roadster

Years of production	1990–1996
Displacement	4601cc (279.3ci)
Configuration	Front-mounted V8
Transmission	Five-speed automatic, rear-wheel drive
Power	225.7kW (305bhp) @ 5800rpm
Torque	405Nm (300lb ft) @ 4800rpm
Top speed	209.2km/h (130mph)
0–60mph (0–97km/h)	4.5sec
Power to weight ratio	183.5kW/ton (248bhp/ton)
Number built	N/A

aluminium extrusions with the joints treated with aerospace adhesives.

While it may have been cringeworthy, nobody could deny that the car had arresting looks and pretty terrific performance – it was just a shame that the design wasn't especially well resolved in some areas.

While the Roadster was obviously inspired by lightweight rockets such as the Lotus and Caterham Seven, it was also something of a pastiche – there were elements from all sorts of classic sports cars in there. Those rear wheel arches were pure AC Cobra for example, although they were even more pronounced thanks to the Roadster's open-wheel design. But the bulge on the bonnet looked crude and the windscreen frame was far too upright – not helped by the fact that it was borrowed from the completely unsuitable VW Super Beetle. That guppy-like grille in the car's nose also did it no favours from an aesthetic point of view – but most of this could just about be forgiven once on the road.

Performance

If the styling was weak, the performance was anything but, thanks to the 4.6-litre (279.2ci) quad-cam V8 that was located in the Roadster's nose. Mounted longitudinally, and driving the rear wheels via a five-speed manual gearbox, the powerplant churned out a healthy 225.7kW (305bhp) at 5800rpm, while torque peaked at 405Nm (300lb ft) at a rather high 4800rpm.

Although the engine had to be used rather hard to get the best out of it (it was red-lined at a thundering 7300rpm), it was still no slouch. Its top speed of 209.2km/h (130mph) was rather academic, because at anything over around 80.4km/h (50mph) it was like sitting in the eye of a storm. The high seating position and relatively low windscreen meant the driver was far too exposed to the elements, but with a 0–60mph (0–97km/h) time of just 4.5 seconds, it was possible to have some fun without having to go especially fast.

Helping the car handle was an all-independent suspension set up at each corner, which used the classic double wishbone system, complete with coil springs and dampers. This, allied to the incredibly stiff chassis, gave predictable handling to the degree that driving the Roadster was more like piloting a single-seater. It could stop too, with disc brakes all round, which in the case of the front items were also ventilated. But there was no need to scrub all the speed off at every corner because there was grip aplenty thanks to the big, sticky 457mm (18in) tyres that were fitted. In fact, considering this was one of the nimblest and fastest sports cars ever to come out of America, it's a shame it's almost always overlooked.

The Roadster's motive power was supplied by a 4.6-litre (280.7ci) all-alloy V8 engine developed by Ford. With four overhead camshafts and 32 valves it produced a healthy 225.7kW (305bhp) and 405Nm (300lb ft) of torque.

Renault Alpine GTA and A610

It may have had only six cylinders, but the A610's powerplant produced a very useful 185kW (250bhp). This, allied to the car's low weight, meant performance was very strong. Top speed was around 257km/h (160mph).

Following the best race-car practice, both ends of the A610 were suspended by unequal length double wishbones along with coil springs and telescopic dampers. There were also anti-roll bars fitted at each end.

The aim of the A610 was to offer practicality with huge performance. That was why there was seating for four people inside the cabin, although luggage space was somewhat lacking at both the front and the rear.

The biggest external difference between the A610 and its predecessors was the use of pop-up headlamps. Earlier cars were fitted with fixed headlamps located behind plexiglass covers.

If only car buyers weren't so precious about the badges on their steeds, the Alpine GTA and A610 could have been so much more successful. Here were two truly talented cars that were handicapped by their branding; had the cars worn Porsche badges, demand would have exceeded supply by a massive margin. But instead, supply exceeded demand and the cars died a lonely death.

Renault and Alpine

The alliance between Renault and Alpine had begun in 1955, when Jean Redélé, founder of the Alpine marque, built his first car using Renault 4CV mechanicals. The A110, launched in 1963, was made with Renault's co-operation, leading to the adoption of Alpine as Renault's competition wing in 1971. In the same year the A310 was introduced and in 1974 Renault bought Alpine. Outside the UK Renault could trade on the Alpine name, but because of Peugeot Talbot's ownership of the name, none of the cars sold there could use the Alpine tag. It was this that was to lead to the car's lack of success – the right badge would have made all the difference.

When the A310 was replaced in 1984, it was by a model called the Alpine V6 GT. In the UK the same car was badged the GTA, and while it was clearly related to its predecessor, the reality was that it was a completely new car, which was longer, wider, better-built and featured a different version of the Douvrin V6 engine that had first been used by the company in the 1970s. There was an all-new bodyshell and the mechanicals and interior were also new. The basic layout was retained, however, which meant there was a steel backbone chassis over which was stretched a glassfibre bodyshell. To keep the car planted to the road there were double wishbones all round and mounted out the back was the familiar 2.8-litre (169.9ci) V6 engine. At first there was just a normally aspirated version available, but within a year a turbocharged version was also on sale. This latter car had a very healthy 148kW (200bhp) on tap, while its lesser sibling had just 118.4kW (160bhp) – although this was still enough to give a top speed of around 241.3km/h (150mph). Although the car was hugely capable, with Porsche-baiting handling and performance, sales continued at a trickle. The car looked stunning and it was practical as well as reliable – it was only the branding that held it back.

The A610 had nearly everything. With reliability, performance, great handling and stunning looks it couldn't fail. Except it did, because potential buyers were frightened of handing over so much money for a mere Renault.

If there was one area that let the A610 down a little, it was the interior. There was too much plastic and it didn't feel special enough – but the same accusations could be levelled at many of its rivals.

The Le Mans edition

In a bid to give the car a boost, a special Le Mans edition was produced in 1990, complete with bigger wheels, flared wheel arches and beefier bumpers front and rear. Available in metallic burgundy only, these cars were fitted with anti-lock brakes and leather trim as standard. Only 300 were built, and because a catalytic converter was standard fare, the available power was cut to 136.9kW (185bhp) – all cars were based on the Turbo rather than the normally aspirated car.

While the GTA was a lot of car for the money, it was its replacement, the A610, that offered truly astonishing value. The A610 was launched at the 1991 Geneva motor show and Renault claimed that over 80 per cent of the car was either completely new or at least heavily revised. Although the silhouette was unmistakably Alpine, the whole thing looked much more aggressive thanks to redesigned bumpers and the judicious use of a few discreet slats and scoops. The biggest difference, however, was a move to pop-up headlamps in place of the previous fixed units which sat behind plexiglass covers.

As was expected, while the basic specification remained the same, stronger brakes and improved suspension were fitted to the A610. The chassis itself was also revised, which made it stiffer, helping to improve the already superb handling. Indeed, as soon as the car was tested by car magazines, it received rave reviews because it couldn't really be faulted. But buyers continued to stay away, spending their money on the Porsche 944 instead.

Renault Alpine GTA and A610	
Years of production	1991–5
Displacement	2975cc (178.5ci)
Configuration	Rear-mounted V6
Transmission	Five-speed manual, rear-wheel drive
Power	185kW (250bhp) @ 5750rpm
Torque	348.3Nm (258lb ft) @ 2900rpm
Top speed	255.8km/h (159mph)
0–60mph (0–97km/h)	5.8sec
Power to weight ratio	133.9kW/ton (181bhp/ton)
Number built	N/A

TVR Cerbera

With all those compound curves and subtle scoops and slats, the Cerbera could only be a TVR. There was one difference between this car and the rest of the family though, in that it was available as a coupé only.

The Cerbera was based on a completely new platform compared with siblings such as the Griffith and Chimaera. To allow for extra seats in the back there was a longer wheelbase than usual.

Another departure for TVR with the Cerbera was an extra pair of seats in the back. While TVRs were usually two-seaters only, this was the company's attempt at a family car – although only small children could be carried in the back.

The all-alloy V8 engine was built in-house, and was TVR's first home-grown powerplant. With a displacement of 4185cc (251.1ci), it was a tough unit but not especially complicated with just two valves per cylinder.

TVR

TVR 100

TVR Great British Sports Cars 01253 356151 ●●●●

There was no anti-lock system for the brakes because TVR couldn't afford it. But with massive ventilated discs all round, gripped by four-pot calipers at the front, there was no shortage of stopping power.

The Cerbera took TVR into a different league, with more performance available than ever before thanks to an in-house engine. The car was also available only as a coupé.

On the face of it, every TVR since the mid-1980s has been a supercar. Always made of glassfibre (so lightweight) and always packed with a potent engine, cars such as the Griffith, Chimaera and the 'wedges' with over four litres have also been terrifically fast. But the Cerbera was different – this was the car that raised the stakes for TVR, with more of everything on offer. There was more power and more speed, but in return TVR asked for more money – this was serious.

In-house engine

Perhaps the key thing about the Cerbera was that it was fitted with TVR's first in-house engine; until this point the Rover V8 had been fitted to the various TVRs, in various capacities and in varying states of tune. But the arrival of the AJP8 meant TVR was now building its own powerplants, with the units designed and built for ultimate power – as well as reliability. The engines were developed within a racing environment (in the Tuscan race series), and if it could survive that, it could survive anything.

Carrying the AJP8 tag, the powerplant wasn't especially advanced, although both the block and heads were made of alloy to keep weight down. To ensure maximum torque at low revs, there were just two valves per cylinder, while to make sure the power was delivered in a linear fashion, there was no

turbocharging or supercharging. What it did feature, which was becoming ever more popular, was a flat-plane crank, which gave the car a very distinctive engine note. At first the Cerbera was available in 4.2-litre (254.9ci) form only, and this first incarnation of the engine was able to develop a healthy 259kW (350bhp) and 435Nm (320lb ft) of torque. That was enough to take the car to 289.6km/h (180mph), while it could also sprint to 97km/h (60mph) in little more than four seconds.

Being a fully fledged supercar meant there was no automatic gearbox option; all cars were supplied with a five-speed manual transmission. This directed all

TVR Cerbera	
Years of production	1996
Displacement	4185cc (251.1ci)
Configuration	Front-mounted V8
Transmission	Five-speed manual, rear-wheel drive
Power	259kW (350bhp) @ 6500rpm
Torque	435Nm (320lb ft) @ 4500rpm
Top speed	289.6km/h (180mph)
0–60mph (0–97km/h)	4.2sec
Power to weight ratio	239kW/ton (323bhp/ton)
Number built	N/A

the power to the rear wheels, and although there was no traction control system, there was a Hydratrak limited-slip differential to help get the power down. This worked by allowing the inside wheel to spin away excess power long before the loaded outside wheel was able to lose traction – crude but effective.

New versions

As if all this wasn't enough, within a year of the Cerbera's launch there was the option of a 4.5-litre (273.1ci) engine, offering even more power. With 310.8kW (420bhp) and 513Nm (380lb ft) of torque, this even swifter version could get to 97km/h (60mph) in just 4.3 seconds before topping out at 287.7km/h (185mph). As if that wasn't enough, it could despatch the standing quarter mile in just 12.6 seconds – this was one seriously fast car.

If all this seemed just a bit too much, from 1999 there was the chance to buy a six-cylinder Cerbera. This was fitted with the straight-six that was to become TVR's next home-grown powerplant. With a displacement of just 3996cc (239.7ci), the Speed Six was slower than its V8-engined siblings – but not by

much. It could still get to 97km/h (60mph) in just 4.5 seconds and it could still do 289.6km/h (180mph). Indeed, its 259kW (350bhp) power output was identical to the 4.2-litre (254.9ci) car, which by now was known as the Speed Eight. Just to put those figures into context, Ferrari didn't have a production car that could get to 97km/h (60mph) as quickly. The Porsche 911, Honda NSX and Nissan Skyline were all slower – it may have been the baby of the family, but the Speed Six was not slow.

In case there were some who felt that TVR had gone soft with the launch of the Speed Six, the Speed Six made an appearance in 2000. With a pair of Speed Six engines mated together to create a V12, the Speed Twelve was a fearsome machine that was likely to kill any unskilled driver as soon as he/she ventured onto the public road in it. With 651.2kW (880bhp) on tap without any tuning, the car would prove to be lethal in the wrong hands – which is why TVR canned it.

Nobody could work out the TVR. The company's cars were very powerful yet not that expensive, and they still featured more bespoke interior fittings than any other supercar maker.

Vector W8

The centre cell of the W8 consisted of a chrome moly steel cage, which Vector claimed featured the strongest roof of any car ever put into production. There was also a three-stage collision protection system at each end.

The body structure was made entirely from carbon fibre and kevlar. Located within this structure there were aircraft-style fuel tanks that were filled with explosion-suppressing foam.

CALIFORNIA
VECTOR

The front suspension was predictable, with double wishbones and coil spring/damper units. At the back there was a De Dion tube with a quartet of trailing arms, a lateral link and concentric coil shock absorbers.

The instrumentation was more than comprehensive – it was like the cockpit of an airliner in there. As well as switches and buttons galore, there was a head-up display and TV screen with various readouts.

At the time those 406mm (16in) wheels were pretty large compared to those seen elsewhere. Made from machined billet aluminium alloy, they were three-piece units which were wrapped in Michelin tyres certified as being safe at 321.8km/h (200mph).

There's a school of thought that says the only proper supercar to ever have come out of America is the Chevrolet Corvette. Luckily for the Americans, that's patently untrue; not only is there the Saleen S7 elsewhere in this book, but during the 1990s there was another contender; the Vector W8. Sadly the W8 is now just a footnote in the history of the supercar, but there was a time when it could have taken on – and beaten – some of its more established rivals. If only the company's founder's feet had been planted a little more firmly on the ground.

Aeronautical technology

As long ago as 1977 the Vector Aeromotive W2 had made an appearance. The company's name gave a clue as to what aspirations its founder (Gerry Wiegert) had. He was obsessed with aeronautical technology, and he reckoned there was a place for it in a road car. While that belief is not completely unfounded, it only really has a place in the commercial world if prices are kept relatively affordable – and they most definitely weren't where the Vector was concerned. Although the project had started in the late 1970s, it wasn't until 1991 that the first car, the W8, was deemed to be ready for delivery. With a price tag of over $450,000, there wasn't much of a queue to buy the cars, but

amazingly, 14 of them did manage to find owners before the car was superseded by the Avtech WX-3 in 1992. If the price tag attached to the earlier car had seemed a bit extreme, the $765,000 cost of the new car was even more outrageous. Unsurprisingly, there were no takers for the car and as a result Vector Aeromotive was taken over by Mega Tech, the Indonesian company which also owned Lamborghini.

The first thing Mega Tech did was to redesign the car and rename it; the M12 was nothing more than an updated Avtech WX-3, but it also cost just $184,000. Considering it now used the Lamborghini V12 engine and a ZF transaxle, this was something of a bargain – especially as the Diablo that used the same powerplant was rather more expensive.

Cost

The reason for the extraordinarily high cost of Gerry Wiegert's cars was the way he built them. He took best practices for aircraft, then replicated them in a road car environment. Even the suspension arms were certified, there was aircraft-grade wiring and fire

This was the final iteration of the Vector, the M12. The car could do 190mph and 0–60mph (0–97km/h) in just 4.5 seconds. It was hoped 100 a year could be sold, but that was just a pipe dream.

You'll have to look pretty closely to see any curves in the W8's design. That rear end was designed with a ruler and set square only, while the rest of the car's styling is predominantly made up of straight lines.

extinguishers were fitted as standard; owners could choose between manual or automatic systems. It was important to Wiegert that he could claim the W8 was the best, fastest and most advanced. To that end he claimed the W8 was the world's fastest car, its central structure was the strongest of any car ever designed, and it featured the world's most powerful engine. Second best was not an option as far as Wiegert was concerned – and supremacy never comes cheap.

At the heart of the W8 was a 90-degree all-alloy V8 that displaced 6 litres (364.2ci). The block was blueprinted and balanced while there were also forged aluminium pistons, a forged crankshaft and stainless steel valves. A pair of Garrett AiResearch H3 turbochargers boosted the air/fuel mix and there was electronic direct port fuel injection. The result of all this was an engine that could generate 444kW (600bhp) at 5700rpm and 810Nm (600lb ft) of torque at 4900rpm; consequently the W8 was capable of topping 321.8km/h (200mph) while dismissing the 0–60mph (0–97km/h) dash in barely four seconds.

While any supercar would usually transmit the power via a manual gearbox, the Vector packed a three-speed automatic. While it didn't need any more ratios thanks to the huge torque levels, it was odd that the driver had little control over which ratio was engaged at any time. There was also little effort put into stripping the car out to keep weight levels to a minimum; on the standard spec sheet were air-conditioning, full leather trim, a sunroof and power-assisted steering. Even with all this the car was no slouch – for all the good that did for Vector's sales.

Although it's not immediately apparent from this photograph, the W8's interior was very much inspired by contemporary aircraft. The dash featured more electronic gadgetry – including a **TV** monitor – than any of its rivals.

Vector W8

Years of production	1991
Displacement	5973cc (358.3ci)
Configuration	Mid-mounted V8, twin-turbo
Transmission	Three-speed automatic
Power	462.5kW (625bhp) @ 5700rpm
Torque	850.5Nm (630lb ft) @ 4900rpm
Top speed	350.8km/h (218mph)
0–60mph (0–97km/h)	4.2sec
Power to weight ratio	366.3kW/ton (414bhp/ton)
Number built	14

The visibility to the front was unrivalled, thanks to that amazing expanse of glass. Despite all the compound curves, there was no distortion when looking to one side or the other. Rear visibility wasn't so good though…

Although ultra-light carbon fibre was becoming de rigueur for low-volume supercars, Yamaha made the decision to build the OX99-011's bodyshell from aluminium. This was hand-beaten with all those glorious curves.

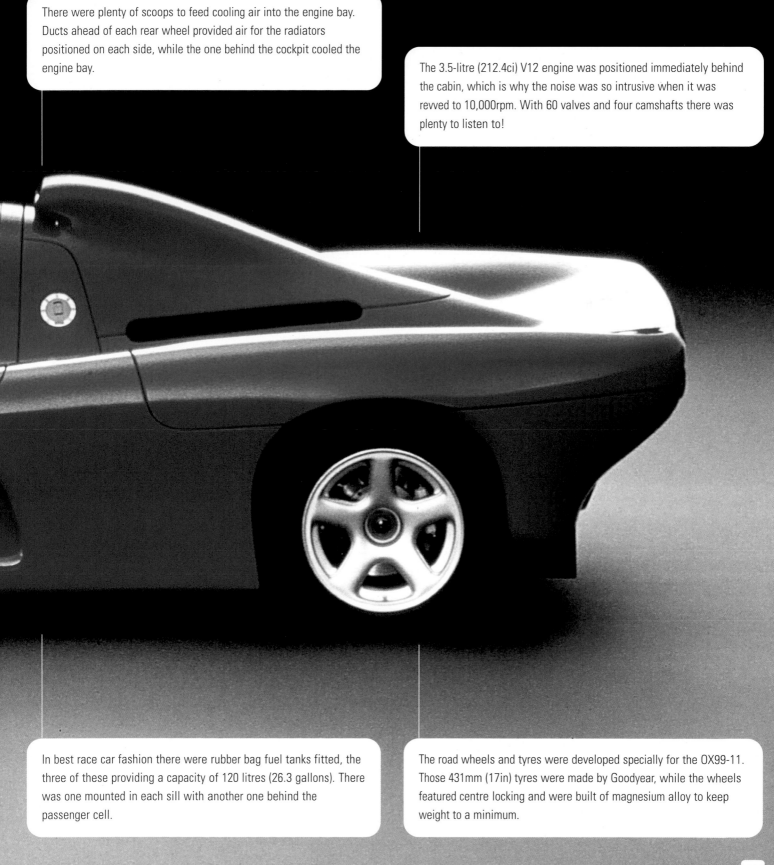

There were plenty of scoops to feed cooling air into the engine bay. Ducts ahead of each rear wheel provided air for the radiators positioned on each side, while the one behind the cockpit cooled the engine bay.

The 3.5-litre (212.4ci) V12 engine was positioned immediately behind the cabin, which is why the noise was so intrusive when it was revved to 10,000rpm. With 60 valves and four camshafts there was plenty to listen to!

In best race car fashion there were rubber bag fuel tanks fitted, the three of these providing a capacity of 120 litres (26.3 gallons). There was one mounted in each sill with another one behind the passenger cell.

The road wheels and tyres were developed specially for the OX99-11. Those 431mm (17in) tyres were made by Goodyear, while the wheels featured centre locking and were built of magnesium alloy to keep weight to a minimum.

It may be one of the greatest supercar clichés ever, but the OX99-11 was supposed to be the closest thing to a racing car for the road. One of the features that allowed it to feel the part was a central driver's seat.

In the world of the supercar, the term 'race car for the road' is usually mere marketing hype. It's a handy line that PR officers coin in an attempt to impress potential buyers and gullible journalists. Few of the supercars that have ever gone on sale have really deserved the tag, but one of those small number was the Yamaha OX99-11. At this point you're probably wondering what on Earth the OX99-11 was, and that's understandable because it never really made the jump from prototype to production. Which is a shame really, because this one car above all others could have given the McLaren F1 a run for its money.

Formula One for the road

The fruits of the OX99-11 project were first made public in 1992, its premise being that this would be the closest thing to a Formula One car for the road. Of course the journalists assembled at the launch had heard it before, but in this case, it was true. There was a 3.5-litre (212.4ci) V12 engine in the middle of the car

– and it was a detuned version of the powerplant fitted to Brabhams and Jordans in the early 1990s. Not only was this bolted directly to the monocoque, but mated to it was a transversely mounted six-speed gearbox – to which was mounted the suspension and various engine ancillaries. Also, the chassis was a carbon fibre honeycomb monocoque, so this really was using the best of the then-current Formula One technology.

As a result of all this high-tech, the car's price was set to be an eye-watering $1 million, but where else could you go to get anything like it? Add a proper bodyshell, air-conditioning, an all-synchromesh gearbox and exhausts catalysts to a Formula One car, and this would be the result. However, after all this ultra-modern technology, there was one throwback to another era, and that was the material chosen for the bodywork. Instead of carbon fibre, it was decided that hand-beaten aluminium panels gave the right impression of exclusivity.

Like its biggest rival, the McLaren F1, there was a central seating position for the driver. But instead of seating for another two occupants, there was merely one other chair, located directly behind the driver. Behind this seat was the bulkhead, and directly behind that was the 70-degree 3498cc (209.8ci) V12.

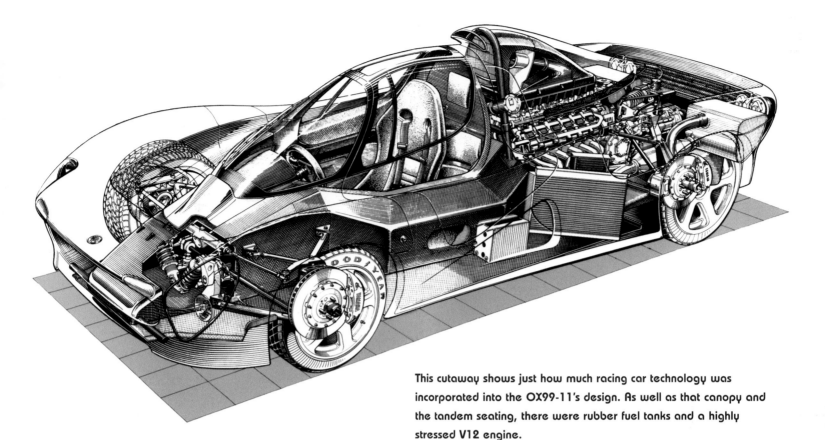

This cutaway shows just how much racing car technology was incorporated into the OX99-11's design. As well as that canopy and the tandem seating, there were rubber fuel tanks and a highly stressed V12 engine.

This was mounted rigidly to the tub of the car, and it was because of this lack of damping that the noise in the cabin as the engine worked its way up to its 10,000rpm red-line was unbearable. With four camshafts actuating five valves per cylinder, there was certainly plenty to listen to once the powerplant was on song!

Low-speed performance

Considering that the engine produced its maximum power of 310.8kW (420bhp) at 10,000rpm, it was amazing how tractable it was at very low road speeds. Even at 1200rpm the engine wasn't peaky, which was a direct result of the electronic control unit having been developed for ultimate usability. It was also a very clean unit, with three-way catalytic converters being incorporated into the stainless steel exhaust system. Transmitting the power to the road was a six-speed manual gearbox, which drove the rear wheels via a limited-slip differential.

The cockpit was very much race-inspired, with carbon fibre all over the place and not too many concessions to luxury. Although there was plenty of room for a conventional steering wheel, a Formula One-style unit was fitted with a squared-off bottom. As if this wasn't enough, it was also removable – completely unnecessary, but all part of building-up the required effect.

Although nobody ever officially tested the OX99-11 for the press, it was clear that it could have sold in limited numbers. But they would have been too limited for Yamaha, which couldn't see a way of making money out of the project. When it was unveiled to the press it was already running late and was over-budget. Even though hardly any more development was needed after testing throughout 1992, the plug was pulled on the project in 1993.

Yamaha OX99-11

Years of production	1992
Displacement	3498cc (209.8ci)
Configuration	Mid-mounted V12
Transmission	Six-speed manual, rear-wheel drive
Power	310.8kW (420bhp) @ 10,000rpm
Torque	N/A
Top speed	305.7km/h (190mph)
0–60mph (0–97km/h)	3.7 sec
Power to weight ratio	270.1kW/ton (365bhp/ton)
Number built	3

2000–2005

As the twentieth century turned into the twenty-first, a whole new supercar chapter was just starting.

Where the breed once meant high speeds at the expense of everything else, the modern supercar owner

can now have complete usability and reliability into the bargain. But that certainly doesn't mean the end

of the supercar as we know it…

Forty years after the introduction of the world's first production mid-engined supercar, the template for ultra-high performance cars hasn't changed. All the various hypercar makers are still building their cars according to the rules written by Marcello Gandini when he styled the Lamborghini Miura. The materials and mechanicals may be constantly evolving, but the cab-forward, mid-engined design reigns supreme.

However, while supercar buyers have their pick of exotica, things aren't as clear-cut as they used to be. For the person who can afford a garage full of expensive cars it's no problem, because the impractical can sit alongside something just as fast that'll carry the kids and a pair of dogs for good measure. The boundaries have certainly blurred, but that only means the choice has widened even further. Where there used to be a choice of established supercar builders and a few others who never really

While heritage is very important to the driver who spends huge sums of money on a car, occasionally something new comes along that bucks the trend. Such a car was the Pagani Zonda, which took on established Italian marques – and won.

stood a chance, there's a whole new range of offerings available which may have little in the way of heritage to draw on, but which can still command stratospheric prices and get away with it. Many of these offerings are far more expensive than cars from companies such as Lamborghini and Ferrari, yet they find buyers because they're so capable and exclusive.

While everyone suspected that Koenigsegg, Spyker and Pagani would prove to be mere flashes in the pan, they've gone on to become as revered as marques that have been with us far longer. And this is in rather less than a decade – who knows what they might achieve once they've been around a while longer.

Meanwhile companies which were already established as purveyors of fine family cars have become equally well known as builders of amazingly practical hypercars. Marques such as Audi, Mercedes and BMW are all building cars that put most exotica built until the early 1980s to shame – and that's on performance alone. When it comes to usability, practicality, comfort and reliability, cars such as the RS6, M5 and E55 are all streets ahead of any 1970s supercar – just where will it all end?

Ascari KZ-1

Sitting behind the cabin was a 4.9-litre (297.4ci) V8 that normally saw service in the third-generation BMW M5. With 370kW (500bhp) and 496.8Nm (368lb ft) of torque, there was no shortage of performance available.

Nothing less than a carbon fibre monocoque would do for the Ascari, which is partly why it was so expensive. Although the car was very highly specified, the car weighed just 1330kg (2933lb) in full road trim.

Stopping power was prodigious, with cross-drilled and ventilated discs fitted at each corner. At the front there were six-pot calipers while four-pot units resided at the back. Anti-lock was standard.

The interior was every bit as bespoke as the exterior, with plenty of colour-matching in evidence. Climate control was standard, along with leather trim, electric windows and lashings of alloy detailing.

There were double wishbones along with coil springs and telescopic shock absorbers at the front as well as the rear. Naturally there were anti-roll bars at each end as well.

The KZ-1's interior was very classy and beautifully built. To justify (or at least attempt to justify) the car's huge cost, most of the switchgear was made specially for the car. The alloy pedals were floor-hinged, in true race-car style.

You can't help but laugh when a company that nobody has ever heard of announces that only a limited number of its outrageously expensive cars will be available. Potential buyers are being told that unless they get their wallet out quickly, they'll miss the chance to buy into the dream – despite the fact that supply is usually guaranteed to exceed demand from the outset.

Such a car was the Ascari, launched in 2005 with the assertion that no more than 50 of the cars would ever be made. The problem was, at three times the price of a Porsche 911, did the company ever stand much chance of finding 50 people prepared to part with that sort of money for a car that had absolutely no badge recognition whatsoever?

Power and weight

While the car's heritage was nil, the fact that Ascari was a new company didn't mean it knew nothing about building sports cars. As is common with such projects, those responsible for fettling powerplants and sorting chassis were drafted in because of their expertise; in this case it was David Minter who was drafted in to make the car handle. With the Lotus

Elise on his CV, he clearly was capable of making cars great to drive. One of the keys to the Ascari's fine handling was its lightweight bodyshell. Created from carbon fibre for exceptional torsional rigidity, the structure was also incredibly light. Even when the car was fully trimmed and ready for the road it weighed in at just 1330kg (2933lb).

Although a low all-in weight was crucial to achieving high speeds, it was also essential that an extremely powerful engine was fitted. Which is where the BMW M5 powerplant came in. Despite the car's

Ascari KZ-1	
Years of production	2005
Displacement	4941cc (297.4ci)
Configuration	Mid-mounted V8
Transmission	Six-speed manual, rear-wheel drive
Power	370kW (500bhp) @ 7000rpm
Torque	496.8Nm (368lb ft) @ 4500rpm
Top speed	321.8km/h (200mph)
0–60mph (0–97km/h)	3.7sec
Power to weight ratio	278.2kW/ton (376bhp/ton)
Number built	50 max

huge price, and the recent introduction of the fourth-generation M5, it was the older model from which the KZ-1 borrowed its powerplant. Therefore, instead of having the latest V10 engine, the Ascari was fitted with a 4.9-litre (297.4ci) V8. However, although it had developed 'just' 296kW (400bhp) in the BMW, it was fettled to produce 370kW (500bhp) in its new home – which was nearly on a par with the new M5's unit.

Peak power was delivered at 7000rpm, while the maximum torque of 496.8Nm (368lb ft) was generated from 4500rpm – which meant there was less than the 540Nm (400lb ft) that the M5 could develop. However, the KZ-1 was hardly lacking in the performance stakes. It was, according to the factory, able to sprint from a standstill to 97km/h (60mph) in just 3.7 seconds, before romping on to a top speed of 321.8km/h (200mph).

Comfort

Despite the performance on offer, the Ascari was no stripped-out race-day special. Supercar buyers in the twenty-first century have come to expect to be able to have their cake and eat it too. They want huge performance without having to forego creature comforts, which is why the KZ-1 had a generous specification sheet. Buyers could expect climate control as standard, as well as a decent hi-fi, electric windows and electric mirrors. Air-conditioning was also included, as were remote central locking and plenty of aluminium detailing. Because of the car's bespoke nature, exterior colour options were limitless, with the interior trimmed to match. Even the carbon fibre bucket seats, supplied by Sparco, were made to measure for individual owners.

For some buyers, Ascari reckoned that even all this wouldn't be enough, which is why it also offered a race spec version of the car. Called the KZ-1R, the engine was tweaked further, so it could develop a thumping 384.8kW (520bhp). Anything that could be stripped out to save weight was removed, so the KZ-1R tipped the scales at 1250kg (2756lb). But the KZ-1R wasn't for sale to just anyone – it came as part of a package which included membership of an exclusive group called the Race Resort. Built in Spain, this was a fully equipped race track where Ascari customers could receive tuition, race against each other or just relax in secluded surroundings. It might sound mad, but nobody else offered anything like it – which is what supercar ownership is all about.

Those teardrop-shaped headlamps were taken from the Peugeot parts bin, but they fitted into the Ascari's design perfectly. Wherever you looked, and from whichever angle, the car was full of sinewy curves and muscular aggression.

Aston Martin Vanquish

While the Vanquish was only an inch or so longer than its smaller brother the DB7, its wheelbase was around 101mm (4in) longer. This gave it much shorter overhangs, to give it a more aggressive look.

By lengthening the wheelbase, there was significantly more cabin space available. This allowed Aston Martin to offer a choice of either two seats or a 2+2 seating configuration; a unique offering in the sector.

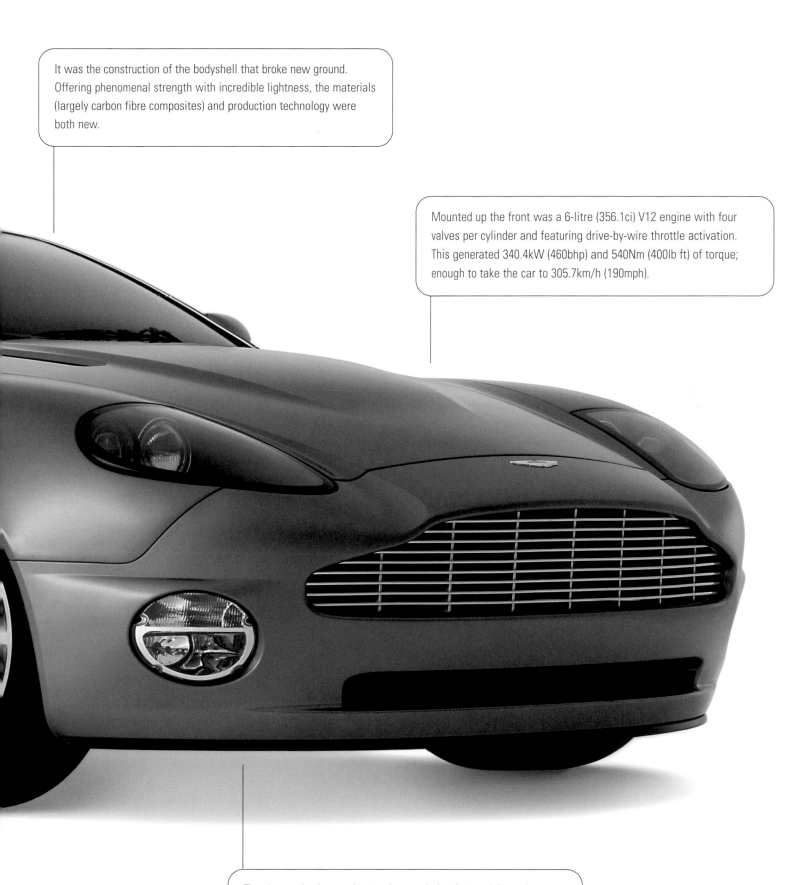

It was the construction of the bodyshell that broke new ground. Offering phenomenal strength with incredible lightness, the materials (largely carbon fibre composites) and production technology were both new.

Mounted up the front was a 6-litre (356.1ci) V12 engine with four valves per cylinder and featuring drive-by-wire throttle activation. This generated 340.4kW (460bhp) and 540Nm (400lb ft) of torque; enough to take the car to 305.7km/h (190mph).

The close ratio six-speed manual transmission featured fingertip-controlled Formula One style paddles which allowed gear changes to be completed in under 250 milliseconds – less than the blink of an eye.

Aston Martin bit the bullet with the Vanquish and produced a thoroughly modern cabin. Although there was still plenty of leather, much of the wood was replaced with aluminium.

When the Aston Martin Vanquish was unveiled in 2000, it was easy to dismiss it as just a DB7 on steroids. After all, this pumped-up supercar featured styling so similar to its smaller brother's that it looked like little more than a top-end version of it. However, the Vanquish was so much more than this, that it really should have had a more distinctive look.

The purpose of the Vanquish was to showcase what Aston Martin was really capable of in the twenty-first century. The company had been under Ford stewardship for over a decade by this point, and it was time to show what it was capable of when it came to cutting-edge technology.

High-tech

Whereas the DB7 featured a steel monocoque clothed in aluminium outer panels, the Vanquish was altogether more high-tech. Its basic platform was an extruded alloy structure, bonded to which were carbon fibre parts in stressed areas such as the door frames, transmission tunnel and screen pillars. The chassis was then built up with composite components using an all-new process for greater strength and

lightness than had previously been possible. All of this was then bonded into a safety cell which was both incredibly strong and astonishingly torsionally rigid. All this was done by hand, and when this process is compared with the mass-produced DB7, it's not hard to see that the cars shared rather less than at first it seemed.

One of the things that the two cars did share was the Duratec V12 engine – or at least the DB7 Vantage was fitted with the same unit, if not the standard car. In the Vanquish the powerplant was developed to produce 333kW (450bhp), which was a 22.2kW (30bhp) advance over its smaller brother. The unit was mounted longitudinally in the car's nose, with all of the power transmitted to the rear wheels only.

Getting that power to the opposite end of the car was a six-speed gearbox which offered fully automatic or sequential manual modes thanks to its steering wheel-mounted paddle shifts. Originally developed by Borg Warner (but produced by Tremec for this car), the transmission was equipped with gadgetry which allowed the driver to select various modes depending on how much traction was available and how fast the gearshifts needed to be. If all this seemed like overkill, Aston Martin was also prepared to build cars to order with a conventional manual gearbox; after all, this was a bespoke car made only to order.

The suspension was developed especially for the Vanquish, with forged alloy double wishbones at each end, these being joined by cast alloy uprights, coil springs and monotube dampers. Anti-roll bars front and rear helped the car to corner in a flatter fashion while at the back there was a limited slip differential which was also fitted with an electronic traction control system to get the power down as tidily as possible. To give the car a contemporary look, nothing

Aston Martin Vanquish

Years of production	2001–
Displacement	5935cc (356.1ci)
Configuration	Front-mounted V12
Transmission	Six-speed manual with semi-auto mode
Power	340.4kW (460bhp) @ 6500rpm
Torque	540Nm (400lb ft) @ 5000rpm
Top speed	305.7km/h (190mph)
0–60mph (0–97km/h)	4.7sec
Power to weight ratio	185.7kW/ton (251bhp/ton)
Number built	N/A

Although the Vanquish looked much like a beefed-up DB7, it was rather more than that. For starters, it was on an all-new platform and its construction was quite unlike its cheaper sibling's.

less than 483mm (19in) alloy wheels would do. In this case they were multi-spoke items and they were wrapped in ultra-low profile 40-series rubber.

Luxury

In true Aston Martin fashion, the Vanquish was fitted with plenty of luxury equipment, taking its weight to a hefty 1820kg (4013lb). Inside the cabin there was satellite navigation, climate control and a domestic-standard hi-fi. Rain-sensing wipers and tyre pressure sensors were standard, as were automatic headlights.

By the end of 2004, Aston Martin released the Vanquish S. As well as engine upgrades to take the power to 384.8kW (520bhp) and the torque to 572.4Nm (424lb ft), there were interior and exterior design revisions along with higher equipment levels. The biggest changes were on the brakes, suspension and wheels, which focused more on sport rather than luxury. All this was a development of the Handling Pack which had become available for the standard Vanquish just before the new S model was launched, and if anybody thought of the Vanquish as merely an upgraded DB7 after all this, they were in need of help.

Bentley Continental GT

The suspension had to be something special to give the right balance between ride and handling. At each corner there were air springs, incorporating self-levelling, with the whole thing controlled by electronic dampers.

Integrated very neatly into the base of the rear windscreen was a pop-up spoiler, which deployed automatically above 193km/h (120mph). This helped to improve high-speed stability without sacrificing low-speed looks.

The transmission was completely up-to-date, with fully automatic or sequential manual modes. Ratios could be manually selected using steering wheel-mounted paddle shifts or the gearlever between the front seats.

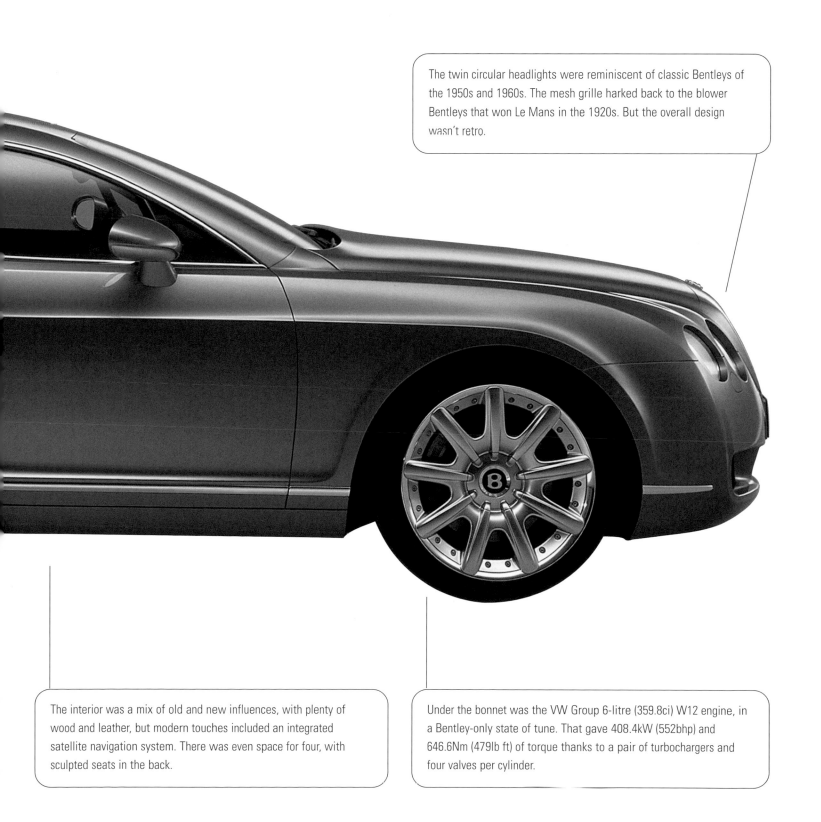

The twin circular headlights were reminiscent of classic Bentleys of the 1950s and 1960s. The mesh grille harked back to the blower Bentleys that won Le Mans in the 1920s. But the overall design wasn't retro.

The interior was a mix of old and new influences, with plenty of wood and leather, but modern touches included an integrated satellite navigation system. There was even space for four, with sculpted seats in the back.

Under the bonnet was the VW Group 6-litre (359.8ci) W12 engine, in a Bentley-only state of tune. That gave 408.4kW (552bhp) and 646.6Nm (479lb ft) of torque thanks to a pair of turbochargers and four valves per cylinder.

If you're unsure of the significance of the Continental GT to Bentley, consider this: it was the first all-new car from the marque in more than half a century. Until the arrival of this car, each time the Crewe company unveiled a new model, there was at least some commonality between it and its predecessor. But the significance was of course even greater than that – this also marked the parting of the ways for Rolls-Royce and Bentley, which had merged back in 1931.

This split offered the perfect opportunity for a fresh start; until this point Bentleys were always based on the same platforms as their Rolls-Royce cousins. And trying to base a sporting coupé on the floorpan of a huge limousine is guaranteed to impose too many compromises for the car to be entirely successful.

Design

The Continental GT's lines were the work of Dirk van Braeckel, who had the brief of making the car look unmistakably like a Bentley, but there was no scope for any retro designs. So while the silhouette was inspired by the 1952 R-Type Continental, the influence wasn't immediately obvious. In isolation some of the details (such as those twin circular headlamps and the mesh grille) harked back to a bygone era, but taken as a whole the new car was definitely a product of the twenty-first century.

The Continental GT was created to mark

The flying B badge that had sat on Bentleys for decades continued to be used. It signifies power, performance and quality in a way that few others can emulate – it's also one of the world's most evocative motoring brands.

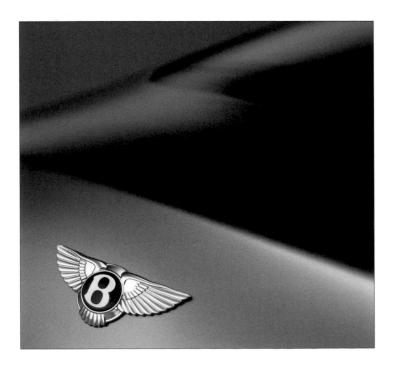

This was the new face of Bentley for the 21st century. With the company under new ownership, it was time to break from the past and start afresh. Having said that, many of the styling cues had been seen before.

Volkswagen's guardianship of Bentley, which is why the car was created using a version of the Phaeton platform. That's also why it featured the all-alloy W12 engine that headed the Phaeton range. Of course Volkswagen went to great pains to point out that the powerplant was significantly reworked, but the basic unit was the same as could be found in VW's slow-selling saloon. In the Bentley it produced 408.4kW (552bhp) at 6100rpm, with a stonking 646.5Nm (479lb ft) of torque available at just 1600rpm. With figures like this, it was no surprise that the Continental GT was capable of nearly 321.8km/h (200mph). Helping to produce such huge reserves of power was a pair of KKK turbochargers, with one for each bank of cylinders. A pair of overhead camshafts actuated a quartet of valves for each cylinder and there was also variable valve timing to increase low-down torque and top-end power.

Transmission

Getting the power onto the road required a state-of-the-art transmission, which is just what was provided. Four-wheel drive (donated from the Audi A8) was standard, complete with a Torsen centre differential that directed the torque to the right end of the car. There was also no shortage of electronic gadgetry to keep the driver out of trouble; anti-lock brakes, traction control, electronic stability programme and electronic brake force distribution were all standard. The ZF gearbox featured six ratios, which could be left to their own devices or the driver could shift them manually.

Air suspension kept the body in check when cornering hard, but also gave a supple ride when needed; each corner was controlled by infinitely adjustable electronic dampers which were managed by sensors scattered all over the car.

The cabin was, unsurprisingly, swathed in wood and leather. Anything else just wouldn't have been right, and the fact that there were plenty of mod-cons thrown in for good measure didn't detract from the desired effect. The multi-media system didn't look at all out of place, and neither did the chromed dash vents which looked at home despite them looking as though they'd come out of a 1960s T-Series. Behind the two front seats was another pair of chairs, which were heavily sculpted and perfectly capable of taking six-footers on trans-continental hauls. After all, this was a Grand Tourer in the traditional sense.

However, the Continental GT wasn't as grand a grand tourer as the four-door saloon derivative that

Mixing old and new with a perfect balance, the Continental GT's cabin used premium materials throughout, but also incorporated the latest technology. So all that wood and leather was joined by satellite navigation.

Bentley Continental GT	
Years of production	2003–
Displacement	5998cc (359.8ci)
Configuration	Front-mounted W12
Transmission	Six-speed auto/sequential manual, four-wheel drive
Power	408.4kW (552bhp) @ 6100rpm
Torque	646.6Nm (479lb ft) @ 1600rpm
Top speed	318.6km/h (198mph)
0–60mph (0–97km/h)	4.7sec
Power to weight ratio	170.9kW/ton (231bhp/ton)
Number built	N/A

broke cover in the summer of 2005. Called the Continental Flying Spur (a reference to a 1960s Bentley), it was capable of travelling at over 334.7km/h (208mph) while also carrying four people and their luggage. If that isn't a grand tourer...

Bristol Fighter

The Fighter's styling was a complete departure from Bristol's usual fare of awkwardly designed saloons. The looks were certainly distinctive, and those gull-wing doors were very unusual in the supercar world of the twenty-first century.

The gullwing doors were opened electrically, by a button that was hidden in the B-pillar. Once opened, the very wide sills were exposed, making entry into the car a bit tricky. These were necessary to give the car its strength.

The visibility from the driver's seat was astonishingly good – better than most superminis. Not only were the windscreen pillars very slim, but the very oddly-shaped rear window also afforded excellent vision behind.

Mounted in the nose was an 8-litre (479.7ci) V10, sourced from the Chrysler Viper. In standard form it offered 388.5kW (525bhp) and 708.7Nm (525lb ft) of torque, but these could be increased if it was felt the standard car was too slow.

Flick through the pages of this book and you'll find that most of the cars featured have one thing in common: they're all advanced in their engineering, design, construction or all three. All their makers wanted to be seen as delivering the best of everything to justify a stratospheric price – after all, carbon fibre monocoques and ceramic brakes don't come cheap. But of course there's always somebody who will try to buck the trend, and when Bristol gets involved, you can bet mainstream won't be anywhere to be seen. That's exactly how it was with the Fighter, a car that owed much of its design and engineering to a previous era – even if it was hugely powerful and consequently massively fast.

V10-powered coupé

Until 1999, Bristol was merely the maker of sober saloons for very rich people who didn't like to flaunt their wealth. Cars such as the Beaufighter, Blenheim and Britannia could swallow continents whole, but didn't shout about it with their understated looks and not especially imposing dimensions. That's the way things were likely to stay as well – until towards the end of 1999 when an announcement was made that

The Fighter's narrow width is apparent, but so is its lack of aerodynamic appendages. Despite the paucity of spoilers and wings, the car can allegedly do over 321.8km/h (200mph) without taking off.

Bristol would be entering into the world of the supercar within two years. The plan was to develop and build a V10-powered gullwing coupé, selling them at a rate of 20 per year from the end of 2001.

It wasn't until the summer of 2003 that a rolling chassis was first shown, the work having been done by Max Boxstrom, who had previously engineered the Aston Martin AMR-1 which took part in the 1989 Le Mans race. Although Bristol had initially talked of a chassis made entirely from aluminium, the end result was one with a massively strong box-section structure in steel, with aluminium honeycomb flooring and a pair of substantial roll hoops. The suspension was pure race car, with double wishbones all round, combined with telescopic shock absorbers and coil springs, plus an anti-roll bar at each end.

The bodywork was typical Bristol, which meant it was all made by hand, mainly from aluminium. The wings, roof and bonnet were all made from alloy while the doors and tailgate were constructed from

In true Bristol fashion the Fighter's cockpit featured a no-frills design, although the materials were first-rate. That strange steering wheel was typical Bristol, just like the gauges fitted above the windscreen.

carbon fibre composite. The bodyshell itself featured very different proportions compared with most other hypercars – the Fighter was narrower and taller than most. Compared with the Viper which donated its V10 engine, the Bristol was nearly 127mm (5in) narrower – and amazingly it was 254mm (10in) narrower than a Ferrari 575M. The Fighter was also much more aerodynamic than most other supercars, with its drag co-efficient of just 0.28 – Bristol avoided addenda to create downforce, knowing that this just creates drag at the same time. Instead, the company designed for stability and slipperiness at high speeds. Indeed, when viewed from above, the glasshouse of the Fighter resembles a teardrop; the ideal wind-cheating slippery shape.

Performance

The most important part of the Fighter was the V10 engine, taken from the Chrysler Viper in 8-litre (488ci) form. Able to develop massive power to give even more massive performance, there was 388.5kW (525bhp) on offer – which Bristol claimed was enough to take the car to well over 321.8km/h (200mph). It could also dismiss the 0–60mph (0–97km/h) sprint in around four seconds because with a six-speed manual gearbox, there was no need to change from first gear before hitting 97km/h (60mph).

As you can imagine, some felt that the 388.5kW (525bhp) and 708.7Nm (525lb ft) of torque offered by the standard Fighter weren't enough. Which is why with such weedy figures as standard, Bristol began to offer an uprated engine from summer 2004. With fettling in various areas such as the engine management system and the manifolding, power was up to a scarcely believable 464.7kW (628bhp), while torque increased to a stump-pulling 783Nm (580lb ft). No independent performance figures were available for either car, but as the company has always said about its cars, the performance on offer is 'adequate'.

Bristol Fighter	
Years of production	2004–
Displacement	7996cc (479.7ci)
Configuration	Front-mounted V10
Transmission	Six-speed manual/four-speed auto. Rear-wheel drive
Power	388.5kW (525bhp) @ 5600rpm
Torque	708.7Nm (525lb ft) @ 4500rpm
Top speed	337.9km/h (210mph) (claimed)
0–60mph (0–97km/h)	4.0sec (claimed)
Power to weight ratio	267.8kW/ton (362bhp/ton)
Number built	N/A

Bugatti Veyron

To achieve over 400km/h (250mph), the Veyron had to be incredibly slippery. That's why there was a panelled undertray to smooth airflow, while there were diffusers built into the underside at the rear and an automatic rear spoiler to create downforce.

Four-wheel drive was deemed essential to getting such huge amounts of power to the Tarmac. There was also a paddle shift-operated seven-speed sequential manual gearbox with a twin-plate clutch.

18·4 EB 67

The W16 engine was basically a pair of V8s fused together with a common crankshaft. Incredibly compact, there were also four turbochargers and two intercoolers in the engine bay; the result was 730.3kW (987bhp).

The wheels were designed for light weight as well as for brake cooling. The light weight came from the use of aluminium alloy, while those 12 spokes were offset from each other to channel cooling air into the brakes.

In the history of the car, has there ever been a model with a more difficult gestation period than the Bugatti Veyron? It didn't help that the targets set were the most ambitious ever for any road car – but then that was the point; this was to be the most audacious supercar ever made. It was to have the most powerful engine and be the fastest car to ever turn a wheel. With 1000PS (987bhp), the aim was to build a car that would be able to top 402km/h (250mph), which brought with it a whole new set of problems in terms of traction, stability and cooling – issues that would dog the project from the very outset.

The Veyron was first shown to the world in spring 2001, at the Geneva motor show. Within months, at the Frankfurt motor show of the same year, there was a redesigned car. As it was unveiled, the word was that by 2003 the EB16.4 Veyron would be on sale. That became 2004, which in turn became 2005 – and then 2006. As this book was being written it was due to make its debut at the 2005 Frankfurt motor show, but once again it wasn't ready for its official debut – would the car ever be available to the buying public?

Engine

The rationale behind the Veyron was to trounce the McLaren F1, with its 463.9kW (627bhp) and 386.2km/h (240mph) top speed. However, where the British car had been all about light weight and aerodynamic efficiency, the Bugatti was more about brute force; ultimately, despite a relatively high kerb

Bugatti gave the Veyron an interior worth writing home about. There was machine-turned alloy all over the place, along with leather and brushed aluminium – this was no parts-bin special.

weight, the massive power on tap would be enough to push the car through the 400km/h (250mph) barrier.

At the heart of the Veyron was an 8-litre (479.5ci) W16 engine, although the initial plan had been to use a 6.3-litre (382.4ci) W18 unit. This pushed out 410.7kW (555bhp), which clearly wasn't anything like enough; the answer at first seemed to be to bore the unit out. But this produced some major reliability

Bugatti Veyron	
Years of production	2005–
Displacement	7993cc (478.5ci)
Configuration	Mid-mounted W16, quad-turbo
Transmission	Seven-speed sequential manual
Power	730.4kW (987bhp) @ 6000rpm
Torque	1244.7Nm (922lb ft) (no rpm available)
Top speed	405.5km/h (252mph)
0–62mph (0–100km/h)	3.0sec
Power to weight ratio	471.3kW (637bhp/ton)
Number built	N/A

issues, which is why a more compact W16 powerplant was developed, the idea being that it could also be used in future Bentleys (the marque also being part of the VW/Audi portfolio).

The W16 that was developed was essentially a pair of narrow-angle V8s mated together with a common crankshaft, with the whole unit being mounted longitudinally ahead of the rear axle on a separate aluminium subframe. With a displacement of 7993cc (478.5ci), the engine was amazingly compact at just 710mm (27.9in) in length and 767mm (30.1in) in width. But by the time a quartet of turbochargers had been bolted in place, the engine bay started to get rather crowded. To help boost power even further there were two water-to-air intercoolers, while direct fuel injection, variable valve timing and dry-sump lubrication were all on the menu as well.

Transmission

The problem with generating 730.3kW (987bhp) and 1244.7Nm (922lb ft) of torque was that this had to be transferred to the road somehow, which meant the transmission had to be something pretty special. Haldex four-wheel drive was taken as a given, while the gearbox was a seven-speed sequential manual

unit developed in conjunction with British transmission specialists Ricardo, the company responsible for engineering the gearbox in the Le Mans-winning Audi R8. Operated by paddle shifts on the steering column, there was a twin-plate clutch and thanks to a series of electronic actuators in place of a conventional clutch pedal, shift times were reduced to a miniscule 200 milliseconds.

To keep the car stable at high speed, the aerodynamics had to be spot on. The underside of the car was as finely engineered as the top, with diffusers at the back to suck the car onto the ground at high speeds. As speed increased, a spoiler at the rear automatically rose to increase downforce levels. Suspension was by double wishbones all round, with electronic damping adjustment as well as variable ride height all included as standard. Brakes were ceramic discs while the tyres featured run-flat technology. And so the list went on – more and more complex technology, which would cause nothing but problems throughout the car's development.

You had to look very closely to find a straight line on the Veyron's bodyshell – it was full of muscle and aggression. Despite having 16 cylinders, there was still just a single exhaust outlet at the back.

Farboud GTS

The GTS had to be practical as well as very fast. That's why the cabin had to feature plenty of leg room and luggage space. Overhangs were kept short and there was a long wheelbase to maximize cabin space.

Wheels were 483mm (19in) in diameter front and rear. Behind these was an AP Racing four-pot braking system, with ventilated discs all round. At the front these were 350mm (13.7in); they were 330mm (12.9in) at the rear.

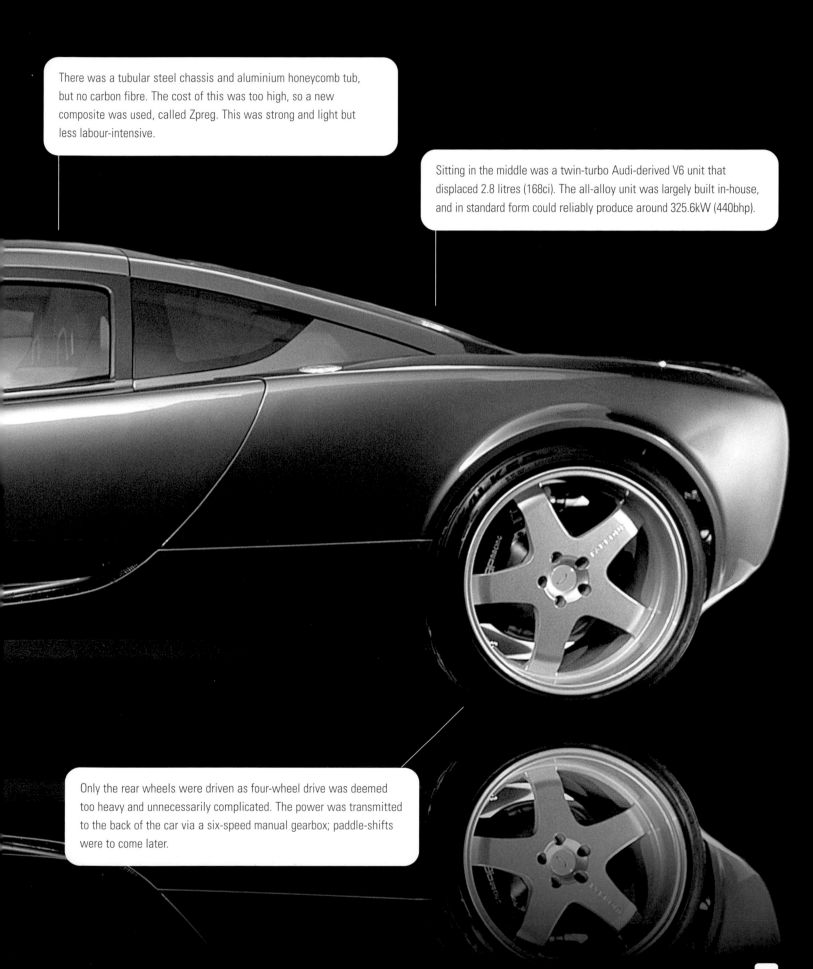

There was a tubular steel chassis and aluminium honeycomb tub, but no carbon fibre. The cost of this was too high, so a new composite was used, called Zpreg. This was strong and light but less labour-intensive.

Sitting in the middle was a twin-turbo Audi-derived V6 unit that displaced 2.8 litres (168ci). The all-alloy unit was largely built in-house, and in standard form could reliably produce around 325.6kW (440bhp).

Only the rear wheels were driven as four-wheel drive was deemed too heavy and unnecessarily complicated. The power was transmitted to the back of the car via a six-speed manual gearbox; paddle-shifts were to come later.

In the great tradition of will-it-succeed-or-not British sports cars, the Farboud is up there with the best (or should that be worst?) of them. As this book went to press, the company had existed for all of four years or so. Yet in that time it had produced a prototype, the design for which was scrapped in favour of an all-new car, then the whole project was sold to somebody with more experience of making specialist cars.

The founder of the company, Arash Farboud, had hatched a plan to go into supercar production after visiting Le Mans in 1998. Still in his early 20s, he was heir to a fortune that would allow him to play supercar-maker and by the summer of 1999 he already had plans on the drawing board for his first car. As far as the outside world was concerned, the Farboud story started with the appearance of the Porsche 911 GT1-inspired GT at the start of 2002. With a bespoke steel chassis, carbon fibre panelling and a 370kW (500bhp), 2.7-litre (162ci) twin-turbo V6 in the middle, the car showed some promise. But Porsche objected to the car's design – although it looks more like the Maserati MC12 that appeared a couple of years later.

V6 powerplant

That first car had looked too much like a racer; what was needed was something that looked more like a road car, which is where the GTS came in. Its project

Farboud GTS	
Years of production	2005–
Displacement	2800cc (168ci)
Configuration	Mid-mounted V6, twin-turbo
Transmission	Six-speed manual, rear-wheel drive
Power	325.6kW (440bhp) @ 5500rpm
Torque	472.5Nm (350lb ft) @ 5500rpm
Top speed	291.2km/h (181mph)
0–60mph (0–97km/h)	3.6sec
Power to weight ratio	248.6kW/ton (336bhp/ton)
Number built	N/A

name of F420 was a clue as to what was expected from the new model; 420bhp (310.8kW) to give the turn of speed Farboud hoped for. It would also be more usable on the road – the GT had been more of a track day car that would be road-legal.

The GT had made its debut in January 2001, and it took just a year to come up with the car's successor, the GTS. Although the GTS was apparently completely new, the powerplant was the same twin-turbo Audi V6 unit that had appeared in the GT. Farboud had been keen not to use a V8 powerplant because it was too predictable. A V10 wasn't something that could be bought in at affordable levels, so a boosted V6 seemed the obvious choice. The company's founder was used to driving Porsche 911s anyway, and knew that a six-cylinder powerplant could be made to produce the sort of power that was needed.

When Farboud started developing the Audi engine it was little more than an RS4 unit with mild tweaks. By the time the prototype was ready to roll, only the cylinder heads and the block were from Audi – everything else had been built in-house. In time, Farboud was also hoping to produce the block and heads – not that the original Audi units were lacking in any way. But by building everything themselves, Farboud could alter design details if necessary – such as a move from five valves per cylinder to four. The first thing that was done was to ditch the standard turbochargers in favour of a pair of Garret T28 units, which were particularly efficient, so able to spool up very quickly. That helped to cut down the lag, making the power delivery more linear – and with around 550 horses on tap that was no bad thing.

There was a single exhaust pipe for each bank of cylinders, with the V6 engine being donated from the Audi stable. It didn't take much tweaking to deliver a reliable 325.6kW (440bhp) – enough to give a top speed of over 291.2km (180mph).

Although there wasn't anything especially unusual about the Farboud's design, everything came together very well. Those faired-in headlamps and clean lines conspired to give the car a very elegant look.

Still in preparation

Power was taken to the rear wheel via an Audi six-speed manual gearbox; there was talk of paddle-shifts becoming available later on. Double-wishbone suspension and a ventilated-disc braking system were par for the course, but the bodywork wasn't carbon fibre – that would have pushed up the build costs too much. Farboud's aim was to build a supercar that was relatively affordable; there were too many companies fighting it out in the upper echelons of the market.

Just as things seemed to be getting going, Farboud sold the whole project to Chris Marsh, of Marcos fame. He started to redevelop the car to improve the quality and reduce the build costs, in a bid to slash the purchase cost by around a third. As this book went to press the car was still being prepared for sale…

If there was one aspect of the GTS's design that didn't quite work as well as the rest, it was the rear view. Although it was a better-looking car than many of its rivals, from this angle it was also a bit bland – but at least it was distinctive.

Ferrari Enzo

When seen in profile the doors are much like any other supercar's in that they're hinged at their leading edge. But on the Enzo they were also hinged on the roof, a large part of which opened up with the doors.

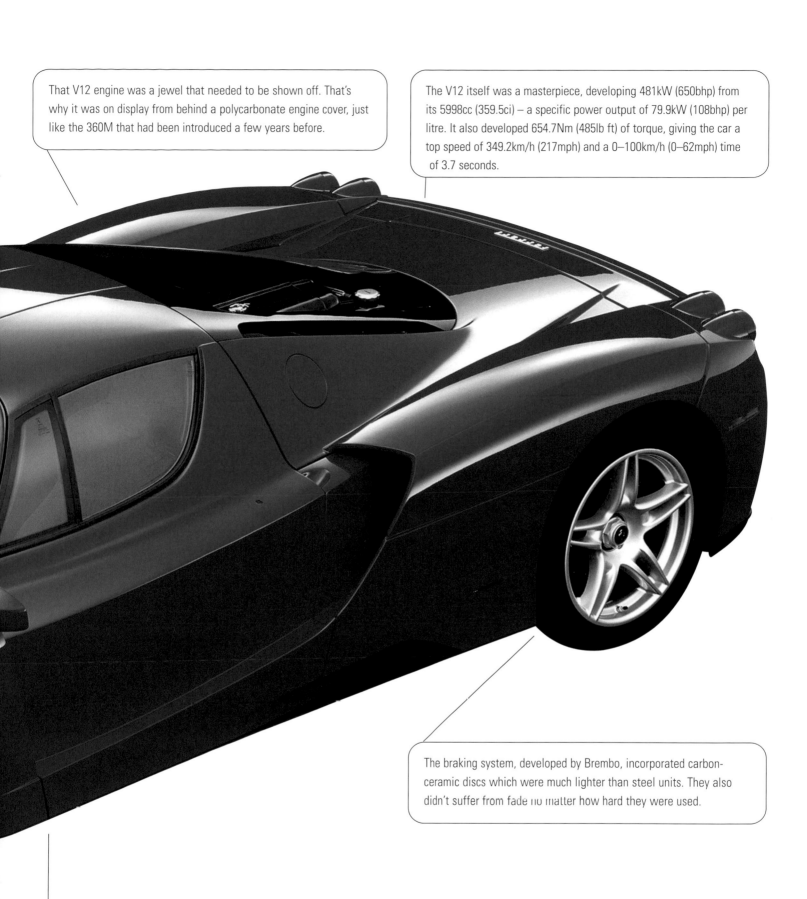

That V12 engine was a jewel that needed to be shown off. That's why it was on display from behind a polycarbonate engine cover, just like the 360M that had been introduced a few years before.

The V12 itself was a masterpiece, developing 481kW (650bhp) from its 5998cc (359.5ci) – a specific power output of 79.9kW (108bhp) per litre. It also developed 654.7Nm (485lb ft) of torque, giving the car a top speed of 349.2km/h (217mph) and a 0–100km/h (0–62mph) time of 3.7 seconds.

The braking system, developed by Brembo, incorporated carbon-ceramic discs which were much lighter than steel units. They also didn't suffer from fade no matter how hard they were used.

With careful attention to detail with the car's underside, there was no need for a huge rear wing to create the massive downforce needed to maintain stability at high speeds. Instead there were diffusers in the undertray that sucked the car onto the road.

It's when seen in profile that the Enzo looks its least spectacular; indeed, when viewed from this angle it would be easy to wonder what all the fuss was about. But see it from any other angle and it's a different matter...

Just like its forebears, the Ferrari Enzo would be the closest thing to a Formula One car for the road, packing the very best technology into the most advanced bodyshell possible. Money would be no object, and production would be limited to just 349 examples. Yet while the Enzo has earned a reputation for being fearsomely quick and massively expensive, it's also one of the safest and cleanest supercars made.

The starting-point for the Enzo was its predecessor, the F50. Ferrari took that car and worked out where its weak points were, addressing them in turn so that the Enzo wouldn't suffer from any of them. The main improvements Ferrari sought were in the refinement and lack of performance at low engine speeds. As was usual, Pininfarina came up with the styling, having been briefed that the new car would be available as a coupé only. Of course the car had to be dramatic, but it also had to be aerodynamically efficient, aggressive and hopefully even beautiful too. Whether the latter was achieved is open to debate, but it certainly scores on all the other points – it would be hard to imagine how a car could pack any more visual drama.

Downforce

Although the car had to be dramatic, its design also had to remain pure. That's why everything was integrated rather than tacked on; there were no wild spoilers here. The whole of the Enzo's underside was designed with generating downforce in mind. Flaps ahead of the front wheels and below the radiators automatically worked in unison with the small adjustable rear spoiler to generate 344kg (758.5lb) of downforce at 201.1km/h (125mph) – this increased to 775kg (1708.8lb) at 299.3km/h (186mph). The bodyshell itself was no less impressive, being both light and rigid thanks to the use of carbon fibre and aluminium honeycomb throughout.

Although the Enzo was meant to be the closest thing to a road-going Formula One car, Ferrari opted not to fit a V10 engine to it. The inherent smoothness of a V12 unit was preferred, and besides, a V10 powerplant didn't offer any tangible packaging benefits. Because it was felt that the F50 hadn't offered sufficient torque because of its relatively small capacity of 4.7 litres (285.2ci), the Enzo's completely new engine had a displacement of 6 litres (372ci). Redlined at 8200rpm, the 65-degree unit featured four belt-driven camshafts, with variable inlet and exhaust valve timing along with a continuously variable inlet manifold to increase torque. This all conspired to produce 481kW (650bhp) at 7800rpm and a peak torque figure of 654.7Nm (485lb ft) at 5500rpm; enough to take the car to a top speed of 349.2km/h (217mph), having despatched the 0–100km/h (0–62mph) sprint in just 3.6 seconds.

With such performance on offer, something special had to be designed in the braking department. Brembo was asked to come up with something suitable; the answer was a carbon-ceramic system that didn't suffer poor performance when cold but also didn't fade when the car was driven mercilessly. With the discs measuring 380mm (14.9in) in diameter, there were six-pot calipers at the front and four-pot at the rear.

The FXX

While all this may sound like more than enough technology and performance in one car, for some it wasn't enough. That's why Ferrari developed the Enzo even further, to come up with the FXX, which was built for track use only – it wasn't homologated for road use. Just 20 were built, with buyers only able to use the cars on tracks around the world. Each car incorporated an advanced telemetry system that allowed Ferrari to monitor how its cars were driven, so even better cars could be developed for the future. To boost power to 592kW (800bhp), the V12 engine was taken up to 6.3 litres (382.4ci) while the paddle-shift gearbox could swap ratios in just a tenth of a second. Bodywork changes improved the downforce by 40 per cent while Bridgestone engineered special 483mm (19in) slick tyres especially for the car. If all this wasn't enough, a real Formula One car was the only answer.

Ferrari Enzo	
Years of production	2002–4
Displacement	5998cc (359.5ci)
Configuration	Mid-mounted V12
Transmission	Six-speed manual, rear-wheel drive
Power	481kW (650bhp) @ 7800rpm
Torque	654.7Nm (485lb ft) @ 5500rpm
Top speed	349.2km/h (217mph)
0–62mph (0–100km/h)	3.6sec
Power to weight ratio	352.2kW/ton (476bhp/ton)
Number built	349

This is the view that does the Enzo the greatest justice. Those gaping grilles, massively wide rear track and huge air intakes for the mid-mounted engine give the Enzo amazing visual drama. Just how will they top this?

Koenigsegg CC8S and CCR

Instead of producing a roadster, the Koenigsegg featured an ultra-light removable roof panel which could be stored in the luggage bay ahead of the cabin.

Although an ultra-low weight was one of the key targets, there was plenty of standard equipment. This included air-conditioning, central locking, electric windows and mirrors with a long options list as well.

Those wheels were made of ultra-light magnesium, and they measured 457mm (18in) across. They were 228mm (9in) wide at the front and 279mm (11in) at the rear, and were wrapped in 40-profile Goodyear F1 tyres.

Ceramic brake discs were shunned in favour of conventional ventilated steel items, with the former deemed to be less reliable as well as less usable. The discs measured 330mm (12.9in) across at the front and 315mm (12.4in) across at the back.

Comfort was high on the list of priorities for Koenigsegg's customers, which is why the seats were truly cutting-edge. They featured carbon shells cushioned with a NASA-developed material called Tempur which moulded itself to the occupant's body.

The mid-mounted V8 powerplant was bought in from Ford, and was the familiar quad-cam unit that became favoured by many low-volume car makers around the world. It was supercharged to give 484.7kW (655bhp) and 746.5Nm (553lb ft) of torque.

Those air intakes just ahead of the rear wheels are reminiscent of the ones seen in Jaguar's XJ220; but Koenigsegg was hoping for a much smoother production and sales run than Jaguar's ill-fated supercar.

While the established supercar manufacturers can trade on their reputations, newcomers have to offer something very special if they want to get so much as a look-in. At this level, customers expect to get a lot of heritage for their (large quantities of) money – and if not that, then something pretty sensational indeed. It's fair to say that while Swedish company Koenigsegg can't claim to have much history, it can build one of the most powerful supercars ever made in the shape of its CC8S and CCR. Buy a full-on version of the latter and you'll have a whole 596.4kW (806bhp) on tap to whet your appetite. Suddenly, all those Lamborghinis and Ferraris look very tame…

The perfect supercar

The rationale behind the Koenigsegg CC was that it should be the car to beat the McLaren F1 – pure and simple. However, while the rationale might be straightforward, producing something that could take on the McLaren and win was no easy task – but it was a challenge that the Swedish company was quite happy to rise to. The goals of the project were a top speed of 389.4km/h (242mph), delivered thanks to a power output of 484.7kW (655bhp), a drag co-efficient of 0.28–0.32 and a kerb weight of just 1100kg (2435.5lb).

The project began in 1994, and was the brainchild of a Swede called Christian von Koenigsegg. So you can think of the Koenigsegg as the antidote to all those tedious Volvos of the 1970s and 1980s… von Koenigsegg reckoned there was a gap in the supercar market, and that instead of waiting for somebody to fill it, he would build the perfect supercar. Considering he was in his early 20s at the time, that's no mean feat!

At the end of 1995, Koenigsegg built its first prototype, with most of 1996 taken up testing it. It had a mere 370kW (500bhp), but the chassis was honed to perfection so that when the power was

Koenigsegg CC8S and CCR

Years of production	2001–
Displacement	4600cc (276ci)
Configuration	Mid-mounted V8, supercharged
Transmission	Six-speed sequential manual
Power	484.7kW (655bhp) @ 6500rpm
Torque	746.5Nm (553lb ft) @ 5000rpm
Top speed	389.4km/h (242mph) (claimed)
0–62 (0–100km/h)	3.2sec
Power to weight ratio	448.4kW/ton (606bhp/ton)
Number built	N/A

When you're building a car that's capable of rather more than 321.8km/h (200mph), it's essential that the car doesn't take off at high speeds. That's why Koenigsegg incorporated ground-effect aerodynamics at the back.

boosted, there would be no problem taming it. By the end of 1998 the first big breakthrough took place, when a carbon semi-monocoque was adopted, along with fully adjustable all-wishbone suspension. By summer 2000 the first production-ready car was finished and in autumn of the same year the car made its world debut at the Paris motor show.

In many ways the car was fairly derivative in that it featured a cab-forward stance, a mid-mounted engine and a fairly standard mechanical specification. Its carbon fibre construction was also something that had been seen before. But nobody had seen anything like this from Sweden – and that door arrangement was something else. But how many people would buy a car purely because of the way its doors opened?

Thankfully, for those who took the time to delve beneath the skin there were plenty of other delights.

The seats featured a material developed by NASA, which moulded to the body shape of the person sitting in it. The paddle-shift transmission was something rarely seen at this point in time, even if it has since become much more common. Then there was the control system that allowed the driver to adjust the chassis, aerodynamics and braking parameters from the cockpit. And the braking system was a true work of art – just like the 457mm (18in) magnesium wheels wrapped in ultra-low profile rubber. The roof arrangement was also extremely neat, as it featured a carbon fibre panel which could be lifted out and stowed in the luggage bay, to give a targa effect.

The CCR

While on paper many of the Koenigsegg's rivals were much the same, the mix was slightly different with the Swedish car. The massive power, superb attention to detail and great design were a pretty impressive mix for a first attempt. It wouldn't take long for the CC to be developed into something even more powerful. When the CCR broke cover in spring 2004 it offered 596.4kW (806bhp) from its supercharged 4.7-litre (285.2ci) V8. Even with around 111kW (150bhp) over its predecessor, Koenigsegg was still claiming a top speed of 389.4km/h (242mph).

Trying to come up with something new in the world of supercars isn't very easy. But Koenigsegg managed a first with the CC8S and CCR – a door with an opening arrangement even more complicated than the norm.

Lamborghini Murcielago

The rear of the car featured two active intakes for the engine cooling air. The system, called VACS (Variable Air-flow Cooling System), allowed the aperture of these air intakes to be varied to suit the driving conditions.

The power was fed to all four wheels, while the gearbox was mounted in front of the engine. The rear differential was integrated into the engine unit, while there was also a central viscous coupling to control the torque split.

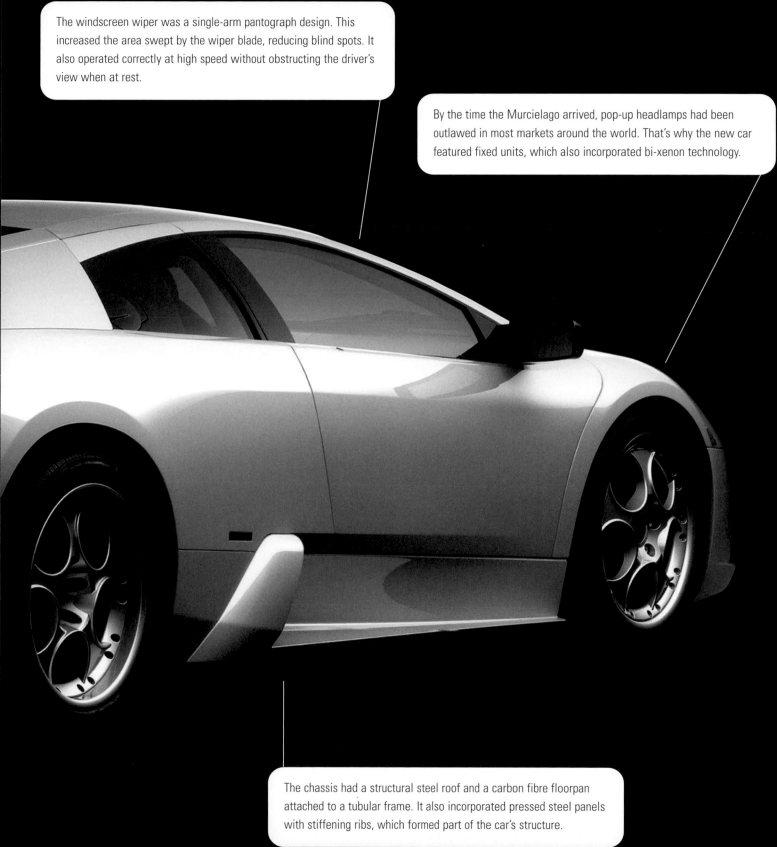

The windscreen wiper was a single-arm pantograph design. This increased the area swept by the wiper blade, reducing blind spots. It also operated correctly at high speed without obstructing the driver's view when at rest.

By the time the Murcielago arrived, pop-up headlamps had been outlawed in most markets around the world. That's why the new car featured fixed units, which also incorporated bi-xenon technology.

The chassis had a structural steel roof and a carbon fibre floorpan attached to a tubular frame. It also incorporated pressed steel panels with stiffening ribs, which formed part of the car's structure.

As if the standard Murcielago coupé wasn't flash enough, there was an open-topped version for terminal show-offs. With the same engine as the closed car, this was the machine to buy for that ultimate wind-in-the-hair experience.

Take a look at a Miura and you don't have to analyze too closely to see that the quality is laughable – along with the usability. As Lamborghini's V12 cars progressed, things got better and better. The Murcielago represented the pinnacle of this development, which was helped in no small way by the acquisition of the company by Audi in 1999.

While some things changed for the better, Audi realized that it needed to allow Lamborghini plenty of opportunity to stick to tradition as much as possible. The Murcielago's arresting design and conventional packaging were the most obvious way of doing this, but the naming of the car clung to Lamborghini's protocol. As was common with the company's cars, the Murcielago took its name from a fighting bull,

whose life was spared after a particularly courageous fight in the nineteenth century.

Usability

While nobody could deny that the Murcielago was a highly dramatic car to look at, many questioned whether it was distinctive enough. After all, its forebears had all broken new ground, but the new arrival was somewhat derivative. It had been penned by Belgian designer Luc Donkerwolcke, and when put next to the Diablo, the Murcielago didn't seem especially revolutionary – despite it being almost entirely new.

Before the car's design had even got underway, one of the key requirements for the Diablo's successor was usability. That meant it had to be comfortable and reliable, while also offering top-notch performance and handling. That meant attention to detail had to be paid where the weight of the clutch was concerned, as well as the cabin's ergonomics and the precision of

the gearchange – among a whole raft of other things.

The only significant component carried over from the Diablo was the V12 engine, although this was heavily re-engineered for its new application. Whereas the last of the Diablos had a displacement of 6.0 litres (364.2ci), the new car had a 6.2-litre (376.3ci) capacity. This was achieved by extending the stroke to give a displacement of 6192cc (371.5ci). The extra capacity, combined with variable valve timing and variable intakes, gave a power output of 429.2kW (580bhp) at 7500rpm – along with a peak torque figure of 646.6Nm (479lb ft) at a rather high 5400rpm.

A new technology was introduced with the Murcielago, to help the engine keep its cool under pressure. Called VACS (Variable Air-Flow Cooling System), it was basically an adjustable flap above the rear wheels, which allowed varying amounts of cooling air to be fed to the engine bay.

Getting such a huge amount of power and torque to the tarmac reliably meant a four-wheel drive system

Although most supercars had become incredibly curvy by the start of the 21st century, Lamborghini resisted the temptation to conform and incorporated lots of straight lines in the Murcielago's design. It still looked great though!

had to be used. While the Murcielago's basic layout was borrowed from the Diablo, it was overhauled for better reliability and driveability. A central viscous coupling allowed the torque split to be varied between the front and rear axles, while the six-speed manual gearbox was once again located ahead of the longitudinally mounted engine.

Because the Murcielago was a clean-sheet design, it was possible to ensure that all the dimensions were optimal. That's why the wheelbase was 15mm (0.6in) longer than the Diablo's, while the length increased by 110mm (4.3in). Because it was also 25mm (1in) taller and 5mm (0.2in) wider (taking it to an outrageous 2240mm / 88.2in), it was also 25kg (55.1lb) heavier than its predecessor.

The Murcielago Roadster

In July 2004 the next phase was announced – the open-topped Murcielago Roadster. Every bit as extreme as its coupé counterpart, the Roadster was designed for sunny climes because it didn't feature a proper roof. More importantly, it didn't feature a speed limiter either, but it was fitted with an even more impressive braking system than the standard car. The brake discs increased in diameter from 355mm (13.9in) to 380mm (14.9in) at the front, and the rear items were 355mm (13.9in) instead of the previous 332mm (13in). The irony of this, of course, was that few drivers would ever explore the car's outer limits so would never appreciate the fitting of such hefty brakes. After all, most owners of the Roadster didn't plan to thrash it mercilessly – they just wanted something eye-catching to pose in…

Lamborghini Murcielago	
Years of production	2001–
Displacement	6192cc (371.5ci)
Configuration	Mid-mounted V12
Transmission	Five-speed manual, four-wheel drive
Power	429.2kW (580bhp) @ 7500rpm
Torque	646.6Nm (479lb ft) @ 5400rpm
Top speed	329.9km/h (205mph)
0–60mph (0–97km/h)	3.6sec
Power to weight ratio	257.5kW/ton (348bhp/ton)
Number built	N/A

Laraki Fulgura/Borac

Get past the ultra-wide sills, and the cosseting cabin was beautifully designed and constructed. Far more minimalist than many of its rivals, the Fulgura borrowed some parts from mainstream cars, but much was bespoke.

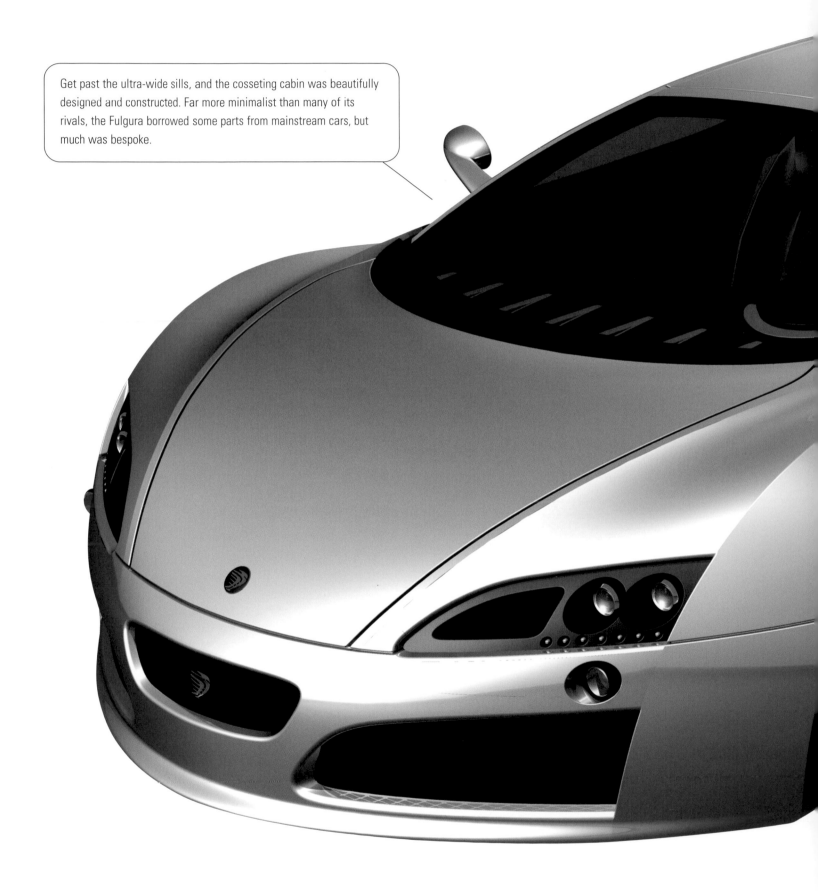

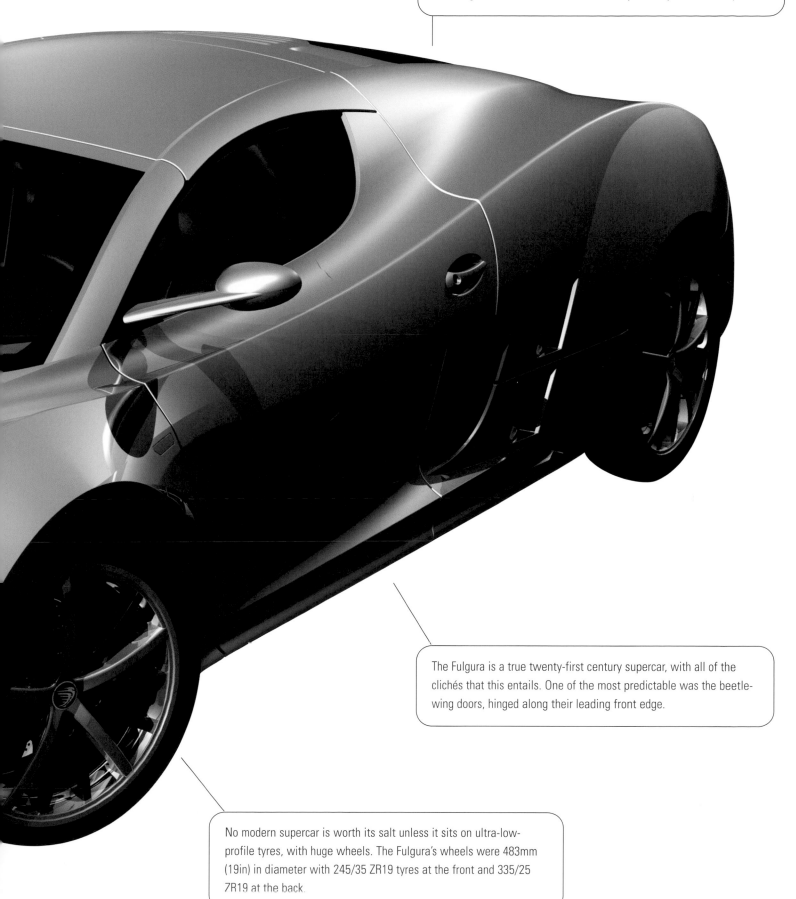

The 6-litre (364.2ci) V12 engine was sourced from Mercedes, but tuned to produce 503.3kW (680bhp). The powerplant was mated to a six-speed manual gearbox, which also featured a sequential (paddle shift) option.

The Fulgura is a true twenty-first century supercar, with all of the clichés that this entails. One of the most predictable was the beetle-wing doors, hinged along their leading front edge.

No modern supercar is worth its salt unless it sits on ultra-low-profile tyres, with huge wheels. The Fulgura's wheels were 483mm (19in) in diameter with 245/35 ZR19 tyres at the front and 335/25 7R19 at the back.

You could be forgiven for never having heard of Laraki Cars. But the next time you're at a quiz and you're asked to name a car that's produced in Morocco, you've found the answer. However, whether or not the car really is in production – as in available to buy – is a debatable question. Various prototypes have been shown and the cars have been restyled numerous times, but production has never really got underway.

The lack of availability is understandable – to compete in the supercar market in the twenty-first century takes a very special car. With Lamborghini offering a V10 370kW (500bhp) supercar at little more than the price of a Porsche 911 Turbo (which in itself is incredibly capable and practical), it's hard to sell a supercar if it doesn't sport a well-known badge. That's why Laraki has thought and rethought its offerings, which are shown here.

Design

The Fulgura is Laraki's full-on supercar, designed to compete with cars such as the Lamborghini Murcielago, while the Grand Tourer is the Borac. When the cars were first shown at the 2002 Geneva motor show, many show visitors must have thought Ferrari had two stands at the event; and no doubt Ferrari must have been on the phone to its lawyers pretty quickly, for breach of design copyright. At first

Laraki threw every styling cue it could think of when designing the Fulgura, with the car looking horrifically overdesigned. Scoops and slats were joined by blisters and spoilers all over the place, to make a nasty mess.

the Fulgura was a carbon-copy of the Ferrari 360 Modena while the Borac was a facsimile of the 550 Maranello. By the 2003 Geneva motor show the cars had been restyled so they were slightly more original – but not much! One year on there had been another raft of minor styling changes and at the Geneva 2005 motor show yet another version of the Fulgura was unveiled. Count that lot up and you'll see there have already been four different versions of the Fulgura and the car has never yet gone on sale!

Despite so many prototypes having been created, Laraki seems to have settled on the design shown here – although whether or not several more derivatives will be produced before a customer takes delivery is anybody's guess. It's also unlikely that customers will be queuing up anyway – with a price tag of 500,000 Euro it's hard to see how the car can be worth it.

At the heart of each Laraki is a Mercedes powerplant; in the case of the Fulgura it's a 6-litre (364.2ci) V12 that would normally see service in the CL600 coupé or S600 limousine. In a bid to outdo anything that Mercedes can offer, Laraki fettled the powerplant to produce a sporting 503.2kW (680bhp), and a no less useful 746.5Nm (553lb ft) of torque. If you're wondering how such figures are possible, the simple answer is by bolting a quartet of turbochargers to the V12. It's no wonder that with figures such as those, Laraki claims the car is capable of 352.4km/h (219mph). The company also claims the 0–100km/h (0–62mph) dash can be despatched in just 3.4 seconds – although so far nobody has been able to drive the car, never mind put those figures to the test.

The Borac

If the Fulgura seems a bit on the extreme side there's always the chance to buy a Borac – although once again, the car has been redesigned more than once and no cars (at the time of going to press) have been delivered to customers. The Borac features the same V12 engine as the Fulgura, but without the aid of any turbochargers. As a result it develops a rather weedy 399.6kW (540bhp) – which is why its top speed is a mere 310.5km/h (193mph) and it takes a painfully slow 4.5 seconds to get to 100km/h (62mph).

You had to hope that your head wasn't any taller than the seat, because if it was you were going to need to get the tin opener out. Getting in and out was a nightmare, but at least the Fulgura was nicely trimmed.

Laraki Fulgura/Borac	
Years of production	2005–
Displacement	6000cc (364.2ci)
Configuration	Mid-mounted V12, quad-turbo
Transmission	Six-speed manual, rear-wheel drive
Power	503.3kW (680bhp) (no rpm available)
Torque	746.5Nm (553lb ft) (no rpm available)
Top speed	352.4km/h (219mph) (claimed)
0–62mph (0–100km/h)	3.4sec (claimed)
Power to weight ratio	411.4kW/ton (556bhp/ton)
Number built	N/A

Like its bigger brother, the Borac sits on 483mm (19in) wheels wrapped with 35-series rubber. They certainly give the car a menacing look, while also displaying the brakes off to great effect. These were 355mm (13.9in) ventilated discs at the front while the rear ones were 320mm (12.5in) across. Ironic then that the car should have such great stopping power when the project itself has never really got started in a commercial sense.

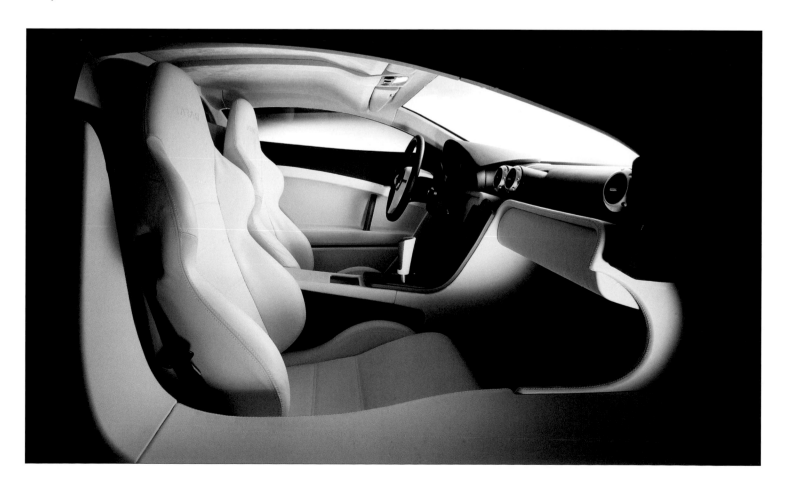

Maserati MC12

Although the 6-litre (359.8ci) V12 engine was similar to that fitted in the Ferrari Enzo, it wasn't identical. Power and torque were both slightly reduced, but there was still 460.2kW (622bhp) on tap, along with 648Nm (480lb ft) of torque.

Lightweight materials were used as much as possible to keep the car's weight to a minimum. This included a carbon fibre bodyshell while the central tub was made of a carbon fibre and nomex honeycomb sandwich.

To haul the car down from huge speeds there were cross-drilled ventilated disc brakes at both ends. At the front they were 380mm (14.9in) in diameter while at the back they were 335mm (13.1in) across. ABS was standard.

The roof panels lifted out, so that the car's two occupants could sample wind-in-the-hair motoring at nearly 321.8km/h (200mph). But there was nowhere to store the panels once removed, so they had to be left behind.

Independent suspension all round was by means of double wishbones. Anti-dive and anti-squat geometry was designed in at both ends while there was also the facility to raise the front of the car for parking ramps.

All MC12s were fitted with Maserati's Cambiocorsa six-speed sequential manual gearbox. This gave the driver paddle-shift control over the transmission, with the choice of Race or Sport modes also selectable.

It doesn't look quite as extreme as the Ferrari Enzo from this angle, but underneath the MC12 is effectively the same car. Yet despite being a little slower, the Maserati was even more expensive – and exclusive – than the Ferrari.

Maserati MC12

Years of production	2005
Displacement	5998cc (359.8ci)
Configuration	Mid-mounted V12
Transmission	Six-speed sequential manual, rear-wheel drive
Power	460.2kW (622bhp) @ 7500rpm
Torque	648Nm (480lb ft) @ 5500rpm
Top speed	329.9km/h (205mph)
0–60mph (0–97km/h)	3.8sec
Power to weight ratio	350kW/ton (473bhp/ton)
Number built	50 approx

For a marque that was founded on motorsport, it was incredible that the arrival of the MC12 marked a return to factory-backed motor racing for Maserati, after nearly half a century's absence. And if it wasn't for the Ferrari Enzo which donated much of the running gear, the MC12 would probably never have happened at all.

Looking like a refugee from a 1980s Group C Le Mans race, the MC12 first broke cover at the 2004 Geneva motor show, where it took the crowds by storm. After the sober cars of recent years, the MC12 marked a welcome return to the heady supercar days of the 1960s and 1970s, with that long, flowing body and the promise of complete impracticality. For Heaven's sake, Maserati had even been toying with the idea of building a people carrier, with its Kubang concept of 2003!

Powerplant

While Maserati didn't want too many parallels to be drawn between the MC12 and Ferrari's Enzo, the latter car donated its central carbon fibre and nomex honeycomb monocoque as well as its engine. The dry-sumped V12 powerplant borrowed much from the Enzo, but it was changed in various ways for fitment to the Maserati. These changes reduced the available power and torque slightly, although 460.2kW (622bhp) and 648Nm (480lb ft) were enough for most of the people who drove the car. With four valves per cylinder (driven by a quartet of gear-driven overhead camshafts), the maximum power was delivered at a screaming 7500rpm. To keep weight down as much as possible the crankcase was constructed from aluminium while

titanium con-rods ensured that even when constantly red-lined, the engine wouldn't self-destruct. The upshot of all this work was a car that weighed just 1335kg (2943.6lb) (less than some small family hatchbacks), which in turn led to a top speed of 329.9km/h (205mph) – which was slower than the Enzo.

With so much power on tap the MC12 needed something pretty special in the braking department, which is exactly what it got. Cross-drilled ventilated discs were fitted at each corner, with huge 380mm (14.9in) diameter items at the front gripped by six-pot calipers. The rear ones were nearly as impressive, being 335mm (13.1in) across and using four-pot calipers. An anti-lock system was also standard, while 483mm (19in) alloy wheels were fitted. These were

The MC12 was born to be raced, but despite this its interior had rather more creature comforts than the typical single-seater. While much of it was welcome, whoever thought the trademark oval clock was a good idea should have been shot...

wrapped in 35-profile rubber all round, the tyres having been developed by Pirelli.

The MC12's cabin was very much a cross between a road and a racer. While it didn't ooze luxury from every pore, it wasn't stripped out either. Trimmed in alcantara and leather, there were also lashings of carbon fibre on hand to lend a suitably high-tech atmosphere. In true race car fashion there was a starter button (finished in blue) but sitting somewhat incongruously in the centre console was the trademark oval Maserati clock. Well, someone must have thought it was a good idea at the time...

Doors

While the MC12 didn't really look much like the Enzo, the basic shape was much the same – although the MC12 had wider tracks front and rear as well as a longer wheelbase (by 150mm / 5.9in). It was also longer by 440mm (17.3in), which meant its overall length was a whopping 5.1m (16.7ft). But with the same monocoque underneath (as the Enzo), a pair of seats and the same engine sitting out the back, there were only so many directions the designers could take. However, there was one very big difference between the two cars and that was the door arrangement. Because the Ferrari was fitted with dihedral doors, it also had to be equipped with a fixed roof. But because the Maserati used conventional units, its roof could be removed to turn the car into a targa. Unfortunately the car's design didn't stretch to providing anywhere to stow the panel once removed though, making it something of a pointless exercise for some of the less-predictable climates. But then what are the chances of anybody buying one of these cars to actually use it?

This was the bit that really mattered – the all-alloy six-litre V12 that pumped out a whopping 460.2kw (622bhp). There were four camshafts and four valves per cylinder along with some exotic materials to maximize strength while minimizing weight.

Mercedes SLR McLaren

The adaptive spoiler at the back provided additional downforce. From 95km/h (59mph) it automatically adjusted, increasing rear downforce. The spoiler also doubled as an airbrake under heavy braking.

The SLR's bodyshell was made entirely from carbon fibre, which is around half the weight of steel and 30 per cent lighter than aluminium. It's also very stiff while being incredibly strong.

The five-speed automatic transmission allowed the driver to choose between three programs with different shift characteristics. These were Sport, SuperSport and Race – the latter significantly reducing the shift times.

The doors were a modern interpretation of those seen on the 1955 SLR race car. They were attached to the front roof pillars rather than to the roof itself and swung forwards and upwards for easier cabin access.

In typical Mercedes fashion, the SLR was designed to be one of the safest cars on the road. That's why there were six airbags fitted, seat belt pre-tensioners and an automatic child seat recognition system.

The carbon brakes offered a life of up to 300,000km (186,416 miles) along with low maintenance requirements. They were also around 60 per cent lighter than conventional brake discs.

That front was an acquired taste, with that bulbous nose and oversized three-pointed star. But while it was easy to argue with the design, nobody could quibble with the engineering or performance on offer.

When the Mercedes SLR McLaren finally burst onto the scene in September 2003, it was all a bit of an anti-climax. It wasn't that the car wasn't hugely capable – it was simply that scoop photos of it had been gracing the pages of car magazines the world over for what seemed like an eternity. The other thing was that by the time the SLR went on sale in spring 2004, Mercedes was offering a choice of cars with nearly as much power but without the massive price tag. Cars such as the CL65 AMG and SL65 AMG offered just 8.1kW (11bhp) less but cost half the money – arguing a case for the SLR wasn't easy.

To justify the huge cost difference, Mercedes crammed in all the technology it possibly could; engine, transmission, construction and equipment were all the best available at the time. But Ferrari, Aston Martin, Porsche and Lamborghini all claimed the same thing – and their cars were typically half the cost of the SLR.

Styling

Perhaps the biggest problem with the SLR, aside from its 500,000 Euro price, was its exterior styling. It was certainly dramatic, but many also reckoned it was unnecessarily ugly. Whatever it was, nobody could deny it was eye-catching. The bodyshell itself was constructed entirely from carbon fibre, which went some way to explaining why it cost so much to build and buy. The twenty-first century SLR took some of its styling cues from the legendary SLR race car of the 1950s, the most notable being the finned gills in the front wings. The doors were also unconventional – although by the time the SLR appeared, unusual door arrangements were decidedly mainstream where supercars were concerned.

Mercedes SLR McLaren

Years of production	2004–
Displacement	5439cc (326.3ci)
Configuration	Front-mounted V8, supercharged
Transmission	Five-speed automatic, rear-wheel drive
Power	463.2kW (626bhp) @ 6500rpm
Torque	776.2Nm (575lb ft) @ 3250rpm
Top speed	331.5km/h (206mph)
0–62mph (100km/h)	3.8sec
Power to weight ratio	269.3kW/ton (364bhp/ton)
Number built	N/A

Those doors had become something of a McLaren trademark, as they were first used on the F1. But once you'd climbed inside, the interior of the SLR was rather sober, borrowing heavily from lesser cars in the Mercedes range.

When it came to the engine, Mercedes and McLaren pulled out all the stops to come up with something with plenty of shove. The V8 powerplant was also positioned quite far back for a front-engined car; Mercedes called it a front-mid-engined design, in a bid to make the weight distribution as balanced as possible. With a capacity of 5439cc (326.3ci) and thanks to a supercharger being strapped to it, the powerplant was able to develop 463.2kW (626bhp) at 6500rpm along with 776.2Nm (575lb ft) of torque at 3250rpm. With numbers like that, it was no surprise that the SLR could touch around 337.9km/h (210mph) while sprinting to 100km/h (62mph) in 3.8 seconds.

Although the powerplant was incredibly pokey, it was also one of the cleanest engines of its kind. With a quartet of catalytic converters on board, the car was able to meet the most stringent emissions regulations applicable at the time.

Gearbox and brakes

By the time the SLR surfaced, gearboxes were expected to be more than just a way of transmitting the power from the engine to the wheels. In the case of the Mercedes, there was a five-speed automatic gearbox which allowed the driver to choose between three programmes, each with different shift characteristics. With manual selected, the five gears could be shifted using buttons on the steering wheel or the gearstick could be nudged backwards and forwards. In this latter mode the driver could also select between Sport, SuperSport or Race – the latter option significantly reducing the shift times.

Naturally there was an eye-popping braking system fitted, which also incorporated an air brake. This was in the form of a rear-mounted adaptive spoiler, which rose to an angle of 65 degrees under heavy braking. This not only created aerodynamic drag but it also increased downforce over the rear wheels to increase traction. The brakes themselves were ceramic discs all round, with anti-lock, brake assist and other driver-aid technologies such as electronic stability programme and traction control.

The performance figures posted by the SLR were even more impressive when the car's standard equipment list was taken into account. Every technology that could be squeezed in was included in the price, from bi-xenon headlamps and satellite navigation to automatic tyre pressure monitoring and a multi-media system. With all this, the kerb weight was a hefty 1768kg (3898.4lb) – which only made the available performance even more impressive.

Noble M12 GTO

The powerplant that allowed the M12 to achieve such amazing performance was nothing more than a humble Ford V6, displacing 2.5 litres (151.7ci). But it was fettled comprehensively, and boosted by two turbochargers.

That huge rear wing looked more like the sort of thing a boy racer would fit to his supermini in a desperate bid to increase street cred. While it allegedly failed to reduce the top speed, it did increase downforce significantly.

There was no automatic transmission option for those who opted to buy an M12 — it was a six-speed manual gearbox or nothing. This was engineered in a collaboration between Ford and Getrag.

One of the criticisms of the M12 was its driving position, with the seats too close to the car's sides. The M400 featured a redesigned floorpan that moved the seats closer to the car's centreline.

The first examples of the Noble M12 featured single exposed headlamps. These became double units which were fared in on later models, to improve the aerodynamic efficiency.

The M12 was suspended by double wishbones at each corner, along with coil spring and damper units. There were also anti-roll bars at each end, along with 330mm (12.9in) ventilated brake discs.

Britain has always been good at producing men in sheds who aspire to changing the course of motoring history. Take a look at the number of tiny car-producing outfits which have set up shop at some point in the UK and you'll be amazed at how many there have been. In recent years, the companies that have managed to break into the established supercar arena are few and far between, crowded out by marques that are able to boast heritage and in many cases, some motorsport success. One exception to this rule was Noble Automotive, set up by ex-racer and engineer Lee Noble.

Noble Moy Automotive

In reality, Lee Noble's first creation should be in here instead of the more familiar Noble. The Ultima GTR was available with Renault V6 or Chevrolet V8 engines, and it was this car that catapulted Noble's name into the limelight – and the history books. With over 444kW (600bhp) it clinched numerous records – and also served as the test mule for McLaren's mighty F1. Could there possibly be a higher honour than that? Whatever the Ultima's merits, Noble felt it was time to move on, which is why he then sold the company to focus on a new car that would carry his

Compare this shot with the similar one of the Lamborghini Miura earlier and you can see that the inspirations are obvious. The Noble was rather more affordable, though, yet it offered even more power and performance.

own name. There were several projects in the meantime though – 250 Ferrari P4 replicas were produced as well as a low-budget track car called the Pro-Sport. Around 50 of those were churned out before Noble's next venture appeared, the MidTec. Focused on the leisure market, this was the precursor to Noble's most ambitious venture so far: the Ascari. Having set up that company, Noble then sold up to focus on his new venture, Noble Moy Automotive, which he set up with Tony Moy.

Ford engine

The first car to be introduced from the new company was the M10, unleashed in 1997 with 2.5-litre (151.7ci) Ford V6 power. It was enough of a car to take on the Lotus Elise, according to many who tested it – the handling was that good. But the styling was awkward and it needed more power because the chassis was barely stretched with the grunt on offer. The result was the M12, which was first seen in 2000, although no customer cars were delivered until the following year.

With 229.4kW (310bhp) and 432Nm (320lb ft) of torque from the V6 engine, there was no shortage of go. It was still the same Ford-sourced 2.5-litre (151.7ci) Duratec unit that had done such sterling work in the M10, but in the M12 the powerplant was boosted by a pair of Garrett T25 turbochargers. The engine's internals were also uprated so it could cope with the levels of power being squeezed from it, and

Noble M12 GTO

Years of production	2004–
Displacement	2968cc (178ci)
Configuration	Mid-mounted V6, twin-turbo
Transmission	Six-speed manual
Power	314.5kW (425bhp) @ 6500rpm
Torque	526.5Nm (390lb ft) @ 5000rpm
Top speed	297.7km/h (185mph)
0–60mph (0–97km/h)	3.5sec
Power to weight ratio	296.7kW/ton (401bhp/ton)
Number built	N/A

(352bhp) was coaxed from the all-alloy unit – dropping the 0–97km/h (0–60mph) time to just 3.8 seconds. The new engine came with a change in designation to GTO-3; this in turn brought with it another derivative called the GTO-3R. A lightly disguised road racer, this later model was fitted with a close-ratio six-speed manual gearbox, along with a Quaife automatic torque biasing differential to help get the power down.

You'd think that all this would be enough for most owners, but those who took their Nobles onto the track said the car needed more power. The result was the M400, launched in 2004. This car brought with it an incredible 314.5kW (425bhp) – this was still just a 3-litre (182.1ci) V6 remember, which was enough to take the car from a standstill to 160km/h (100mph) in just eight seconds. The M400 also incorporated various revisions to the rest of the running gear, such as more direct steering and improved cooling. But the best bit was the low price – which was just the tonic for blowing away all those Lamborghinis and Ferraris.

with a power to weight ratio of 237.5kW/ton (321bhp/ton), the car certainly delivered. The 100km/h (60mph) mark came up from rest in just 4.1 seconds, with 160km/h(100mph) flashing past just 6.1 seconds later.

At the beginning of 2003, the M12's engine capacity was increased to 3 litres (183ci). Still sporting a pair of Garrett turbochargers, a whopping 260.4kW

For such a low-volume production car, the Noble's interior was very impressive. Not only was it well designed, but the standard of fit and finish were extremely good too. Not quite up to Porsche standards though...

Pagani Zonda

With such huge speeds possible, it was essential that the Zonda's basic structure was incredibly strong. To that end there was a carbon fibre centre cell, from which were hung chrome moly steel space frames.

In predictable supercar fashion, there was double-wishbone suspension fitted at both ends, made of aluminium to reduce the unsprung weight. Coil springs and dampers were joined by anti-roll bars front and rear.

Massive ventilated discs were fitted at each corner, although there was no anti-lock at first (but it came later). Each disc measured 355mm (12.9in) across; to house such brakes, 457mm (18in) wheels had to be fitted.

The original V12 engine used was the 6-litre (364.2ci) unit seen in various Mercedes models. In time this grew to a massive 7.3 litres (443ci), with the powerplant coming straight from Mercedes' tuning division, AMG.

Although the Zonda's structure had to be strong, lightness was also essential. Extensive use of carbon fibre for the bodyshell kept the weight down to a tiny 59kg (130lb). The doors were made of carbon fibre too; they tipped the scales at just 4.5kg (9.9lb) apiece.

The first Zondas were fitted with a ZF five-speed manual gearbox, complete with awkward dog-leg first gear. In time this transmission was updated to a six-speed manual.

Everywhere you looked on the Zonda there were exquisite details that delighted – despite the car's design looking relatively clean at first glance. When you consider this was the company's first effort, it's even more impressive.

There are dozens of failed supercar attempts, all of which could potentially have made it into these pages. Because of a lack of funding, poor management or unrealistic business plans, history is littered with supercars that might have been. But occasionally a company comes along that succeeds where everybody else has failed. It puts the cat among the pigeons for a while, then everything settles down and suddenly the car is accepted as one of the establishment. That's exactly what happened to Pagani, which burst onto the scene in 1999, seemingly from nowhere.

Carbon fibre

The reality was that Horacio Pagani already had a track record in specialist car design and manufacture. Born in Argentina, he was a friend of legendary racing driver Juan Manuel Fangio. This connection won him an introduction to Lamborghini's Giulio Alfieri, who consequently offered Pagani a job with the company. Pagani immediately started experimenting with carbon fibre – he knew what an impact this incredibly light but strong material would have in the supercar world. Besides helping to engineer the Countach Evoluzione prototype, Pagani also styled the Countach Anniversary's monstrous bodywork modifications – which just goes to show that he didn't get it right all of the time.

In time, Pagani set up a company specializing in carbon composites and engineering. Called Modena Design, clients included Ferrari and Lamborghini, which looked pretty good on the CV. The obvious next step was to launch a whole car, which occurred in 1999. Pagani's initial idea was that the car would be named after Fangio, but when the great racing driver died before the project was completed, the new car was called the Zonda, after a wind from the Andes. Fangio had already approved of the project, having been told of it in its early stages. He immediately insisted that a Mercedes engine should be used in it, which is why Pagani chose to fit a V12 powerplant produced by the Stuttgart-based company.

Pagani Zonda

Years of production	1999–
Displacement	7291cc (437.4ci)
Configuration	Mid-mounted V12
Transmission	Six-speed manual, rear-wheel drive
Power	410.7kW (555bhp) @ 5900rpm
Torque	746.5Nm (553lb ft) @ 4050rpm
Top speed	321.8km/h (200mph) approx
0–60mph (0–97km/h)	3.7sec
Power to weight ratio	333.7kW/ton (451bhp/ton)
Number built	N/A

The basis for the Zonda was chrome moly steel space frames, which were attached to a carbon fibre centre section. A chrome moly steel and carbon fibre roll bar was then bolted and heat-bound to the chassis – the whole structure offering incredible stiffness while also being remarkably light.

There was independent suspension all round that consisted of aluminium wishbones, coil springs over dampers and anti-roll bars at each end, with the whole lot incorporating anti-dive and anti-squat geometry. As you'd expect, the braking department was pretty special. The system was engineered by Brembo, with servo-assisted 355mm (12.9in) ventilated discs at front and rear. Initially there was no anti-lock option though, as this robbed the system of feel. Although the Zonda was an incredibly modern car in its engineering and design, the interior wasn't quite as cutting-edge. While there was alloy detailing and Alcantara, the toggle switches and swathes of leather were very traditional – but also extremely comfortable.

Variants

By 2002 a 7.3-litre (443ci) version of the Zonda had been launched. Called the C12S it offered 410.7kW (555bhp) and a top speed of over 321.8km/h (200mph). Even more spectacular was the Roadster,

which arrived in 2003. Mechanically the same as the C12S, with a kerb weight of just 1280kg (2822.4lb) there was still a top speed of over 321.8km/h (200mph). Compare that weight with Lamborghini's Murcielago Roadster (1715kg / 3781.5lb) and you can see how effective the carbon fibre bodyshell was.

The ultimate incarnation of the Zonda appeared at the 2005 Geneva motor show, with the arrival of the Zonda F (for Fangio). With a 7.3-litre (443ci) engine breathed on by AMG, there was a storming 439.5kW (594bhp) – and an even more storming 756Nm (560lb ft) of torque. Despite such figures though, just 0.1 seconds was shaved off the 0–100km/h (0–62mph) time (to bring it down to 3.7 seconds). But it wasn't all about power; 50kg (110.2lb) was taken from the weight, bringing it down to 1230kg (2712lb). Another major innovation was the ceramic braking system, which used composite discs that measured a huge 380mm (14.9in) across. The other key feature of the new car was a one-piece rear spoiler that dramatically increased rear downforce at high speed. And with such power, the car was eminently capable of very high speeds…

With serious opposition from the likes of Porsche (Carrera GT) and Lamborghini (Murcielago Roadster), Pagani had to offer an open-topped Zonda to compete. Naturally the detailing was streets ahead of its rivals.

Porsche Carrera GT

Bose was drafted in to build a 100-watt amplifier that fed a lightweight subwoofer which fired into the hollow chassis tub to create better bass. As if the engine didn't provide enough aural entertainment…

Ceramic brakes had to be fitted from the very start of the project, because Porsche was very keen to prove their worth. It had to be proved that they were durable and efficient, as well as being lighter than steel items.

For the first time ever in a road car, the Carrera GT was fitted with a twin-plate ceramic clutch. This was capable of transferring more torque than was usual; up to 1012.5Nm (750lb ft) could be transmitted, at speeds up to 20,000rpm.

By using plenty of carbon fibre, magnesium and aluminium alloy in the Carrera GT's construction, Porsche managed to keep the car's weight down to just 1380kg (3042.9lb). For an open-topped car this was extraordinarily light.

Although Porsche was well known for its boxer engines, a V10 unit was used in the Carrera GT because of its lower centre of gravity. For the ultimate in handling, this was essential.

The suspension was taken from Porsche's aborted Le Mans race car project. As a result it featured double wishbones with inboard spring and damper units at the front as well as the rear.

The lines of the production Carrera GT remained faithful to those of the concept. While the car looked very dramatic when seen as a whole, when viewed from this angle it's rather uninspiring.

Ah, the irony of it all. Knowing that a crop of supercars would be arriving not long into the twenty-first century, Porsche decided the time was right to build its most innovative – and fastest – road car ever. This would be the supercar to show everybody else how it was supposed to be done. However, it wasn't just the established supercar makers that Porsche wanted to upstage; the company also claimed that some of the supercars due out around the time the Carrera GT would debut, weren't going to be from companies that were 'connected with sports cars'. And this was coming from a company that around the same time would be introducing an off-roader – which was about as far removed from the supercar world as it was possible to be. Or at least that was the case until Porsche entered the arena with the Cayenne...

Cutting-edge

Knowing that there would shortly be some very hot competition from the likes of VW, Audi, Mercedes and Ferrari, Porsche started the project rolling with the appointment of Michael Hölscher. He was one of the company's most promising engineers, and his brief was to come up with something that offered massive performance thanks to an advanced

There were no fixed-head Carrera GTs, as they all featured a lift-out roof panel. This was an odd decision, as open-topped cars are less rigid than closed ones – not that stiffness was a problem...

powerplant, cutting-edge transmission and the best construction techniques available anywhere. That meant the car had to be capable of at least 321.8km/h (200mph), pack a minimum of 444kW (600bhp), and be built from the most advanced composites anywhere. It would also have to have a very low centre of gravity, to ensure that even under the most arduous of conditions, the handling would remain pin-sharp.

The Carrera GT was first seen as a design study at the 2000 Paris motor show. It was very clear even at this stage that the car would be going into production, although Porsche didn't reveal this officially until early in 2001. While there were many detail changes between the design study and the production car, at first glance there were very few differences. The most obvious one was the complete absence of any weather protection for the concept; the road car was to be as usable as possible, which meant engineering some form of roof.

Porsche didn't hold back with any aspect of the Carrera GT – this car would prove that the company could produce cutting-edge supercars where no expense was spared. Mounted behind the passenger cell was a normally-aspirated V10 engine, with a closed-deck light-alloy crankcase that featured nickel/silicon liners and titanium connecting rods. There were also alloy cylinder heads with four valves per cylinder, four overhead camshafts, variable valve timing (which Porsche called infinite VarioCam control) on the intake side, mechanical valve play compensation, dry sump lubrication – this was no mere shopping trolley.

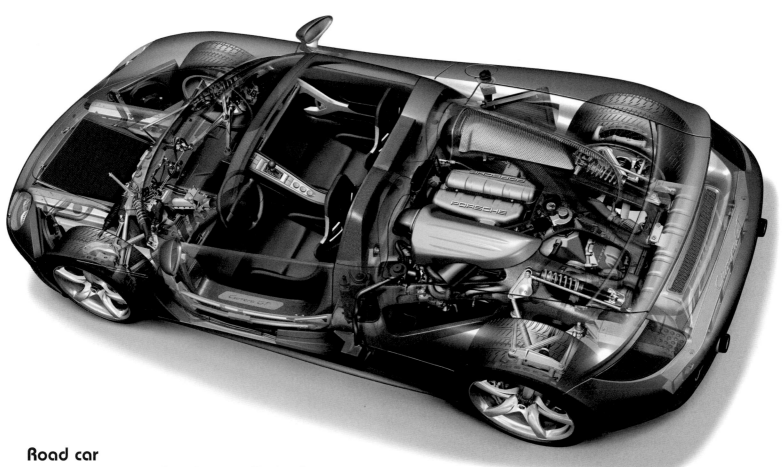

Road car

The V10 wasn't developed especially for the Carrera GT though – its origins lay in a stillborn race car project that had been begun to win Le Mans. Much of the car's construction and suspension had also been designed for that car, but because the Carrera GT was to be built for the road, things would have to be changed significantly so the car was usable on a day to day basis. Not that many owners would actually live with the car on a day-to-day basis of course…

Porsche threw everything that it could at the Carrera GT, in terms of mechanical engineering and construction. There were lightweight composites and astonishing levels of technology in that mid-mounted V10. Despite this, production was cut short because of a severe lack of demand.

Although tubular steel and aluminium structures were experimented with during the Carrera GT's development, it was carbon fibre that was used because of its strength and lightness. As well as a central tub made of this wonder-material, there were various components manufactured from it, then bonded to the tub. Most components mounted to the central structure were made of alloy or magnesium, but where strength was really crucial (such as in the crash structures) there was plenty of high-strength stainless steel.

As Porsche had pioneered the use of ceramic brakes, it was no surprise that they were fitted to the Carrera GT. The aim was to reduce unsprung weight while increasing the available braking capacity; as the heat built, this system increased in efficiency rather than faded away. Which is just what Porsche was hoping for with the whole project; a car that did anything but fade away in the annals of supercar manufacture.

Porsche Carrera GT

Years of production	2003–6
Displacement	5700cc (342ci)
Configuration	Mid-mounted V10
Transmission	Six-speed manual, rear-wheel drive
Power	452.8kW (612bhp) @ 8000rpm
Torque	587.2Nm (435lb ft) @ 5750rpm
Top speed	329.9km/h (205mph)
0–62mph (0–100km/h)	3.9sec
Power to weight ratio	327.8kW/ton (443bhp/ton)
Number built	1500 projected

Saleen S7

The seats were fixed and the pedal box was set up to suit each individual driver. But this wasn't done on a DIY basis – it had to be done by the factory, so fast driver changes often weren't an option!

The underside of the S7 was as carefully designed as the bodywork. There was so much downforce at 257.4km/h (160mph) that Saleen claimed the car could theoretically be driven upside down!

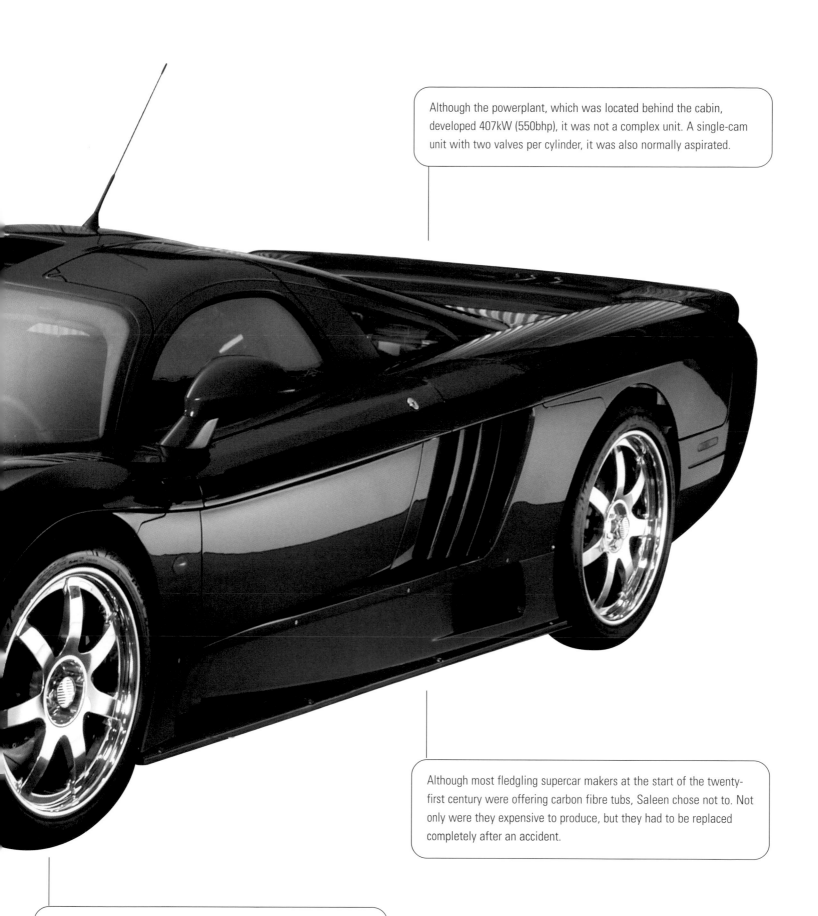

Although the powerplant, which was located behind the cabin, developed 407kW (550bhp), it was not a complex unit. A single-cam unit with two valves per cylinder, it was also normally aspirated.

Although most fledgling supercar makers at the start of the twenty-first century were offering carbon fibre tubs, Saleen chose not to. Not only were they expensive to produce, but they had to be replaced completely after an accident.

The brake discs were the size of dinner plates; they were 381mm (15in) in diameter at the front and 356mm (14in) at the rear. Conventional steel items were used, with six-piston calipers; there was no anti-lock option initially.

If you're going to take a car to ultra-high speeds you need some serious aerodynamics to keep it firmly on the ground. That's why the S7 featured venturis at the rear – to keep the car glued to the road.

There's nothing like a good track record in racing to boost the credibility of any supercar – a fact that wasn't lost on Steve Saleen, who set up supercar maker Saleen, based on the west coast of America. However, while the car was conceived and styled in the US, much of its development was carried out in the UK by Ray Mallock Engineering. The reasoning behind this was that if the car was to succeed in GT racing, it needed to be developed by engineers who knew exactly how to produce a competitive car – and the UK leads the field when it comes to motorsport expertise.

New car

Saleen made its name by tuning Mustangs for the road and track, but it was only a matter of time before a full car was designed and engineered by the company. The idea came about after the arrival of the Mustang-based SR, a car which used only the glazing and airbags with the donor vehicle. Saleen reckoned that if it was going to change the car so much, a new model created from scratch was the next logical step. And if a completely new car was going to be developed, it may as well be a hypercar.

At first glance, and especially when viewed from

head on, the S7 has strong overtones of the McLaren F1. That central air intake above the windscreen and those faired-in headlamps are the biggest reminders, but as soon as you view the car in profile it's easy to see that the main influences were long-tailed GT racers. This car is nothing like as compact as the F1. All those scoops, spoilers and gills also gave it amazing presence, just like the cab-forward stance and low roofline.

The S7's construction was unusually low-tech in some ways, although it made up for it in others. There was no carbon fibre central tub, because in the event of an accident that would automatically have to be replaced – which meant rebuilding the entire car. Saleen instead preferred to go for a tubular steel spaceframe, which could be repaired in the event of an impact. However, around this was wrapped glassfibre and carbon fibre bodywork that was lightweight but tough.

Usability and maintenance

Where the S7 scored over its rivals was in the usability and maintenance stakes. Hypercars aren't meant to be easy to live with, and a pre-requisite is usually hideously high running costs – but Saleen wanted to change all that. Instead of a highly-strung V12 powerplant with oodles of camshafts, valves and turbochargers, there was a simple all-alloy V8 positioned behind the cabin. With just two valves per

Saleen S7	
Years of production	2001–
Displacement	6998cc (419.8ci)
Configuration	Mid-mounted V8
Transmission	Six-speed manual, rear-wheel drive
Power	407kW (550bhp) @ 6400rpm
Torque	708.7Nm (525lb ft) @ 4000rpm
Top speed	386.2km/h (240mph) (claimed)
0–60mph (0–97km/h)	3.3sec
Power to weight ratio	330.7kW/ton (447bhp/ton)
Number built	N/A

Saleen didn't try to pare everything down to a minimum in a bid to shave every last kilo off its weight. At this level, buyers expected to have luxury as well as massive performance – which is exactly what they received.

cylinder (which were actuated by pushrods), and normal aspiration, this wasn't a complicated engine. But it was very effective because it was capable of pushing out 407kW (550bhp) and 708.7Nm (525lb ft) of torque. Although it was based on a Ford unit, it was so heavily reworked by Saleen that there was little evidence of the powerplant having started out with a blue oval on it.

The first development cars also featured a very straightforward six-speed transaxle, designed by ZF but engineered by American firm RBT. There was also no four-wheel drive or anti-lock braking system, but the parts that were fitted came from the best suppliers around the world. Brakes were courtesy of Brembo and the wheels were made by Enkei, shod with Pirelli tyres.

In 2005, Saleen added a pair of Garrett turbochargers to the S7 to produce a 555kW (750bhp)

monster. With a huge 945Nm (700lb ft) of torque on tap as well, the car was claimed to be capable of despatching the 0–100km/h (0–62mph) sprint in just 2.8 seconds – as well as the quarter-mile in a mere 10.7 seconds. Just in case this wasn't enough for some owners, there were rumours circulating that a 740kW (1000bhp) intercooled version was being developed. At the same time as the mechanical changes there were also some bodywork revisions to cut drag by 40 per cent while increasing downforce by 60 per cent.

Taking the cab-forward stance to extremes, the S7 featured an amazing amount of bodywork behind the cabin. This was to allow for some luggage space while also offering a mid-engined layout.

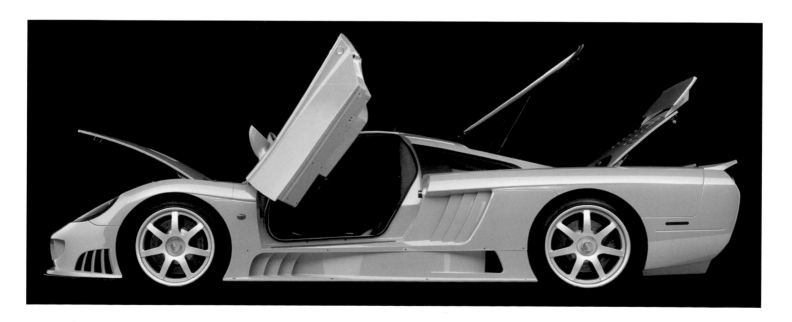

Spyker C8

Each of the alloy body panels was stamped with the chassis number of the car it was built for, so it could always be traced back to when it was made and who the car's original owner was.

In true racing style there was an adjustable balance built into the braking system. With six-pot calipers at the front and four-pot at the back, along with ventilated discs all round, there was plenty of stopping power.

Mounted behind the cockpit was a 4.2-litre (254.9ci) V8 engine with a pair of turbochargers. Sourced from the Audi S8, it could generate 310.8kW (420bhp) and 477.9Nm (354lb ft) of torque — enough to take the car to 300.9km/h (187mph).

C8 Laviolette

If you're going to resurrect a brand, it makes sense to pick one that used to be known for innovation and quality. That's exactly what the original Spyker company represented, but as it died in 1925, by the time the new version appeared everybody had forgotten that the earlier company ever existed. Then of course you have to consider that when you're looking around for innovative Dutch brands, there aren't very many to choose from...The first Spyker company, which started up in 1898 in Holland, had built cars using Mercedes engines. Its 44.4kW (60hp) of 1903 was the world's first grand prix racer with six cylinders and four-wheel drive.

'Jewellery on wheels'

The Spyker company was set up by Maarten de Bruijn and Victor Muller – neither of whom had a background in car design or engineering. But they did appreciate the finer things in life, and their aim was to produce a car that was effectively jewellery on wheels. It would be a piece of art that could be passed down through generations; a family heirloom like an expensive watch or antique furniture.

Taking the Bugatti Veyron on at its own game, the Spyker offered an interior that looked more as though it was a piece of jewellery. Everywhere you looked there was machine-turned metal and polished stainless steel.

Spyker C8	
Years of production	2001–
Displacement	4172cc (250.3ci)
Configuration	Mid-mounted V8, twin-turbo
Transmission	Manual or sequential six-speed, rear-wheel drive
Power	310.8kW (420bhp) (no rpm available)
Torque	477.9Nm (354lb ft) (no rpm available)
Top speed	300.9km/h (187mph)
0–62mph (0–100km/h)	4.5sec
Power to weight ratio	310.8kW/ton (420bhp/ton)
Number built	25 per year

Although de Bruijn had trained as a lawyer, he had aspirations of becoming a supercar maker. While doing his studies, he read up on car design, construction and engineering, before creating his own steel-bodied coupé using a 185kW (250bhp) Audi engine. In time this would evolve into the C8, but that meant getting some financial backing. Family friend Victor Muller came to his rescue, and between them they set up the new Spyker company, with the aim of producing high-quality supercars.

The Spyker came from nowhere and immediately captured supercar buyers' imaginations around the world. It wasn't as good to drive as most of its rivals, but its engineering was quite exquisite – inside and out.

The first Spyker to break cover was the C8 Spyder which made its debut at the 2000 Birmingham motor show. With this new car, there were few parallels with the original Spyker company. There was no four-wheel drive, but the engine was borrowed from a German manufacturer; this time round it was Audi that donated a V8 powerplant, in this case from the S8. That meant there was a displacement of 4172cc (250.3ci) and with the aid of a pair of turbochargers a healthy 310.8kW (420bhp) was produced. The all-alloy unit featured four overhead camshafts and there were five valves per cylinder to ensure the unit could breathe easily at high revs.

The power was transmitted to the rear wheels via a six-speed gearbox, which could be specified with sequential or manual operation. Only the rear wheels were driven and if the car was going to be caned regularly, Spyker recommended the fitting of a limited-slip differential to help get the power down. The suspension was Formula One-derived, which meant it was fully adjustable all round. The Koni dampers were mounted in-board while the uprights were machined from solid billets of aluminium alloy – much of the rest was constructed from stainless steel. There was no cost-cutting here!

The Laviolette

The next Spyker to appear was the Laviolette, which made its debut at the 2001 Amsterdam motor show. This car was the closed version of the C8 that was already on sale, and it took its name from the Belgian engineer Joseph Valentin Laviolette who had engineered the first Spykers nearly a century before. Thanks to a more slippery shape, the coupé was capable of a marginally higher top speed (305.7km/h / 190mph) while also being fractionally quicker to 100km/h (62mph) – 4.2 seconds.

Because of the bespoke nature of its cars, Spyker offered customers the chance to see its car being built via a webcam; the factory was based in Holland, but most cars were exported. As the car was built, each alloy panel was stamped with the vehicle's chassis number, so everything could be traced back to who made what, and when. It was also possible to tailor the car to the customer's exact specifications, which included the stage of tune for the engine, the colour schemes, the equipment levels and the type of transmission. With such personalization available, and with the factory able to create just 25 cars a year, Spyker was very keen that no two examples should be the same.

The future

An environmentally friendly supercar may seem like a contradiction in terms, but if the breed is to survive, a way will have to be found of greatly reducing fuel consumption. If that seems like a depressing prospect, it needn't necessarily be as there are solutions at hand – it just depends on how much of a will the exotic car makers have to adapt to the changing conditions.

In an environmentally aware world, cars that squander the Earth's resources are increasingly frowned upon. But as long as there are enough wealthy enthusiasts to sustain the various supercar makers, exotic cars will continue to be churned out. What will have to change is how those cars are made and how much of the available resources they're allowed to consume. The supercar technology bar has been raised to such a high level after over a century of development, the goal for the future must surely be to allow supercar drivers to enjoy the same level of performance while also using as little fuel as possible. That is assuming that the motive power continues to be petrol – perhaps the first diesel supercars are still to be built? Maybe the first hybrid hypercar is on its way? Now that all of the established supercar builders are in the hands of large corporations, these are distinct possibilities – assuming they don't dilute the values of the brand in question too much.

Whether or not Chrysler will have the courage to produce the ME412 is open to debate. What can't be denied though is that if it did happen, Chrysler's image would go through the roof.

One small British marque that was already pushing the boundaries as this book went to press was Connaught. Nothing to do with the sports car company that existed in the 1950s, the new outfit was working on a V10-engined 1.5-litre (91ci) hybrid car that promised massive performance with respectable fuel economy. While it was merely the work of a small operation, with the might of a company such as DaimlerChrysler or General Motors.

The other key way in which supercars will evolve is their construction and exclusivity. As the standard of living around the world increases, and expectations increase exponentially, there will always be the lucky wealthy few who can afford to indulge their passions. While companies such as Porsche, Lamborghini and Aston Martin will continue to offer powerful cars at relatively affordable prices, there will be a level above this that far more exclusive companies will inhabit. After all, for the super-rich, nothing less than a stratospherically priced car (or two) will do. And that means one thing – the established names just won't be distinctive enough. Could Pagani and Koenigsegg be the new Ferrari and Aston Martin?

Audi Le Mans

The windscreen was given a hydrophobic (water-repellent) coating to keep it clean. A similar coating was also used to help reduce the penetration of ultra-violet and infra-red rays to keep the cabin cool.

The car's full name was the Le Mans Quattro, which, as the name suggests, meant it was equipped with Audi's famous four-wheel drive system. The torque split was 60:40 rear:front in normal driving.

There were plenty of light-emitting diodes (LEDs) around the exterior, although these probably won't make production. The headlamps were made up of 17 LEDs while the rear lamps also utilized LED technology.

An aluminium space frame formed the central structure. The outer skin was constructed from aluminium and carbon fibre, offering enormous torsional rigidity while also keeping weight down to 1530kg (3373.6lb).

The 5-litre (303.5ci) V10, borrowed from the Lamborghini Gallardo, showcased Audi's FSI direct fuel injection technology. It also sported two turbochargers

Those gorgeous multi-spoke alloy wheels measured a whopping 508mm (20in) across. That gave everyone a better view of the massive brakes behind while also stiffening up the ride at the same time.

The beauty of Lamborghini being bought by Volkswagen/Audi is that completely irrelevant image-boosting cars like the Audi Le Mans are born. If it hadn't been for the Lamborghini Gallardo, the Le Mans would never have been shown in concept form at the 2003 Frankfurt motor show. That car was displayed to test the waters and see if there would be any demand for a V10 mid-engined supercar wearing Audi badges – and the decision was taken that the sums did add up.

It was about time Audi bit the bullet, because this was the fourth mid-engined supercar to be exhibited by the company in little more than a decade. The Quattro Spyder and Avus, both shown in 1991, should really have been put into production, if not the rather ugly Rosemeyer of 2000 – but none of them ever saw the showroom. Fourth time round Audi decided it may as well go for it, with the first cars expected to be delivered in 2006.

Engine

It was the Lamborghini Gallardo which donated the engine as well as the basic structure for the Le Mans. That meant there was a V10 powerplant nestling behind the driver, boosted by a pair of turbochargers to produce 451.4kW (610bhp). With a crazy 746.5Nm (553lb ft) of torque also on tap (from just 1750rpm) the

It's all gone full circle, with Audi buying Lamborghini, then building its own mid-engined supercar based on the Gallardo. It's a far cry from the Miura that launched the mid-engined layout four decades earlier.

car could easily clear 321.8km/h (200mph) while also getting to 100km/h (62mph) in under four seconds. The fuelling for this engine was by Audi's recently-introduced FSi direct fuel injection system, which offered much greater efficiency than a standard fuel injection set-up. Thus equipped, the Le Mans developed even more power without using any more fuel.

With Audi's quattro four-wheel drive system being one of the most advanced transmissions in the world, it made sense to use it in the Le Mans. In normal driving conditions the torque would be split 60:40 with a bias towards the rear wheels. But if traction was better at the front the balance could be adjusted within a fraction of a second, so that it was anywhere between 20:80 and 70:30 front:rear. The gearbox featured six ratios, these being selected sequentially using steering wheel-mounted paddle shifts.

For the first time ever on an Audi, ceramic composite brakes were fitted. Costing horrific amounts of money, and usually lasting a very short time (although they're supposed to last much longer than conventional steel items), this system is lighter and far more capable than a normal braking system. It's really only suitable for racing cars because the system has to be warmed up before it's truly effective – but once up to temperature the braking distances can be slashed because the brakes can dissipate so much heat so quickly.

Helping to dissipate the heat were 508mm (20in) alloy wheels, which were of a slimline spoked design. The wheels were shod with 255/30 tyres at the front and 295/30 rubber at the back; with such low-profile tyres the car was capable of generating even higher cornering forces than it would otherwise have done.

Wheelbase

Audi was very keen to establish a link between the Le Mans and its highly successful R8 endurance racer. The R8 was equipped with buttons on the steering wheel to allow the driver to set a speed limiter as well as to adjust the damper settings. It was also possible to change the angle of the rear spoiler – although whether any owner would ever bother with manually over-riding the automatic systems is pretty unlikely.

One of the key areas where the Le Mans differed from the Gallardo was in its wheelbase, which was stretched by 90mm (3.5in). This allowed a more luxurious cabin to be offered, with a bit of extra room behind the seats for luggage to be carried. Whether or not this will be enough of a difference for buyers to choose an Audi over a Lamborghini remains to be seen, but as this book went to press there was already talk of the production car possibly being fitted with a 3.2-litre (194.2ci) V6 to make it more affordable...

It's unlikely that the interior of the production version of the Le Mans will be as imaginatively engineered as the concept. What is certain though is that the car will be great to drive as well as being quick.

Audi Le Mans

Years of production	2006/7–
Displacement	4961cc (297.6ci)
Configuration	Mid-engined V10, twin turbo
Transmission	Six-speed sequential manual
Power	451.4kW (610bhp) @ 6800rpm
Torque	746.5Nm (553lb ft) @ 1750rpm
Top speed	344.3km/h (214mph)
0–62mph (0–100km/h)	3.7sec
Power to weight ratio	295.2kW/ton (399bhp/ton)
Number built	None

Cadillac Cien

The Cien consisted of a central monocoque made of carbon fibre, which offered immense strength with the minimum of weight. Inside the cabin, and in true supercar fashion, there were just two seats.

The bodywork was punctuated by scoops all over the place, some to cool the brakes and others to either cool the engine or help feed it. One of the more subtle scoops was positioned immediately behind the doors.

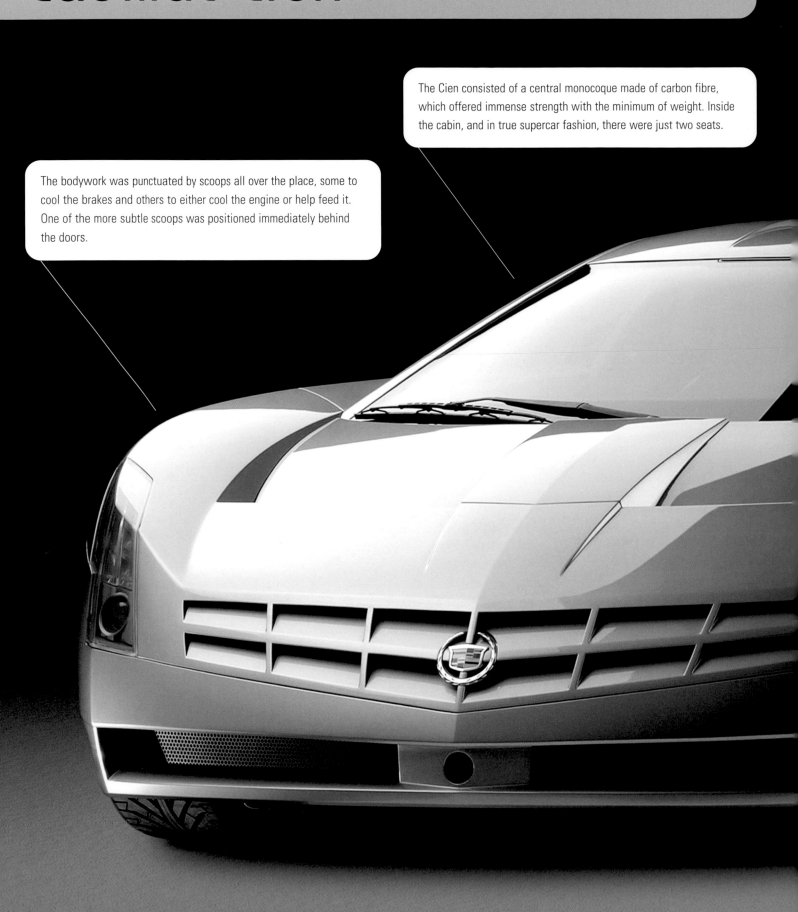

Although the V12 powerplant was massively powerful, it was smaller than the typical V8 thanks to its compact 60-degree angle. It was fitted with two overhead camshafts and 48 valves.

The 7.5-litre (445.2ci) V12 engine made its debut in the Cien, but it was built for real as it was to power Cadillac's flagship models. SUVs such as the Escalade were to be fitted with it, but not in the 555kW (750bhp) form the Cien featured.

Apart from the brakes and dampers, all of the Cien's mechanicals were made especially for it. The alloy double wishbone suspension was bespoke, as were the wheels and tyres.

The problem with big businesses such as General Motors is that they tend to be run by bean counters. Everything comes down to pounds, shillings and pence with them, because they know the price of everything but the value of nothing. That was the problem with GM's management; they knew the Cien would do a great job of lifting Cadillac's image – but nobody could work out by how many dollars' worth. If somebody had been able to put a price on how much the halo effect produced by the Cien would have been worth, it just might have made production.

When the Cien was unveiled at the 2002 Detroit motor show, there was serious talk of the car making production. Cadillac's image needed a major boost because it had become a maker of cars for old people. What the company needed was a younger target audience, which would latch onto the cars at an earlier age and buy one after another. Instead, customers were buying what would perhaps be their last car before they shuffled off this mortal coil. The problem was, how could Cadillac tempt buyers into showrooms when all it had to offer was deathly dull cars that nobody wanted? The answer lay in a car that would wow people – it didn't matter that it wouldn't make any money. Except to the holders of the purse strings it did matter…

Centenary celebrations

The Cien was the start of Cadillac's centenary celebrations, which kicked off at the start of 2002. The

This was just the shot in the arm that Cadillac needed, to attract younger buyers to the brand. Although the much edgier styling did make it into the company's regular range, there was no room for a mid-engined supercar, sadly.

name Cien came from the Spanish word for one hundred, and this concept was hopefully going to mark a fresh start for the American giant, which had seen better days. Styled by British designer Simon Cox, the car was assembled by English company Prodrive while the 7.5-litre (445.2ci) V12 engine was also created by a British company – Cosworth. While Cadillac had developed an image for luxury, what it really wanted was a name for performance. And what better way was there than to unleash a 321.8km/h (200mph) no-holds-barred supercar?

There were several pieces of big news with the Cien, the first one being that dramatic bodywork. At the heart of the car was a carbon fibre monocoque, for strength, rigidity and lightness. Of course it was all bespoke, but more surprisingly, so was the aluminium double-wishbone suspension, the semi-automatic six-speed gearbox with paddle shifts and even the 533mm (21in) Michelin tyres – although the front items were a mere 482mm (19in) across. In fact, of all the mechanical components, only the shock absorbers and Brembo brakes were taken off the shelf.

The next big news was the all-alloy Northstar XV12 engine, which was engineered to power the most expensive Cadillac production cars. It wouldn't

With such visual drama going on outside, it's a shame that Cadillac didn't follow it up with something more exciting for the cabin, especially as this was just a one-off anyway. Where was all the futuristic technology?

generate the 555kW (750bhp) that the Cien did, but it did feature Displacement on Demand, which was a fuel-saving technology developed by GM to make its cars more environmentally friendly. This allowed the engine to run on six cylinders instead of 12, if the car wasn't being driven especially hard. As a result, and also thanks to its direct fuel injection, the V12 unit delivered fuel consumption figures on a par with a typical V8.

First outings

In a bid to test public reaction, General Motors paraded the Cien in front of massive crowds at the 2002 Le Mans 24 Hours, and then again at the Goodwood Festival of Speed the same summer. Each time the crowds went wild; it was clear that this car had the impact the company wanted. Ford had done something similar with the Ford GT, which had been given the green light within a few weeks of its first

public showing. People were asking how Ford could afford to miss such an opportunity – and that's just what was said about GM and the Cien. But of course there was a huge difference between the two companies – Ford put the GT into limited production and GM chickened out.

Cadillac Cien	
Years of production	2002
Displacement	7500cc (445.2ci)
Configuration	Mid-mounted V12
Transmission	Six-speed semi-automatic
Power	555kW (750bhp) (no rpm available)
Torque	607.5Nm (450lb ft) (no rpm available)
Top speed	321.8km/h+ (200mph+)
0–60mph (0–97km/h)	N/A
Power to weight ratio	N/A
Number built	1

Chrysler ME412

The bodyshell was as high-tech as they come, being produced of carbon fibre around an aluminium honeycomb tub. For a supercar it was slippery too, with a drag co-efficient of 0.36.

To keep weight down there were cast aluminium wishbones at each corner, along with driver-adjustable pushrod spring/damper units.

The braking system featured 381mm (15in) ventilated carbon ceramic composite discs with six-piston aluminium monoblock calipers. The discs were 65 per cent lighter than comparable cast-iron units.

Despite the huge reserves of power, only the rear wheels were driven so that weight could be kept to a minimum. Power was transmitted to the back end via a seven-speed manual gearbox.

The V12 engine had seen service in various AMG versions of Mercedes' line up. It displaced 6 litres (364.2ci) and could produce 629kW (850bhp) and 1147.5Nm (850lb ft) of torque thanks to four turbochargers.

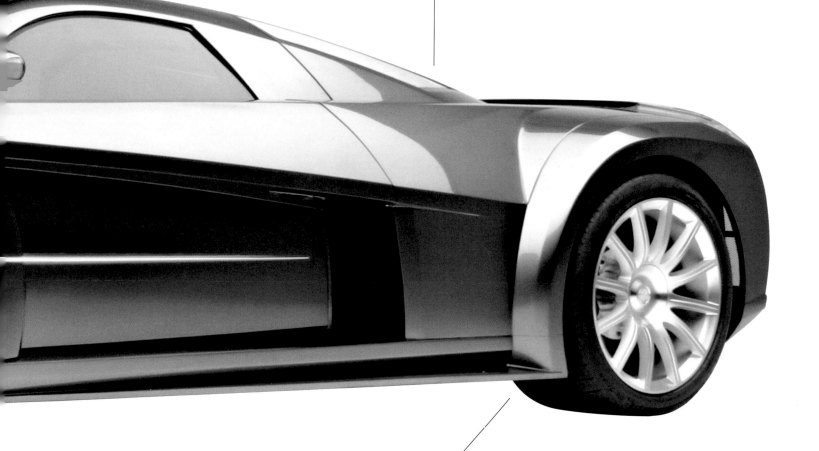

Those gorgeous wheels were cast aluminium and measured 482x254mm (19x10in) at the front and 508x317mm (20x12.5in) at the rear. Michelin high-performance tyres were 265/35ZR19 at the front and 335/30ZR20 at the rear.

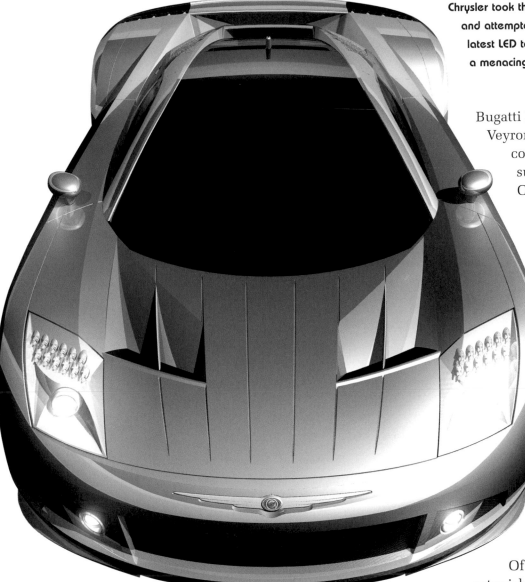

Chrysler took the tried and tested mid-engined layout and attempted to put a new spin on it. Using the latest LED technology, those headlights gave the car a menacing look while also being highly effective.

Bugatti having been working on the Veyron for several years, and with completion of the project supposedly not too far away, Chrysler didn't want to be left behind. The Veyron was set to offer 730.3kW (987bhp), but Chrysler reckoned that with 'just' 629kW (850bhp) it would be able to produce a car that would give the Bugatti a run for its money in terms of top speed and acceleration. Based on computer modelling, it was reckoned that the ME412 was capable of a frankly ludicrous 399.1km/h (248mph), as well as a 0–60mph (0–97km/h) sprint of just 2.9 seconds.

Engine

Of course, to offer such astonishingly high levels of performance, the ME412 had to be fitted with something pretty special in the engine stakes. The basis of the powerplant was the AMG-produced 5980cc (358.8ci) V12 powerplant that was available in various Mercedes models. Capable of developing around 444kW (600bhp) when used elsewhere, Chrysler's engineers needed to beef it up considerably if it was to offer serious competition to Bugatti. To that end, no fewer than four turbochargers were bolted onto it, to produce a completely insane 105kW (142bhp) per litre. Of course it's relatively easy to generate huge amounts of power from an engine, and also to produce massive amounts of specific power (horsepower per litre), but the trick is to keep everything tractable at low engine and road speeds. With modern electronics this didn't prove too much of a problem for the spannermen, and peak torque of 1147.5Nm (850lb ft) was available from just 2500rpm.

When Chrysler unveiled its ME412 at the 2004 Detroit motor show, the company went to great pains to point out that this was not a concept. Instead, it was a prototype which could have been ready for the road within six months. Not only that, but the company was also seriously considering putting the car into production with anywhere between 10 and 2000 examples being available. There was also talk of 100 cars being built each year for a couple of years – but whatever happened, Chrysler really wanted to see this car hit the road. But it never happened of course. It may have had a halo effect and lifted the reputation of the rest of Chrysler's range, but the price was simply far too high. Trying to engineer and sell the car just wouldn't have made sense in a world that was fast becoming choked with ultra-expensive supercars which had little prospect of finding owners.

The reasoning behind the ME412 was that anything that Bugatti could do, Chrysler could also do. With

If keeping the engine tractable at low speeds seemed like a hurdle, it was nothing compared to getting all

Chrysler ME412	
Years of production	2004
Displacement	5980cc (358.8ci)
Configuration	Mid-engined V12
Transmission	Seven-speed manual, rear-wheel drive
Power	629kW (850bhp) @ 5750rpm
Torque	1147.5Nm (850lb ft) @ 2500rpm
Top speed	399.1km/h (248mph)
0–60mph (0–97km/h)	2.9sec
Power to weight ratio	480.2kW/ton (649bhp/ton)
Number built	1

Chrysler has produced some truly great concept cars, pulling out all the stops to make them look imaginative. The ME412 was no exception, with a floating dash and aircraft-style flat-bottomed steering wheel.

that power down without drama. The obvious thing to do would have been to install a four-wheel drive system, but that would have added weight and complexity. So a rear-wheel drive layout was used instead, which Chrysler claimed was perfectly capable of putting the power down without lighting up the rear tyres every time the throttle was dabbed. The transmission, built by Ricardo, was fitted with seven speeds, and featured a pair of clutches to enable faster gearchanges than usual. The result of all this was a kerb weight of 1310kg (2888.5lb), which was little more than the typical small family hatchback – and somewhere around half a ton less than most equivalent supercars.

Lightweight materials

The weight was also kept down by using lightweight materials as much as possible. The suspension was built largely of aluminium alloys, while the bodyshell was constructed of carbon fibre, with the whole thing being based on an aluminium honeycomb tub. Even the brakes were carbon, giving awesome stopping power while weighing only a third of comparable steel units. It was through this intelligent design that Chrysler intended to beat Bugatti – not by ever higher power outputs, but by reducing weight to the absolute minimum. It could have done it too, perhaps forever changing the image of the company, so what a shame it never happened.

The derivative styling of the ME412 is most obvious when the car is viewed in profile. That dramatic cab-forward stance and huge door-mounted scoop are classic supercar clichés – but those angular lines means the car still looks stunning.

Maybach Exelero

The huge grille certainly jars, but it also makes the car look even more menacing. Some observers claimed it carried strong overtones of Darth Vader's mask, from the *Star Wars* series.

While the standard Maybach engine isn't exactly lacking, it wouldn't be able to propel the Exelero at speeds of up to 350km/h (219mph). That's why it was reworked to give 518kW (700bhp) and 1015.2Nm (752lb ft) of torque.

Those wheels were built specially for the job. Measuring a monstrous 584mm (23in) in diameter, their design is based on that of a turbine. That's why they're unidirectional; one side is a mirror image of the other.

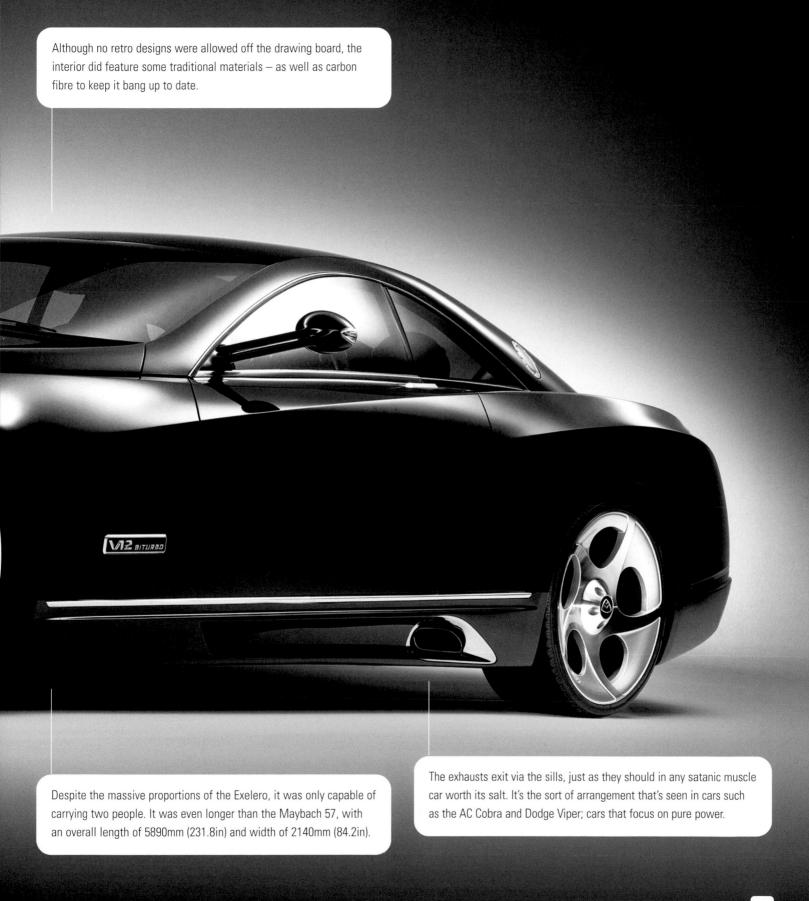

Although no retro designs were allowed off the drawing board, the interior did feature some traditional materials — as well as carbon fibre to keep it bang up to date.

Despite the massive proportions of the Exelero, it was only capable of carrying two people. It was even longer than the Maybach 57, with an overall length of 5890mm (231.8in) and width of 2140mm (84.2in).

The exhausts exit via the sills, just as they should in any satanic muscle car worth its salt. It's the sort of arrangement that's seen in cars such as the AC Cobra and Dodge Viper; cars that focus on pure power.

The Exelero may have used plenty of parts from the Mercedes parts bin, but the cabin was no less worse off for it. Those electro-luminescent dials were futuristic while the rest of the cockpit was fairly low-key.

While it looks like a refugee from a Batman film, the Exelero was never designed for a starring role on the silver screen. Instead it was designed as a mobile test bed for high-speed tyres, bankrolled by tyre maker Fulda and based on the platform of the Maybach 57 limousine. This wasn't the first time that Fulda had teamed up with the Maybach marque, nor was it the first time that the tyre maker had built a vehicle specially for the purpose of demonstrating its tyres.

Back in 1938, Fulda commissioned Frankfurt-based coachbuilders Dörr & Schreck to build a one-off version of the Maybach SW38, to enable high-speed tyre testing on Germany's autobahns. That car was completed in July 1938 – just before the outbreak of World War II. During the hostilities the car disappeared and was never seen again. In the meantime, Fulda commissioned a madly modified Porsche 911 (by Gemballa) to demonstrate its 1996 range. When an all-new line up of tyres was unveiled

in 2005 the company wanted to pull out all the stops and commission something unique. As the Maybach marque had been revived by this point, the decision was made to team up with DaimlerChrysler, custodians of the Maybach brand, to build a show-stopping car that had as much go as it did show.

Maybach Exelero	
Years of production	2005
Displacement	5908cc (354.4ci)
Configuration	Front-mounted V12, twin-turbo
Transmission	Five-speed auto
Power	518kW (700bhp) @ 5000rpm
Torque	1015.2Nm (752lb ft) @ 2500rpm
Top speed	350km/h (219mph)
0–60mph (0–97km/h)	4.4sec
Power to weight ratio	194.6kW/ton (263bhp/ton)
Number built	1

Tyre showcase

The whole Exelero exercise was carried out so that Fulda could show off its new Carat Exelero range of tyres – the largest of which had a diameter of 584mm (23in). The tyres were capable of running at speeds of up to 350km/h (219mph), so the Exelero's top speed needed to match this. But while the standard Maybach range was hardly lacking in terms of available performance, something special would have to be done to achieve the level of speed that Fulda required.

In a bid to extract as many horses as possible from the twin-turbo V12 powerplant, its capacity was increased from 5.6 to 5.9 litres (339.9 to 358.1ci). That liberated an extra 111kW (150bhp) or so, taking the tally up to 518kW (700bhp), which was enough to take the Exelero up to its 350km/h (219mph) target speed. To make sure the car was capable of achieving this pace, it was driven around the Nardo test facility – where it notched up a maximum velocity of 351.45km/h (219.6mph). However, it wasn't capable of attaining such velocities in the form shown here. To improve aerodynamics and add a few kilometres per hour to the top speed, the wheels were enclosed with panelling – adding around 4km/h (2.4mph) in the process.

Design

While the mechanical side was clearly crucial to getting the car up to the required velocities, its design and construction were also important. To come up with a suitably menacing look, Fulda teamed up with the students of Pforzheim Polytechnic's Department of Transport Design. It wasn't the first time the two had collaborated – in the mid-1990s they had teamed up to create a futuristic truck to showcase Fulda's products. This time round the work of 24-year-old Fredrik Burchhardt was chosen as the basis for the project; his menacing study was just what Fulda reckoned it needed to grab plenty of column inches in the world's media.

Despite the Exelero being even longer than the Maybach 57 that donated its platform – its length was 5890mm (231.8in) while its width was 2140mm (84.2in) – it featured seating for just two people. Italian specialist vehicle maker Stola built the car at its base in Turin and by the summer of 2005 the car was ready to be unveiled. Although there were few definite requirements for the exterior styling (the main one being that no retro suggestions would even get out of the starting blocks), there were some very specific demands where the interior was concerned. On the list of required materials were natural leather, neoprene and coated punched aluminum sheet along with carbon fibre finished in glossy black and red. Whether it looked classy or like a tart's boudoir is a matter of interpretation...

Satanic is the word that best describes the Exelero, whether it's viewed from in front or behind. The black coachwork and aggressive curves gave the car a menacing look that was purely intentional.

GLOSSARY

A/B/C/D-pillars

Each of the pillars supporting the roof are named in sequence, from front to back. So the leading pillar – usually the windscreen surround – is known as the A-pillar. The B-pillar is the one between the front and rear doors and the C-pillar usually sits behind the rear door. It is normally only estates that have a D-pillar, as only this type of car has four roof supports.

Active ride

By using electronics it is possible to calculate the loadings at each corner of a car as it travels along. By measuring the various forces acting on the car at any given point, it is possible to prevent the car from rolling in corners as well as to counteract the dive and squat that are inherent in braking and accelerating respectively – thus levelling out the ride and making it corner, accelerate and brake in a more flat manner.

Brake horsepower (bhp)

The measure of an engine's horsepower without the loss in power caused by the gearbox, alternator, differential, water pump and other ancillaries. The horsepower delivered to the driving wheels is always less than the engine is capable of generating because of these transmissions and ancillary losses. It's the power output divided by the aerodynamic drag which dictates a car's top speed.

Cab-forward

Usually a characteristic of two-door, two-seater supercars, a cab-forward design is one that puts the car's occupants towards the front of the car, normally with the engine tucked away behind them.

Drag co-efficient

How aerodynamic a car is, and also known as the drag factor; an unusually slippery car will have a drag

With a bigger brother that packed 600bhp, the entry-level Aston Martin V8 Coupé seemed rather tame. But it still had 350bhp and was capable of over 150mph (241.4km/h), which was enough for most people. But at £140,000 in 1996, it was fabulously expensive.

factor of, say, 0.25. Things such as flush-fitting glazing and tighter shutlines between panels have reduced the air resistance around a car – the limiting factors are now accommodating people and mechanicals.

Drive by wire

Most of the controls of a car are connected to mechanical linkages. For example there is the pedal box for the accelerator, brakes and clutch as well as a steering column from the steering wheel. By getting rid of all these linkages and relying on electronics instead, huge advances can be made. Cars become safer, better packaged and easier to tailor to a driver's individual requirements. But the technology needs to be failsafe, and so far it rarely is.

Fastback

A car that has an unbroken line from the top of the rear of the roof to the rear bumper; this line is usually at a relatively shallow angle.

Glass house

The amount of glass within a car – that is, the volume of window space taking into account the windscreen, back window and side windows. It also often refers to the depth of the side windows, and the proportion of them relative to the overall height of a car.

GT/Grand Tourer

From the Italian Gran Turismo. A car combining saloon and sports car qualities in which effortless power is the dominant feature. Combines excellent road handling with high levels of comfort and is the perfect type of car to enjoy a long-distance (usually fast) journey.

Header rail

Usually only applicable on a convertible, the header rail is what runs across the top of a windscreen. In an open-topped car, the folding roof will close flush with the header rail.

Kamm Tail

If a car features an abrupt ending it has a Kamm tail, named after the German aerodynamicist W. Kamm. He discovered that drag begins to increase after the rear of a car's cross-sectional area is reduced to 50 percent of the car's maximum cross section.

The XJ220 never achieved the status of rivals from Italy and Germany – yet it was very powerful and fast. It looked fantastic from any angle, so it was a shame that it packed only six cylinders.

Lean burn

An engine runs on fuel mixed with air. The ratio in which the fuel/air mixture is burned depends on various things such as the operating temperature of the engine and how much load the unit is under (i.e. whether or not the car is accelerating or cruising). A lean burn engine attempts to reduce the amount if fuel being burned while still allowing enough power to be produced for the car to accelerate cleanly.

Monobox design

In profile a car is made of varying numbers of boxes. For example, the classic saloon is a three-box design while the typical hatchback or estate is a two-box design. By sloping the bonnet sharply, at roughly the same angle as the windscreen, it is possible to create a monobox design. The most common cars that feature this are people carriers and the new breed of hatchbacks.

Monocoque

Whereas cars used to be built with a separate chassis (and some specialist cars still are), for many years the standard method of car construction has been the monocoque. Otherwise known as unitary construction, this way of building a car features a bodyshell onto which everything is attached directly; engine, suspension and transmission.

Normally aspirated

The opposite of turbocharged (also known as forced induction). Instead of forcing the fuel/air mixture into an engine, it is injected in at atmospheric pressure.

You couldn't argue with looks like those – and the Viper was definitely not a case of just looking good. This second-generation car packed 500bhp and 676Nm (500lb ft) of torque as well as 8193.5cc (500ci) to give phenomenal performance.

Pillarless construction

Cars do not generally have a truly pillarless construction, as there would be no protection in the event of a roll over accident and there would be no way of supporting a roof or holding a windscreen in place. Some cars sometimes have no B-pillar behind the front doors. This is popular with two-door coupés and is becoming increasingly common on four-door saloons; especially those with rear-hinged back doors.

Roadster

An open car of sporty appearance, also known as a convertible, cabriolet or drop head. Rag top, drop top and spyder are also names for these open-topped cars. While originally they were all slightly different, they have tended to be lumped together in recent years.

Targa

A removable-roof body style popularised by Porsche that is similar to a convertible, except that it incorporates a fixed rear window.

Torque

It's the amount of available torque that determines a car's acceleration. The torque at the wheels dictates how quickly a car can accelerate; this is a result of the available torque from the engine and the gearing used to transmit it to the driven wheels.

Transmission

This refers to the gear shifting system through which engine power is transferred to the wheels. The purpose of the transmission is to keep maximum engine power applied to the wheels at all times for all conditions, from start-up to high speeds. Most transmissions have 3-6 ratios or 'speeds'. The engine (via the crankshaft) spins too fast to drive the wheels. The transmission reduces the revs and allows the engine to drive the wheels. Generally speaking, the fewer ratios a transmission has, the less efficiently the engine operates.

Tumblehome

This term that describes the convex curvature on the side of a car body, when viewed from straight ahead or directly behind.

Wheelbase

The distance between the centres of the front and rear wheel axles as viewed from the side of the vehicle.

INDEX

PICTURE CREDITS

All pictures supplied by Richard Dredge except the following:

Giles Chapman: 50
TRH: 24–25, 26–27, 40–42, 44–45, 48–49, 74–75, 86–87, 124–125